Rebellion Against Victorianism

REBELLION AGAINST VICTORIANISM

The Impetus for Cultural Change in 1920s America

STANLEY COBEN

New York   Oxford
OXFORD UNIVERSITY PRESS
1991

Oxford University Press

Oxford   New York   Toronto
Delhi   Bombay   Calcutta   Madras   Karachi
Petaling Jaya   Singapore   Hong Kong   Tokyo
Nairobi   Dar es Salaam   Cape Town
Melbourne   Auckland

and associated companies in
Berlin   Ibadan

Library of Congress Cataloging-in-Publication Data
Coben, Stanley.
Rebellion against Victorianism :
the impetus for cultural change in 1920s America /
Stanley Coben.
p. cm. Includes bibliographical references and index.
ISBN 0-19-504593-9
1. United States—Civilization—1918–1945.
2. United States—Social conditions—1918–1932.
3. United States—Intellectual life—20th century.
I. Title. E169.1.C583 1991
973.91′5—dc20   90-39823

973.915
CoB

c, 1

2 4 6 8 9 7 5 3 1

Printed in the United States of America
on acid-free paper

For Herminia

ACKNOWLEDGMENTS

While preparing this book, the largest debt by far of the many I incurred was to my wife, Herminia Menez Coben. She took time from her own research, writing, and teaching to assist my research and to criticize every chapter in the book.

I am extremely grateful also to William E. Leuchtenburg, who read and criticized an early draft of the manuscript. His suggestions led me to revise what I had written about many important matters. However, we still disagree about some of these. Henry F. May, who also read and criticized an early draft, helped most by urging me not to change my peculiar perspectives. Suggestions from my editor, Sheldon Meyer, improved critical portions of the manuscript. His confidence in the importance of this book sustained me throughout my work.

Others whose criticism helped me improve sections of this book include Arthur S. Link, Otis L. Graham, James H. Billington, Reinhard Bendix, Thomas S. Kuhn, Nathan Reingold, Daniel W. Howe, Joyce A. Appleby, Kathryn K. Sklar, Robert A. Hill, Gregory H. Singleton, Elizabeth M. Teague, Clyde C. Griffen, and Richard M. Abrams.

Research assistants who provided significant aid included Joyce D. Goodfriend, Leonard J. Moore, Peter Akin, Thomas A. Mertes, Emory J. Tolbert, Ellen A. Slatkin, Jan Grittelfeld, Boyd James, Eleanore Breese, Kenneth D. Rose, William Barth, Damon Woods, and Barbara Smith.

Numerous philanthropic institutions made possible research, contemplation, and writing which otherwise would have been postponed. Foremost among these was the Woodrow Wilson International Center for Scholars, which, for a calendar year, provided me with research assistants, clerical aid, intellectual stimulation, and the opportunity to use these as I chose. Assistance for this work was provided also by grants from the

John Simon Guggenheim Memorial Foundation; the Social Science Research Council; the American Philosophical Society; the Rockefeller Foundation Archives; the Herbert Hoover Presidential Library; the Center for Afro-American Studies, University of California, Los Angeles; the University of California Humanities Institute; and the Committee on Research, Academic Senate, University of California, Los Angeles.

Los Angeles, Calif.   S. C.
June 1990

CONTENTS

INTRODUCTION

The themes of this book can be viewed clearly through the eyes of one Victorian woman. She participated in the early stages of the assaults on Victorianism—by intellectuals, blacks, feminists, and dissident economic and political groups—with which this book deals. She considered her reform activities attempts to eliminate the contradictions between American ideals, such as those expressed in the Declaration of Independence, and the realities of Victorian life. The opponents she encountered resembled closely the defenders of Victorianism in the early twentieth century.

Very early in her life, Elizabeth Cady realized that Americans valued boys more than girls and that her father wished that she were a boy. She resolved to become more like a boy "and thus delight my father's heart." She learned horseback riding, advanced mathematics, Latin, and Greek and won a prize her school offered to students of Greek.

"One thought alone filled my mind after winning the prize. Now... my father will be satisfied with me." Elizabeth ran home from school and placed her award, a new Greek Testament, before her father. "There," she exclaimed, "I got it!" Her father leafed through the book, impressed. He asked her questions about the class and teacher. Obviously pleased, he kissed Elizabeth on the forehead and sighed, "Ah, you should have been a boy."[1]

Nevertheless, Elizabeth's resolve to excel at learning and to participate in physical activities continued. She declared that her resolutions served to "mold my character anew." After graduating from a seminary for females (no college in the country admitted women), she devoted a period to daily reading of her father's law, history, and fiction books. Her son and daughter wrote later that "she enjoyed that rare combination, bodily vigor and temperamental inclination to the sedentary life of the scholar."[2]

Cady joined the early nineteenth-century woman's rights movement. Because she believed that slaves suffered at least as much as women from the tyranny of the white, middle-class males who dominated America, at first she devoted most of her energy to the antislavery movement. Cady met her husband, Henry Stanton, at an antislavery meeting.

Soon after their marriage in 1840, the Stantons traveled to London, where Henry served as a delegate to an international antislavery conference. After male delegates refused to admit the female delegates, Elizabeth Cady Stanton and Lucretia Mott decided to organize the world's first woman's rights convention. It met in Seneca Falls, New York, where the Stantons lived, in July 1848. Stanton wrote the final draft of the resolutions that the convention approved, modeling them and their preamble on the Declaration of Independence.[3]

During the second half of the nineteenth century, Stanton served as the chief theorist and political leader of the woman's rights movement, including the fight for woman suffrage. She argued for cooperative housekeeping, easier divorce, and equality between husbands and wives in the home. She acted also as a leading advocate of rights for African-Americans. In addition to other efforts for that cause, she led a woman's organization which collected 400,000 signatures on a petition asking President Lincoln to free all slaves.

Stanton fought for workers' rights. She defended unpopular strikes and the idea that labor created all wealth. She served as a delegate to the third annual congress of the National Labor Union in 1868. She urged workers, blacks, and woman's rights advocates—members of the three great nineteenth-century reform movements—to join forces in a new political party. These movements, she asserted in 1868, could form "a triple power that shall speedily wrest the sceptre of government from the non-producers." Meanwhile, Stanton took care of a home and raised seven children.[4]

The three broad reform currents that Stanton joined continued into the twentieth century. So did the developing discontent of intellectuals, including Stanton, with many aspects of Victorian life.

Until her death in 1902, Stanton continually criticized American society in speeches, articles, and books, as well as in her letters and diary. In 1885, she declared that "I am weary seeing our laboring classes so wretchedly housed, fed and clothed. . . . The strikes, mobs and discontent of the people warn us that, though we neglect and forget the interests of the people, we do it at our peril." She wrote in 1887: "Of one thing men may be assured. . . . The next generation will not argue the question of equal rights [for women] with the infinite patience we have displayed during half a century." In 1899, she added: "The battle [for woman's rights] is not wholly fought until we stand equal in the church, the world of work, and have an equal code of morals for both sexes." She asked women to support the People's Party (Populists).

Stanton counted black abolitionist Frederick Douglass among her close friends. He encouraged her to present her radical resolutions to the Seneca Falls convention. He attended the meeting and spoke in favor of the woman suffrage resolution that Stanton introduced. After Douglass died, she wrote in 1897 that "I loved him as he loved me because of the indignities we both alike endured."

Stanton wrote a letter to President Theodore Roosevelt the day before she died. In it, she urged him to transform his statements in favor of woman suffrage into political action.[5]

By the 1920s, the reform movements which had preoccupied Stanton had expanded sufficiently to become clear dangers to Victorianism. Values of intellectuals shifted in the direction of Stanton's; the numbers of intellectuals multiplied, as did their financial support from publishers, philanthropic foundations, and universities. The sizable intelligentsia created by these changes attacked and weakened the intellectual foundations of Victorianism, including the justifications for racial, class, and gender hierarchies.

The migration of blacks to the North unleashed elements of black culture on white Americans. These ranged from well-developed concepts of black nationalism to jazz and dances which allegedly were conducive to immorality among whites.

A political coalition in 1924 brought together workers, farmers, Socialists, ethnic groups, intellectuals, black leaders, and many feminists. That coalition threatened Republicans enough to cause the party's vice-presidential candidate to charge continuously that it constituted a Communist effort to take over the United States.

Despite these powerful assaults, the contradictions which Stanton tried to resolve between American ideals and practice continue to be the source of major conflicts in the final decade of our century. These continuing conflicts become much more comprehensible when the essence of Victorianism—within which the contradictions are embedded—is understood.

Rebellion Against Victorianism

1

VICTORIAN CHARACTER

The home served as the vital institution of Victorian culture, incorporating functions performed by other agencies both earlier and later. Ideally, it provided men a haven from a ferociously competitive society. It gave women a well-established place in that society and assurance that they played a crucial role as wives and mothers. The physical house itself held a place in Victorian culture reminiscent of the central position for families as well as for the community of the church building in seventeenth-century Puritan New England.[1]

In the home, children received training which enabled them to develop the ideal "character" that marked a successful Victorian. "Character" connoted some different traits and nuances for females than for males, but its attainment was crucial for middle-class respectability among both sexes.[2]

William Dean Howells, born in 1837, who understood his fellow Victorians as well as anyone and who earned a reputation as a leading American realist author, in *A Modern Instance* (1882)—the novel that he considered his best—made an especially perceptive individual in that novel say:

Character is a superstition, a wretched fetish. Once a year wouldn't be too often to seize upon sinners whose blameless life has placed them above suspicion, and turn them upside down before the community, so as to show people how the smoke of the Pit had been quietly blackening their interior. That would destroy character as a cult.[3]

The most significant aspect of this statement lay not in Howells's cynical accusation about widespread hypocrisy—a common charge in any era— but in the confident assumption that readers would understand that a quality called "character" obliged Victorians who otherwise would have engaged in sinful behavior to live an outwardly blameless life.

The configuration of virtues which formed this cult of character went far toward defining an American Victorian, certainly in their hypothetical state. An analysis of hundreds of statements about character from a great variety of sources indicates that a male or female person of character was dependably self-controlled, punctual, orderly, hardworking, conscientious, sober, respectful of other Victorians' property rights, ready to postpone immediate gratification for long-term goals, pious toward a usually friendly God, a believer in the truth of the Bible, oriented strongly toward home and family, honorable in relations with other Victorians, anxious for self-improvement in a fashion which might appear compulsive to modern observers, and patriotic.[4]

However, not everyone who conformed to the Victorian ideal of character was accepted as a Victorian. The association of Victorian culture with "American" by the British-American ethnic group, which still dominated United States society between 1830 and 1890, enabled Victorians to exclude certain other ethnic groups perceived as alien from full membership in either the established culture or the nation. Blacks and American Indians, whose ancestors had lived in America longer than almost every Victorian's, some of whom exhibited most Victorian character traits, were among those regarded and treated as "foreign." So were almost all Asians, Jews, and Catholics—especially those Catholics of Irish, Italian, or Mexican descent.

❧ | ❧ | ❧

In an angry response to hostile reviews of her first novel, a romantic[5] story entitled *Moods*, which some reviewers charged made light of adultery, Louisa May Alcott vowed in her diary that her next book would have "no ideas in it, only facts, and the people shall be as ordinary as possible. . . ."[6]

Prior to publication of that subsequent volume, the author confided to her diary that if the novel succeeded, it would be because it was "not a bit sensational, but simple and true, for we [she and her family] really lived most of it."[7] *Little Women* (published in installments in 1868 and 1869) quickly became one of the best-sellers of the Victorian era. Encouraged by public acclaim and publishers' advances, Alcott repeated the formula of combining the writing skill she had been honing since an early age with her rich knowledge about Victorian youth. Americans of school age, especially girls, and many of their parents regarded her books and stories as reflections of their own lives; though the tales often were more than slightly sentimentalized to meet the tastes of the age.[8]

Alcott drew upon a diverse background to interest her readers and to understand them. She grew up in a home with three sisters, in an atmosphere that encouraged serious writing—which she began at age seven. Her father, Bronson Alcott, wrote copiously, and his close friends included Emerson, Hawthorne, Thoreau, and Margaret Fuller.[9] She benefited from "home" tests conducted by her educator-father of his theories about indoctrinating children with Victorian values in which she served as an experimental subject. Incidents in her stories showed that she had grasped the essence of success in Victorian child rearing, and the character of children in her novels was molded by techniques which resembled those in her father's books and diaries and in mid-nineteenth-century child-rearing manuals.

Alcott had at her disposal a wider knowledge about men and boys than available to her "little women." She never married, which left her free to form many acquaintances with males, at least one or two of which led to proposals of marriage that she rejected. She probably had enjoyed a high-spirited but, she claimed, "quite proper" flirtation in Italy and France for several months with a young Polish musician-composer, who served as the primary model for Laurie, the chief male character in *Little Women*. Working as a nurse in a Washington hospital for wounded soldiers during the Civil War, watching closely the development of her sisters' children, experience as a teacher and as a governess, participating as an Alcott and as a successful author in Boston's—and to a lesser extent in New York's—upper-middle-class society life, evidently equipped Alcott exceptionally well to portray in fiction a wide spectrum of America's Victorian domestic society.[10]

Alcott soon earned a reputation as the foremost chronicler of Victorian America's youthful generation. When her father returned from a speaking tour in the West, he reported that he no longer enjoyed fame chiefly as an author, educator, founder of the utopian community Fruitlands, and friend of Emerson and Thoreau. Now Bronson Alcott claimed that he found himself "adored as the grandfather of *Little Women*." Almost immediately after publication of the novel, Louisa Alcott recorded in her diary: "Reporters haunt the place to look at the authoress." Persuaded in 1870 to visit Vassar College, the most zealously academic college for females, she found herself pursued in a style associated more recently with movie stars and idolized musicians. Surrounded by most of the student body throughout her stay, she spent almost all her time signing autograph books and receiving kisses from ardent admirers. A student recalled that "A group of us took names from 'Little Women' and 'Little Men'. . . . Even today, 'Meg,' 'Amy,' and 'Laurie,' are more familiar forms of address than the true names of those members of our 'March family.' "

While attending a woman-suffrage convention in Syracuse, New York, Alcott had to be rescued from mobs of girls who chased her in the streets, tearing her clothes for souvenirs. Alcott complained in her diary that she had been "kissed to death by gushing damsels." And she protested to her diary also that "One energetic lady grasped my hand in the crowd, exclaiming, 'If you ever come to Oshkosh, your feet will not be allowed to touch the ground: you will be bourne in the arms of the people! Will you come?' 'Never,' responded Miss A., trying to look affable. . . . " After publication of her second domestic novel, *An Old-Fashioned Girl* (1870), Alcott recorded: "Trainboy going to New York put it into my lap; and when I said I didn't care for it, exclaimed with surprise, 'Bully book, ma'am! Sell a lot; better have it.' "[11]

Alcott grew increasingly sensitive to the obligations that she felt accompanied her role as chief novelist of America's youth. "Fathers and mothers tell me that they use my books as helps for themselves," she stated, "so now and again I slip in a page of instruction for them." She defended her frequent replication of adolescent slang: "I feel bound to depict my honored patrons as faithfully as my limited powers permit; otherwise I must expect the crushing criticism, 'Well, I dare say it's all very prim and proper, but it isn't a bit like us.' "[12] Alcott's attempts to represent Victorian family life authentically caused Henry James, Jr., to repent his suggestion made in criticizing her first novel that she write only about "what she has seen." Now he complained in a review of her *Eight Cousins* that her novels were *too* realistic; they undermined the traditional image and therefore the authority of parents: "Miss Alcott," he charged, "seems to have a private understanding with the youngsters she depicts, at the expense of their pastors and masters."[13]

❧ | ❧ | ❧

Henry James's fears seem largely misplaced. The central themes of Alcott's stories deal with the struggles of parents to create homes in which the basic Victorian virtues would be imparted. Alcott did depict most urban, wealthy parents unfavorably and therefore perhaps undermined their authority. She did so because these parents had fallen away from the "old fashioned" Victorian character she continued to admire. Her stories were subversive only in that she reported accurately the diminution of most Victorian girls caused by their training for limited roles, some of the price paid by Victorian males for the stunted development allowed females, and certain vital changes inexorably overtaking Victorianism.

Alcott demonstrated an awareness of tensions within Victorianism and of the changes in values and behavior brought about by such new conditions as urbanization and the materialism accompanying increased leisure time and wealth. She refused to disguise her own preference for the older virtues, including most elements of Victorian character: especially focusing one's life on the home, cooperation within the family, self-control, and the intrinsic value of hard work. She declared in the preface to *An Old-Fashioned Girl*:

> The "Old-Fashioned Girl" is not intended as a perfect model, but as a possible improvement upon the Girl of the Period, who seems sorrowfully ignorant or ashamed of the good old fashions which make women truly beautiful and honored, and, through her, render home what it should be,— a happy place, where parents and children, brothers and sisters, learn to love and know and help one another.[14]

A poignant but unstated attitude permeated the book: an awareness that in urban areas particularly, new values—and therefore a different kind of family and home—threatened to overwhelm the older Victorian virtues, then still prevalent in the predominantly rural nation as a whole. Qualities that the author considered of immense value for society's cohesion and for individual happiness appeared doomed in the fast-growing cities.

Alcott seems to have realized that she served as part of a holding action—or perhaps a counterattack—as she attempted to describe with slightly sentimentalized realism a village girl's response to modern urban life. The heroine of *An Old-Fashioned Girl*, Polly, informed her wealthy but bored Boston friend and hostess: "A little poverty would do you good Fan; just enough necessity to keep you busy till you learn how good work is; and when you once learn that, you won't complain of ennui any more."[15]

In *An Old-Fashioned Girl*, Alcott described a common result when the material rewards of work became its chief objective. Polly wondered why the Shaws, with whom she was living, were not a happier family, why they displayed frequent unkindness and impatience toward each other rather than love. Despite abundant money, they seemed more discontented than her own relatively poor but close-knit family and friends. She detected that Mr. Shaw, Fan's father, although intelligent and devoted to his family, "was a busy man, so intent on getting rich that he had no time to enjoy what he already possessed." She observed Mrs. Shaw arriving home from a visit wearing a fine costume, greeted by her younger daughter Maude, who ran to hug her affectionately. Mrs. Shaw "gathered up her lustrous silk and pushed the little girl away, saying impatiently, 'Don't touch me child, your hands are dirty.' "[16]

Not only were Mr. and Mrs. Shaw indifferent parents, but their attitudes had infected their children. Fanny's chief interests in life were expensive new clothes, fashionable plays, gossip about real or potential love affairs, and flirtations carried on chiefly to arouse approbation or jealousy among other young ladies. Six-year-old Maude, already as vain as her mother and apparently proud of the characteristic, held her doll, Alcott noted, "in a most unnatural manner." Maude and her friends commented about each others' clothes, imitating their mothers: "Was your dress imported?" asked one little girl during a party. "Yes," replied another six year old, "and it cost—oh, ever so much." Maude protested against pressure from her peers to choose "a beau." "The girls all do, and say I ought to have Fweddy Lovell; but I don't like him as well as Hawry Fishe;" however, "Hawry" evidently was reluctant to tie himself down. Mrs. Shaw added to the pressure on Maude by replying, "Oh yes, I'd have a little sweetheart, dear, it's so cunning." Soon afterward, Maude announced her "engagement" to "Fweddy" after "Hawry" declined her overtures.[17]

Although readers, over a century after the characters' creation, might share Fanny's occasional disgust with "old-fashioned" Polly, Alcott's contemporary audience admired the story and its heroine. The author reported good sales, and she claimed that after publication of the early chapters, she decided to double the novel's projected length because of "beeseeching little letters that made refusal impossible."[18] Nevertheless, Alcott understood that her (and Polly's) attachment to Victorian character and to related old-fashioned Victorian values of feminine modesty and simplicity in dress were attitudes on the wane in her society.

Even in *Little Women*, the fictionalized story of her own family, Alcott described unassuming, hardworking Meg developing an immoderate desire for luxury. In Alcott's novel, however, the values imbibed in the March home overcame the budding love of ease and luxurious possessions that wealthy friends were encouraging in the beautiful young girl. Meg married gentle John Brooke, a hardworking, talented young man, who demonstrated no evidence of a competitive drive to accumulate wealth.

Brooke, trained in accounting, found a job in the office of a man engaged in business chicanery. Although trying desperately to support his wife and young children in a middle-class fashion, Brooke refused to participate in the deception despite the offer of a greatly increased salary. "You will never get on in business with such strict principles," he was told. "I never will try to get on *without* them," he replied, and left the position for "a much harder and poorer one." Brooke died young, his friends suggesting that his end may have been hastened by overwork and constant anxiety about his family's welfare. Alcott displayed unmistakable admiration for Meg's husband and his unstained character, but she showed awareness also that he was an exceptional man in an increasingly materialistic society.[19]

Even Brooke's detractors admitted that the man had displayed character, entitling him to almost full respect despite his lack of material success. In a somewhat different fashion from the males in Alcott's stories, females, such as Meg and Polly, took part in real-life morality plays in which the strength of the individual's character was tested. The trait of self-control made it possible for individuals like Brooke to resist temptations toward those dangerous diversions which interfered with work and family obligations. Extramarital sex, idleness, alcohol, gambling, and inability to control unproductive emotions (such as anger) were among the most destructive of these. Meg surrendered a potential life of ease for what Alcott portrayed as the hard, sometimes boring task of caring for a family and home. Alcott's bourgeois men and women constantly fought their baser impulses, succumbed occasionally, felt powerful remorse, and vowed never to give in again. Loss of respectability, perhaps for one's entire family, and other harm caused loved ones had replaced God's wrath as the punishments most feared by Victorians. However, as in the case of Brooke, too strict a character in the business world could bring a family close to financial disaster and thereby also threaten respectability.

Even Mrs. March acknowledged the necessity of constant struggle with the expectation of incomplete success. That nearly ideal woman claimed that she suffered from an unquenchable temper, potentially a destructive element in family life: "I've been trying to cure it for forty years," she confessed to Jo when the girl despaired of overcoming an identical fault, "and have only succeeded in controlling it. I am angry nearly every day of my life, Jo; but I have learned not to show it; and I still hope to learn not to feel it, though it may take me another forty years to do so." Only her calm husband's example, Mrs. March explained, enabled her to exercise the degree of control she had achieved.[20]

Alcott wrote from long and arduous experience, not only with her mother's well-documented temper but also with her own. In one of her earliest diary entries, written at age nine, she confessed: "I was cross today, and I cried when I went to bed. I made good resolutions and felt better in my heart. If I only *kept* all I make, I should be the best girl in the world. But I don't, and so am very bad." In a notation beneath the entry, made when she reviewed the diary for use in a projected autobiography, Alcott wrote "(Poor little sinner! She says the same at fifty— L. M. A.)."[21] Such battles for self-improvement to the point of perfection never could be won completely. The result was perpetual stress within Alcott's Victorians and constant efforts to help friends and family members mobilize self-control to conquer their faults and cultivate their virtues.

Few children's consciences had acquired sufficient strength for adequate protection against wrongdoing. A parent's duty included the establishment of barriers between their susceptible offspring and dangerous temptations. Behind these protective walls, children could develop powers of self-discipline and restraint, foundations on which true character might be built. Whatever parents left undone, or found it impossible to accomplish, a good man or woman might still correct in the adult. Just as Mrs. March credited her husband and his example of restraint for the control she won over her temper, so Jo would owe a similar debt to her wise husband. In most cases, however, females were expected to act as the agents of cultural conformity. Victorians assumed that women "naturally" found it easier to remain virtuous and to teach purity to men—women having an innate righteousness reinforced by protection from the consequences of participation in the venal business world.

Alcott's nobler women sometimes carried out their obligations in a fashion that might seem objectionable now. Meg, first of the "little women" to marry, took advantage of her wedding day to extract from her friend Laurie, then a college student, a pledge of perpetual abstinence from alcoholic beverages. Similarly, sister Jo, in an incident recounted in Alcott's *Jo's Boys*, took on an even more ambitious project of rehabilitation and prevention of vice in young men. During a visit by two Harvard students formerly in her care when they attended the boarding school she and her husband directed (in Alcott's *Little Men* (1871)), Jo discovered signs of incipient sinfulness: they had been drinking wine, enjoying French novels and plays, and had accompanied actresses from the plays to supper. She informed the boys that "I'm going to talk to you now like a mother" and then delivered an inspirational sermon. Unless they declined altogether the company of women like the actresses and ceased drinking wine, Jo warned, they would soon be unfit for the society of "good" women; they would live in "sin and shame." Only if they avoided these "two . . . great things that curse the world and send so many men to destruction altogether" would they be able to kiss their mothers "with clean lips" and have the right to ask innocent girls to marry them. The unfortunate boys seemed chastened. In incidents like these, we can find the wellsprings of later Progressive reform efforts, such as Prohibition.[22]

Such apparently gentle but potent weapons as Jo's sermon and Meg's plea were the Victorians' chief means of obtaining conformity. Painful awareness on the transgressor's part of a loved one's disappointment and unhappiness usually worked better than direct punishment (although the latter still served as a last resort) to activate the nonconformist's Victorian conscience.

An example from Louisa May Alcott's childhood illustrates the types of child-rearing practices which produced such responses, although few parents adopted or recorded these processes so systematically. Bronson Alcott, father of Louisa and the other three models for her "little women," retains some reputation as a pedagogical innovator. When testing his educational theories on his young daughters, Alcott recorded the results in great detail. His chief object was to instill in the small children such conventional Victorian virtues as self-control, respect for others' property, and the habit of positive responses to requests from their parents. In a typical exercise aimed at achieving these objectives (recorded in his journal), he left an apple on the wardrobe in the nursery occupied by Louisa and her older sister Anna, then about two-and-a-half and four years of age respectively. Both girls, but Louisa especially, enjoyed apples inordinately.

As he left the room Alcott inquired, "Anna, should little girls take things that do not belong to them without asking their fathers and mothers?"

"No, they should not."

"Do you think you shall ever do so—take an apple, or such thing if you should see one, without asking for it?"

"No."

"And shall you, Louisa?"

"No, Father."

After dinner, Alcott found the apple core's remains on the nursery dining table. The two girls quickly confessed that after a period of restraint, they had rushed for the apple and eaten it, while telling each other that they must not.

"I was naughty," Anna acknowledged. "I *stole*, didn't I? I did not ask you, as I ought to. Shall you punish me, Father, for it?"

Alcott explained that he had left the apple intentionally as a trial. No punishment would be exacted, but he was disappointed—the most severe penalty that he could have inflicted on the two adoring young girls.

"Did you think you were doing right when you took it?" he asked his daughters.

"No," replied Anna, "my conscience told me I was not."

"Well, Anna, always mind that, and then you will do right, whether Father be by or not."

Taking the younger child on his knee, Alcott inquired, "Louisa, you ate some of the apple. Why did you take it before Father said you might have it?"

"I wanted it," she replied with a grin; then noting the expression of disapproval on her father's face, she added, "but I was naughty."

The next day Alcott left another apple on the children's wardrobe. Mrs. Alcott reported that Louisa picked it up several times, looked at it wistfully, and seemed about to bite it; but each time she stopped and said, "No. No. Father's. Me not take Father's apple. Naughty! Naughty!" By afternoon, temptation overwhelmed the two-and-a-half-year-old girl. When her mother left the room, she ravished the apple. Upon her mother's return, she exclaimed, "Me could not help it. Me *must* have it." Nevertheless, her father and mother were pleased. The child had withstood intense temptation for an entire morning and then had struggled with her developing conscience even as she yielded. Obviously, with aid from the most powerful weapon available for the purpose, manipulation through affection by a close-knit team of father and mother, Louisa's true character was emerging.[23]

Louisa May Alcott demonstrated in her novels an intuitive understanding of the psychological techniques used to nourish virtue in Victorian youngsters.[24] Yet she suffered from acute awareness that despite such intense early training, only constant internal strife thereafter enabled most Victorians to consolidate the emotional victories which built character. Alcott's own severe turmoil caused her to confide in her diary at age sixteen: "So every day is a battle, and I'm so tired I don't want to live; only it's cowardly to die till you have done something." Twenty-seven years later, at the height of Louisa's fame as a novelist, her mother— whom she had helped support with her writing—died, and she wrote: "My duty is done, and now I shall be glad to follow her."[25] Her eulogy for John Brooke in *Little Men*, delivered by his brother-in-law and dearest friend, included the comment that in order to accumulate savings for his family, Brooke "lived so plainly, denied himself so many pleasures . . . and worked so hard that I fear he shortened his good life." Describing a successful female novelist in *An Old-Fashioned Girl*, a perceptive young lady observed that she "looked sick, tired, and too early old."[26]

❣|❣|❣

Alcott's novels showed the author's sensitivity to contradictions inherent in the roles granted females by Victorian culture. Hers may be the most unambiguous fictional depiction of the cooperative form of marriage urged by most American marriage manuals after mid-century. Yet Alcott also described the thwarting of emotional and intellectual growth in girls expected to carry heavy responsibilities later as partners in marriage and child rearing.

Reality undoubtedly differed from the ideal even more often than it did in Alcott's tales, but other evidence indicates that, as usual, she captured the essence of contemporary tendencies. The advice about marriage given Meg, first of her daughters to marry, by Mrs. March in *Little Women* coincides with that given by the most popular contemporary manuals. Mrs. March suggested: "Don't shut him out of the nursery, but teach him how to help in it. His place is there as well as yours, and the children need him; let him feel that he has a part to do, and he will do it gladly and faithfully, and it will be better for you all." Meg received counsel also to take greater interest in her husband's affairs. When Meg continued to sound disconsolate about her marriage, her mother reassured her further. "That is the secret of our home happiness: he does not let business wean him from the little cares and duties that affect us all, and I try not to let domestic worries destroy my interest in his pursuits. Each do our part alone in many things, but at home we work together always." Finally Meg took her mother's advice, and her marriage flowered even more than in its early years. Some scholars have explored the place of men in Victorian culture without sufficient consideration of references like Alcott's to "those sacred words, husband and father."[27]

However, Alcott's ideal cooperative home did not resemble a commune, with every individual free to choose among all possible roles. When Meg counseled her own son indirectly by praising one of his schoolmates, she declared, "Now there's a girl after my own heart. Pretty, well-bred, educated and yet domestic, a real companion as well as a helpmate for some good and intelligent man."[28] These companions and helpmates of both sexes were trained for sharply different lives based largely on gender—one almost entirely domestic, the other concentrating on affairs outside the home. In superior marriages, they came together as partners within the confines of the family, but as partners with separate and prescribed patterns of behavior. Also, because of their early training for these different behavior patterns, neither men nor women were prepared for certain facets of the cooperation in marriage urged upon them.

One of the period's most widely read books of etiquette and marital advice, published in Chicago during 1873 and popular throughout the country, offered advice to readers similar to that given by Mrs. March. The author, Thomas E. Hill, suggested that marriage partners display the utmost affection and tact in every matter, thus creating an atmosphere conducive to a cooperative marriage: "Consult and advise together in all that comes within the sphere of each individually," he urged. Hill instructed men: "Let your wife understand fully your business. In nearly every case she will be found a most valuable adviser when she understands all your circumstances." The manual warned, "Do not be dictatorial in the family circle. The home is the wife's province. . . . You would not expect her to come to your shop, your office, your store or your farm, to give orders how your work should be conducted. . . . " Finally, the author admonished husbands: "Endeavor to so regulate your household affairs that all the faculties of the mind shall have due cultivation. . . . The wife should not be required to lead a life of drudgery. . . . The good husband will so control his business that he may be able to accompany his wife to various places of amusement and entertainment. Thus the intellectual will be provided for, and the social qualities be kept continually exercised."[29]

Catharine Beecher and her sister Harriet Beecher Stowe, in their volume of advice, *The American Woman's Home* (1869), on the "principles of domestic science," declared in a related spirit:

> It is far more needful for children that a father should attend to the formation of their character and habits, and end in developing their social, intellectual and moral nature, than it is that he should earn money to furnish them with handsome clothes and a variety of tempting food.[30]

Beecher and Stowe understood that reality appeared to contradict their opinions about the crucial importance of a homemaker's duties. In *The American Woman's Home*, they acknowledged: "It is generally assumed and almost as generally conceded, that a housekeeper's cares are contracted and trivial; and that the proper discharge of her duties demands far less expansion of mind and vigor of intellect than the pursuits of the other sex." In addition to urging appreciation of the man's role as father, Beecher and Stowe attempted to reinforce most women's satisfaction with their work in the home. "She who is the mother and housekeeper in a large family," they declared, "is the sovereign of an empire, demanding more varied cares, and involving more difficult duties, than are really exacted of her who wears a crown and professedly regulates the interests of the greatest nation on earth [that is, Queen Victoria]." Such statements found an already persuaded audience, largely because most middle-class women, who had thoroughly assimilated Victorian ideals of character and who understood the distinctions between male and female character, bore primary responsibility for instilling this crucial system of characteristics in their children.[31]

William Dean Howells, born only five years after Alcott and reared in small Ohio towns, described these Victorian marriage relationships from a Victorian male's perspective. In *A Modern Instance*, he declared that the female around whom most of the novel revolved entered into her husband's business affairs "with the keen half-intelligence which characterizes a woman's participation in business." Her activity was determined by a female's superior intuition and concern with personal relationships rather than a male's calculation of a situation and its probable effects: "Whatever could be divined, she was quickly mistress of; [but] she failed to follow him in matters of political detail, or of general effect; she could not be dispassionate or impartial; his relation to any enterprise was more important than anything else about it."[32] Howells captured also the ultimate incompatibility between the Victorian woman in the home and the man forced to be "sensible" if he wished to support his family and to take part effectively in community affairs. Most men could not afford to indulge in John Brooke's ethical standards, and because of early training as tough competitors, as well as work experience, most men did not want to do so. In a moment of reverie about her husband, who acted as an attorney of lofty morality when judging the actions of others, a wife in *A Modern Instance* thought: "He seemed to tell her everything, and to be greatly ruled by her advice, especially in matters of business; but she could not help observing that he often kept matters involving certain moral questions from her till the moment for deciding them was past." When she accused him of this fault, he confessed that she was right "but defended himself by saying that he was afraid her conscience might sway him against his judgment."[33]

Members of the two sexes received different socialization in important respects. Girls were specifically trained to preserve the sanctity of the Victorian home, while boys were prepared for business and political competition. As a result, girls, who later would bear primary responsibility for rearing families and for the smooth functioning of households, did not receive adequate physical or emotional preparation for those jobs. Instead, as in Alcott's stories, girls learned to prize themselves for their beauty, passivity relative to males, and skills most useful for manipulating men into marriage.

Almost all the young women in Alcott's tales seemed to enjoy their position as barterable property, with the attendant gossip about the relative advantages of their own and their friends' possible matches. One of the few exceptions, Meg, accustomed to treatment as a mature and talented individual in the March home, received a shock when she discovered accidentally that as a girl of marriageable age she was regarded by those outside her home as a sort of commodity and that the special abilities she had developed held little value in the marriage marketplace.[34]

From an early age, boys were encouraged by parents and teachers to engage in active play, while girls were directed toward more quiet activities. Louisa May Alcott, a sturdy six-footer who loved running and rough play throughout her life and even dressed as a boy at every opportunity when young, inserted propaganda in her stories against the conventional limitations on girls' activities; but she also reported the contemporary situation accurately. A high proportion of the author's heroines—Jo in *Little Women* and *Little Men*, Polly in *An Old-Fashioned Girl*, Rose in *Eight Cousins* and *Rose in Bloom*, Jill in *Jack and Jill*, and Nan in *Jo's Boys*—tried unsuccessfully to break the established pattern. Only Jo and Nan would not respond to pressure for conformity, and even they recognized their behavior as unwomanly. For example, at age sixteen, Jo finished running a race against her friend Laurie just as her older sister Meg appeared, who then chastized her: "You have been running Jo; how could you? When will you stop such romping ways?" In reply, Jo pleaded: "Don't try to make me grow up before my time Meg . . . ; let me be a little girl as long as I can."[35]

After marriage, one or more servants usually lightened the tasks of middle-class Victorian girls who had been consistently discouraged from physical preparation for the arduous tasks of homekeeping and child rearing. In the upper middle class, as in the case of Fanny's mother, Mrs. Shaw, practically all physical duties except stepping in and out of a carriage and dancing were carried on by servants. Beecher and Stowe regretted the consequences:

> Our land is now full of motorpathetic institutions to which women are sent at a great expense to have hired operators stretch and exercise their inactive muscles. They lie for hours to have their feet twigged, their arms flexed,

and all the different muscles of the body worked for them because they are
so flacid and torpid. . . .

Beecher and Stowe recommended women's traditional types of exercise
as a remedy: "sweeping, sewing, dusting, ironing. . . . Our grandmothers
in a week went over every movement that any gymnast has invented, and
went over them to some productive purpose too." Howells observed in
1872 that Americans seemed to be turning their society into a hospital for
invalid women.[36]

A tacit understanding also permitted a double standard of premarital
sexual morality. Although women such as Jo, members of female reform
societies, and males who took their moral precepts seriously resisted this,
the differences in sexual training, degree of repression, and, consequently,
in sexual activity continued. The large number of mostly lower-class
female prostitutes in American as well as in European Victorian cities
served as one of the landmarks of the age.[37]

Attempting to recapture for readers in the 1930s his impressions of
Wilmington, Delaware, during his adolescence in the 1880s and early
1890s, Henry Seidel Canby, editor of the *Saturday Review of Literature* and
professor of literature at Yale, devoted much of his attention in his memoir
The Age of Confidence to the lives of parents and grandparents—the generations described by Alcott and Howells. His account is in remarkable
accord with Alcott's portrayal of Victorian New England and with Howells's depictions of eastern and midwestern businessmen, their families,
acquaintances, and friends. Canby found that young men and women in
his generation enjoyed greater freedom than their predecessors for close
premarital friendships; but the double standard remained in practice. Boys
learned early that society would allow them to take sexual pleasure from
prostitutes and "easy women." When choosing a wife however, Canby
observed, "According to the perhaps somewhat naive belief held in my
town, she could not, if she were the right girl, be won by sexual appeal
alone. If she was so won, she was not the right girl. And some went so
far as to put it to the test!" Some responsibility for developing these
"natural" differences between aggressive males and passive, home-oriented
females fell partly upon the formal education system in which boys and
girls received different treatment and opportunities, but primary responsibility still rested on the heavily burdened home.[38]

Alcott recorded, and regretted, some consequences of these discrep-
ancies between the roles of males and females in Victorian culture. Before
marriage, American girls enjoyed an independence and degree of freedom
unknown in virtually any other civilization—except in the area of sexual

relations. These same young ladies married young and usually bore children within a year or two. "Whether they like it or not," Alcott observed,
"they are virtually put upon the shelf as soon as the wedding excitement
is over, and most of them might exclaim, as did a very pretty woman the
other day, 'I am as handsome as ever, but no one takes any notice of me
because I'm married.' "[39]

Canby recalled the Victorian life cycle as "A golden age of free companionship for youth, but for the middle-aged it drew the cork and let
the wine flatten. The tone, the touch, the ingredient that was lacking in
our society for those past their twenties was so subtle, so formless, that
I despair of getting it accurately into words..." He summarized his
impressions, however, by stating: "We were restless in our genial social
life because we had tacitly agreed that except in sin or in the reticence of
marriage, sexual desires [among middle-class women] did not exist. And
hence that subtle interpretation of the special knowledge of each which
can make an ideal glow between a man and a woman, was frozen at the
source of its rays." In that busy age, men found many satisfying topics
to discuss among themselves, Canby maintained, but "Women past their
twenties, or married, suffered dumbly from an imagination that made
them sexless, because they did not know what was wrong and would not
have admitted the truth if it had been told to them. But men suffered too
by a kind of vivacious dullness which was the note of the period."[40]

Even in the most companionate marriage depicted in his novels (that of
Basil and Isabel March in *A Hazard of New Fortunes*), Howells subtly
implied a similar development. He described the husband as thinking that
some of the "pretty, feminine inconsistencies and trepidations, which had
once charmed him in his wife," now seemed "very like those of less
interesting older women." This perception, Howells wrote, "moved him
with a kind of pathos, but he felt the result hindering and vexatious."[41]

Nevertheless, most observers cited in this chapter discerned something
admirable about American Victorian marriages and the homes they created. In Alcott's stories, in Canby's memoir, in most accounts by Howells
of Victorian marriages, and according to Nancy F. Cott's summary of the
recent historical literature dealing with Victorian women, males and females had acquired a sure sense of their gender-determined roles which
enabled them to act with confidence as husbands and wives.[42] This result
of gender stereotyping left serious casualties, of course. In some cases,
severe anxiety occurred when unusual home training, or innate tendencies,
caused conflicts between temperament and prescribed gender roles. Years
of respectful friendship among unmarried boys and girls, free from sexual
storms, may have left some sexual strangers after their marriage cere-

monies. Nevertheless, the bulk of available evidence indicates that this experience also encouraged a high degree of enduring friendly affection among most married couples.

In Wilmington, as much as in Alcott's New England, existence revolved around the home, "the most impressive experience in life," Canby declared. Home could be "profoundly dull," and the "weight of routine, oppressive," he acknowledged. However,

It had a quality which we have lost. We complain today of the routine of mechanical processes, yet routine in itself is very persuasive to the spirit, and has attributes of both a tonic and a drug. There was a rhythm in the pre-automobile home that is entirely broken now and whose loss is perhaps the exactest index of the decline of confidence in our environment.

Our houses moved with felt rhythms, not set, nor identical, yet so sensible that what one felt first in a strange home was the tempo of life there. We were away for brief intervals only, at home long enough to be harmonized, and even the heads of families, whose working hours were incredible in their length, seemed never to lose their conditioning by the home. If business and the home lived by different ethical standards, as was commonly said, it may be because the worker was a different man outside the rhythm of the house. And women lived almost exclusively within.[43]

This domestic rhythm and the confidence it engendered were maintained, Canby believed, only because both parents sacrificed their youth to their children: "When children came, young men and women gave up the right to be young and assumed the responsibility for a home with no reservations, physical or mental. They did it well or badly, but with no more protest than a tadpole makes in becoming a frog. . . . And the children felt this—it would be too much to say that they knew it." Among the consequences was a respect among children for their parents, even when younger family members held ideas drastically different from their elders.

Canby's account of the conditioning achieved in the Victorian home aids our understanding of the powerful attachment to their communities that a high proportion of Americans retained into the twentieth century. "You belonged," Canby declared. Middle-class youngsters knew that they possessed a secure position in their families and that a secure place in the community awaited them: "There has been no such certainty in American life since." He admitted that

Our confidence was illusion, but like most illusions it had many of the benefits of a fact. Because of our confidence there were values in living . . . which are simply unpurchaseable now. . . . We can put our children on wheels to see the world, but we cannot give them the kind of home that any town provided. . . . [44]

Contemporary writers noted frequently, and often with fervor, that the character of the nation's future businessmen, statesmen, soldiers, and scholars, as well as of the mothers who would shape following generations, was being formed in the country's homes, principally by the female custodians of Victorianism's highest values. Paeans to that effect, mostly written by men, contained notes of caution against disturbing this sensitive arrangement, suggesting some fear of potential discontent or rebellion. Female writers agreed, except for a handful of feminists. Enough of these female authors concentrated so passionately upon woman's *duty* to exert her superior moral influence for society's benefit, not only as wife and mother but also as teacher, nurse, and philanthropist, to suggest a conscious attempt to extend women's authority. Radical feminists carried the argument further. Should not morally superior females occupy the highest positions of power in a Christian democracy? However, such extreme views threatened more modest advances and received only slight open support. [45]

Beecher and Stowe's statement of the popular argument for augmenting the stature and role of the home's preeminent member was a classic of the type. They dedicated their manual "To the Women of America in whose hands rest the real destinies of the Republic, as moulded by the early training and preserved amid the maturer influence of home. . . . " Such appreciations helped females ease their way into positions requiring skills related to those exercised in the home: as teachers and nurses, especially. Women virtually took over those professions during the late nineteenth century, with an accompanying decrease in salary for the work relative to other professions. [46]

Alcott, too, envisioned a new but limited enlargement of women's position. She reserved special praise for a young lady—part of a new race of female pioneers Alcott described in the 1880s—who refused to be deterred by the sexual bigotry of America's physicians, which closed almost all medical schools and hospital internships to women. The girl studied for four years in London, Paris, and Prussia, fortunately able to pay for private lessons "when the doors of public institutions were shut in her face because she was a woman." After completing her training, she found a post as resident physician in an American hospital for women. Then she developed a private practice. Unwilling either to allow marriage to interfere with her career or to miss the joys of motherhood, the physician adopted a daughter. Alcott expressed pride that the young woman had "so quietly and persistently carried out the plan of her life, undaunted by prejudice, hard work, or the solitary lot she chose."[47] It should be noted, however, that Alcott also praised this woman for refusing to surrender her feminine qualities during her struggle. Alcott had performed many of a physician's duties when she served as a wartime nurse, and she had described these duties as extensions of those already exercised by women in the home.[48]

Alcott disclosed her fullest hopes for new relations between men and women when she resumed the story of Polly in *An Old-Fashioned Girl*. She returned the young lady, now twenty years of age, to Boston, installed her in a rented room of her own, and gave her a job as a music teacher. She also awarded Polly new female friends, almost all of whom supported themselves. One worked as an engraver; and her roommate, as a sculptor. The latter was completing a large statue when Polly brought Fanny to the girls' studio. The great clay figure had been created as a result of a recent conversation about what women should be, during which the artist had promised to illustrate her idea—clearly Alcott's also—of "the coming woman."

> There she is . . . , bigger, lovelier, and more imposing than any we see nowadays; and at the same time she is a true woman. See what a fine forehead, yet the mouth is both firm and tender, as if it could say strong, wise things, as well as teach children and kiss babies . . . [She is to be] strong-minded, strong-hearted, strong-souled, and strong-bodied; that is why I made her larger than the miserable, punched-up woman of our day. Strength and beauty must go together. Don't you think these broad shoulders can bear burdens without breaking down, these hands work well, these eyes see clearly, and these lips do something besides simper and gossip.

Certain problems remained to be resolved by these independent girls. Marriage threatened the close friendship of the two artists, for the engraver was engaged to be married in the spring. Alcott's solution did not appear to hold high promise of permanence. The sculptress was to live with the newlyweds. A further possibility included marriage of the second artist. Children were not discussed. Also, the female author, who seemed to be based on Alcott herself, did not present an entirely optimistic vision of the "coming woman's" future. Fanny, looking at her closely, observed on the writer's face evidence of the heavy price women paid for a little success and money.[49]

Catharine Beecher and Louisa May Alcott did not serve as leaders in their era's radical feminist movement, though Alcott considered herself a member of that movement. They might better be characterized as leaders in an effort to define Victorian family life for contemporary readers and to expand the role of its female members. Yet when discussing the traditional role of females outside the home, Beecher and Alcott expressed protest almost as deep, though not so consistent, as that of militants like Susan B. Anthony, Lucretia Mott, and Elizabeth Cady Stanton. The fact that commentators on Victorianism such as Beecher and Alcott objected so strongly against restraints placed on women indicates that broad dissatisfaction existed, ready to be tapped. Their continued devotion to Victorian ideals of femininity and domesticity, however, suggests the limitations of that dissatisfaction and helps explain why Anthony, Stanton, Mott, and their allies enjoyed so little success when they demanded real and full equality in and out of the home for women.[50]

Furthermore, the success of moral arguments like Alcott's or Beecher's for enlarging woman's occupational sphere meant that the extension could not easily encompass positions obliging females to engage in those activities that lowered the moral stature of Victorian men. Places as entrepreneurs and executives in highly competitive industries, soldiers, United States senators, or aggressors in sexual relations, for example, ordinarily remained the prerogatives during the nineteenth century of the admittedly less-pure sex.

$$\maltese \mid \maltese \mid \maltese$$

Alcott and Howells both understood the price exacted from males as they attempted to live up to their ordained roles. For instance, boys were expected to express tender emotions much less readily than girls, and displays of such feelings were apt to be regarded as unmanly. Warned that blindness threatened him, sixteen-year-old Mac, in Alcott's *Eight Cousins*, barely stifled a sob. His friend Rose ran to the sofa on which he lay, knelt, and spoke "with the motherly sort of tenderness girls feel for any sorrowing creature." Mac "felt her sympathy, but, being a boy, did not thank her for it. . . . " His greatest fear, possibly excepting the blindness, prompted him to plead: "Don't you tell the other fellows that I made a baby of myself, will you?" After Mrs. March persuaded Meg to let her husband care for their young children occasionally, Alcott described him as treating their infant son with "womanly patience."[51]

Boys were expected to understand from an early age that at some point in the future the welfare of a family—a devoted wife and trusting children—would depend on their success at earning money in a highly competitive society; no task for a "baby" or for an individual with womanly traits (unless, of course, he had inherited a great deal of money). In Howells's *The Rise of Silas Lapham*, the self-made millionaire Lapham observed a young Boston dilettante of whom his daughters were fond and commented, "I like to see a man *act* like a man. I don't like to see him taken care of like a young lady." He declared about the same person: "I could make a man of that fellow, if I had him in the business with me. There's stuff in him." Another father, an attorney, unhappy with the economic situation of his daughter's fiancé, asserted in *A Modern Instance* that "editing a newspaper ain't any work for a *man*. It's all well enough as long as he's single, but when he's got a wife to look after, he'd better get down to *work*." Another self-made millionaire in Howells's *A Hazard of New Fortunes* practically bought his son a respectable and demanding executive position because "he can't bear to have his boy hanging round the house doing nothing, like as if he was a girl." Howells's stories contain a great deal of representative evidence that respect for Victorian males was contingent in large part on evidence of success in their society's economic warfare.[52]

Training of boys in "manliness" supplemented other values connected with character to produce the archetypal stern and diligent Victorian businessman. These businessmen set the standard for what a man should be. The necessities of business often created circumstances in which the actions required for success conflicted with domestic values. A recurrent theme in Howells's novels about businessmen is the perplexed reaction of wives faced with evidence of their husbands' apparently unethical behavior in business. In almost every case, they grasped desperately at any excuse offered to explain that behavior in a fashion that would allow them to forgive and forget. The author, March, in Howells's *A Hazard of New Fortunes*, described the mean qualities of a successful businessman and commented to his wife, "I am not very proud when I realize that such a man and his experience are the ideal of most Americans. I rather think they came near being mine, once." His wife protested that the suggestion of even such a possibility in himself was mistaken.[53]

If a business opponent or employee seemed an outsider, especially a racial inferior, Victorian men could more easily take advantage of the distinction they had been trained to make between the values connected with the home and those of the business world. This separation of cherished values from certain areas of behavior resembled the fashion in which the pure girls one married were divided from what Canby referred to as the "chippies" with whom one played unscrupulously. It resembled also the ease with which the Victorian conscience could be put aside when men dealt with foreign "heathens" in imperialistic ventures.

❡|❡|❡

The Victorian synthesis depended heavily upon faith in a higher being. By 1870, he asked of his white Protestant chosen people only that they believe in him and in his Bible and that they live virtuously according to his laws, which bore a remarkable resemblance to the values already described as those imbued in the Victorian home.[54] The terrible God of the Puritans, always ready to punish sinners with a vengeance, no longer remained a popular conception.

In exchange for virtuous behavior and unquestioning faith, a friendly God eased the worst burdens of his children. When gentle Beth died at the age of twenty in *Little Women*, her merciful God relieved both the girl's pain and the family's grief. As Alcott described it, the transition to death seemed part of a natural and peaceful cycle: "Beth . . . , like a tired but trustful child, clung to the hands that had led her all her life, as father and mother guided her tenderly through the Valley of the Shadow, and gave her up to God." Thereafter, the family found solace in the belief that Beth remained with them spiritually, watching all that they did, and that eventually they all would join her in a better world.[55]

Later, another extraordinarily virtuous person, Meg's beloved husband John Brooke, failed to survive a sudden illness. Jo wondered how Meg, even on the day of the funeral, retained "the same beautiful serenity" that had shone in her face as a bride ten years before. "The sweet resignation of a truly pious soul made her presence a consolation to those who came to comfort her." Again, a faithful Victorian family was consoled by certainty that their deceased loved one continued to exist among them in spirit. John and Meg's son Demi, after nights of sobbing in his bed "I want my father! Oh, I want my father!" slowly came to feel that his father was not lost, "only invisible for a while, and sure to be found again, well and strong and fond as ever," although it would be many years before they met. This belief, the author observed, "led him unconsciously, through a tender longing for the father whom he had seen to a childlike trust in the father whom he had not seen. Both were in heaven, and he prayed to both, trying to be good for love of them."[56]

Alcott intentionally shifted the balance in loyalties to family members and to God when she described the attitude toward God of the older generation, represented by Mrs. March, whose affection for her husband equaled the love of Demi for his father. When Jo asked her mother how she bore up so well when her loving husband was absent during the Civil War, the bulwark of the family replied,

> It is because I have a better friend even than father, to comfort and sustain me. . . . The more you love and trust Him, the nearer you will feel to Him, and the less you will depend on human power and wisdom. His love and care never tire or change, can never be taken from you, but may become a source of lifelong peace, happiness and strength.[57]

A scholar who studied New England Puritan attitudes toward death concluded:

> Like the Puritan child, the child of the Romantic and Victorian eras was instructed to spend a good deal of time thinking about death. But the similarity . . . ends there. The child of the Puritan was told to "think how it will be on a deathbed"; to consider the terrors of certain separation from and even betrayal by, parents and loved ones; and to imagine what his well-deserved torments in Hell would be like. The instruction of the nineteenth-century child involved the precise opposite of all this. . . . Eternal and heavenly reunion [with family members] was stressed. . . . Indeed, instead of death a new life was emphasized—death as a lonely finality or a grim eternity of torment was simply willed out of existence.[58]

It should not be difficult for modern Americans to understand the long attractiveness to Victorians of a family whose members wished for union throughout eternity and of a God with whom they wanted and expected a close eternal relationship. What else but fierce resistance could be expected from Victorians toward those who attempted to tamper with that united family and that benign religion?

Domestic values interfered in practice only slightly with ruthlessness in economic affairs. The Victorian conscience was appeased by knowledge that God wanted production in industry and on fertile land increased and the accepted virtues spread throughout the continent—indeed, the world—by those strong enough to do his will. A significant proportion of the incredible confidence Americans (and other Western peoples) demonstrated in exploiting resources and "heathens" derived from their belief that they carried out the wishes of their merciful Lord. In this society, ruthless oil-refining magnate John D. Rockefeller, Sr., taught Baptist Sunday school; the king of railroad-stock manipulators, Daniel Drew, endowed a Methodist theological seminary that still bears his name; and international financial buccaneer J. Pierpont Morgan frequently devoted hours of his working day to saying prayers and singing hymns at St. George's Episcopal Church in New York City.[59]

The same Lord who promised true believers reunion in death with their loved ones also condemned as sinful any behavior that might injure the Victorian family—such as fornication or drunkenness. When people outside of white Protestant congregations engaged in such behavior, they gave evidence to Victorians of the sinfulness to which disbelief led. God honored Victorians above all others, appreciated their hard work and their efforts to be virtuous and to improve themselves, but he understood the necessity for occasional unscrupulous behavior in the interests of the sacred home, religion, or nation, and showed his approval by providing material wealth and power for his followers.

However, starting late in the nineteenth century, intellectual challenges to established dogma often received a warm reception, particularly within the younger generations and among intellectuals who had learned to value scientific evidence above religious beliefs.[60] Howells, a professed agnostic, nevertheless struggled—and suffered—with the problem of religious belief throughout his adult life, illustrating the conflicts within Victorian intellectuals. Kenneth S. Lynn asserted that when Howells's mother, whom he adored, died in 1868, "religious issues took on a new urgency for him." Throughout the 1870s, according to Lynn, Howells "continued to reveal, by the anger he generated at its apostles, how badly he himself was shaken by the new science," especially Darwinian biology.[61] Howells demonstrated empathy in his novels for those who agonized over contemporary intellectual currents of disbelief until tension overcame them and they returned to their religion. In *A Modern Instance*, he described a young minister who previously had thrown off all religious creeds:

> He freely granted that he had not reasoned back to his old faith; he had fled to it as a city of refuge. His unbelief had been helped, and he no longer suffered himself to doubt; he did not ask if the truth was here or there, any more; he only knew that he could not find it for himself, and he rested in his inherent belief. He accepted everything; if he took one jot or tittle away from the Book, the curse of doubt was on him. He had known the terrors of the law, and he preached them to his people; he had known the Divine mercy, and he also preached that.[62]

Evangelical Protestantism, a strong component of Victorianism at the height of its influence, retained its hold on a large proportion of those who continued their belief in the other Victorian virtues. Religion became a rallying point for the defense of Victorianism during the 1920s. A large part of the staying power of Victorian religious ideas, however, emanated from the association of Protestantism with the emotions tied to the Victorian home and cohesive community of homes, which also seemed besieged in the 1920s.[63]

❢|❢|❢

Victorianism in the United States was basically the culture of an ethnic and religious group: a confederation of Protestants of British-American descent. Gregory H. Singleton has shown most clearly how the consociation which united various Protestant denominations that had British origins helped perpetuate Anglo-American social and political dominance in the United States and maintained the prominence of that group's cultural values.[64] The high degree of eventual assimilation of Victorian values by nineteenth-century immigrant groups from virtually every part of Europe, and by middle class African-Americans, assisted the conscious effort by Anglo-American Protestants to retain cultural and economic dominance.[65]

The largely British-American Victorians received a rich heritage of ethnic and religious bigotry from their forebears. The early colonists considered blacks barely human. According to most evidence, in the mid-nineteenth century this attitude remained a common one, and perhaps regard for blacks as people had deteriorated even further. Although nineteenth-century English and American Victorians granted the possibility of progress to inferior races, most Victorians set limits on that possibility for those of African descent; and soon late nineteenth- and early twentieth-century science produced both evidence and theories verifying that the majority of Victorians was correct. The Victorians established the late nineteenth-century color bar which separated them from blacks, Asians, and American Indians and embedded this concept and the social structures it supported deeply into Victorian culture.[66]

Hostility to Catholics also reached far back into English and American colonial history. Again, a sizable literature describes how Victorians rationalized and systematized these attitudes.[67] Lyman Beecher, a representative early Victorian American, after helping to inflame public opinion in the East against an alleged Catholic conspiracy threatening American institutions and traditions, successfully aided the effort to organize the West against this menace. Beecher issued one of the quintessential expressions of Victorian anti-Catholicism, *A Plea for the West*, in 1835. These ideas reverberated through the potent Know-Nothing movement which disturbed the established political-party system in the early 1850s, the American Protective Association in the 1890s, the Prohibition movement, the Ku Klux Klan of the 1920s, and a large portion of the immigration-restriction movement which finally achieved success during the 1920s. Beecher warned Victorian Americans against the rapid influx of certain foreign immigrants who were "unacquainted with our institutions, unaccustomed to self-government, inaccessible to our education, and easily acceptable to prepossession, and inveterate credulity and intrigue, and easily embodied and wielded by sinister design."[68] Such fears were exacerbated by the huge immigration of "wild" Irish victims of famine, which began in the late 1840s. The widely noted Irish affinity for alcohol and alleged disinterest in their homes, added to their loyalty to a foreign pope and their insistence upon educating their children in a Catholic school system, earned them a status in some areas below those of blacks or Asians.

Blacks seldom appeared in Alcott's stories, except occasionally as domestic servants. However, among the first students in the school started by Jo and her husband, Professor Friedrich Bhaer, in *Little Women* was "a merry little quadroon, who could not be taken in elsewhere." Townspeople predicted "that his admission would ruin the school."[69] Alcott did not find it necessary to explain why the boy was not welcome elsewhere or why the presence of this lad should have caused such forebodings. Her statements serve, however, as a commentary on attitudes toward blacks in relatively tolerant rural New England.

The Irish presented a far more serious threat than did blacks (over 90 percent of whom lived in the South) to northern cultural coherence, and in Alcott's stories, they were objects of blatant animosity. Alcott's most vicious creation, and the only developed Irish character in her stories, was Pat, a red-headed servant in *Under the Lilacs*. He came on the scene when asked by his employer to take a twelve-year-old orphan, Ben Brown, to the cows he had just been hired to drive to and from their pasture. Pat responded with a variety of English in which he was obsequious to his master and rude to Ben: "Yis, your honor. Come out o' this b'y, till I show ye the bastes." Alcott informs us that "Pat, who made a great show of respect for Duke [his employer's horse] in public, kicked him brutally in private." Pat gave further evidence that he belonged to a slightly different species than Alcott's other characters. He scowled, grumbled, displayed a sneaking greediness, threatened to whip Ben, and showed no redeeming qualities.[70]

Canby described remarkably similar attitudes in border-state Wilmington—though there the social shackles on blacks and Irish Catholics seemed more equal. Blacks constituted a distinct caste within the lower class. In the border-state city, as in New England, this peculiar role could prove advantageous, although it did not permit movement into the respectable white middle class or, with few exceptions, into the white lower class. Because of the large number of blacks and a paternalistic heritage toward them with a history reaching deep into the colonial period, black servants and their affluent white employers enjoyed a symbiotic relationship, which the latter believed was treasured by most members of both groups. After describing the city's unskilled labor force, Canby continued:

> The Negroes were different. We all had Negro "waiters" in our houses, who were good friends to boys. They would steal little things and lie, but in important matters they could be trusted. They sang spirituals while they polished the knives in the pantry, and only ha-ha-ed when a watermelon rind found a mark in the wool. Their wives, who did the washing, helped when we had company, filling the kitchens with chuckles when they came. They were part of us, moulded to our needs, a powerful element in that easy good humor which ran all around the town. When they were sick or destitute we took care of them if they were our darkies, but of course what they thought, if they thought, and what they wanted, if they wanted more than we gave them, was not significant.[71]

As in Alcott's New England, the Irish seemed to constitute a more direct cultural menace. Foreign in speech, manner, and appearance, poor, almost all Catholic, frequently educated in parochial schools, organized into juvenile gangs and adult political clubs, the Irish suffered hatred which they vigorously returned. "The fighting word with us," Canby recalled, "was not 'liar' or 'bastard,' but 'mick.' " Canby fondly remembered walking to school along quiet shaded streets, but at a point in the daily trip, peace and quiet ended: "Then came the Catholics. There was a school of them at Sixth Street . . . and they had to be passed before you reached safety and the gates of our school. . . . The best way was to butt through them in the new football fashion." The Irish, Canby perceived, helped verify and vitalize the values taught to white, Protestant children at home and school. "The micks had no code. They put stones in their snowballs, which was unethical, and jumped on a small boy. . . . They spat in faces and kicked below the belt. . . . They were the evil, the disorganizing principle, which roused the opposite in us, and made us believe that there was something real in the precepts of our elders which usually droned above our heads."

Occasionally the "micks" had to be taught a lesson, and the intrinsic Victorian superiority reaffirmed, Canby remembered:

> We would assemble the fighting strength of the neighborhood and drive the micks into their school yard . . . ; or we would burst like a storm upon the

massed Catholics and send them scurrying behind fluttering sisters who came to rescue. . . . No relations but combat were possible or thought of between our gangs and the micks. . . . They were still the alien, and had to be shown their place. But this was America; if they would adopt our manners (such was our arrogance) we would tolerate them.[72]

Canby regarded these as boys' wars, yet he sensed the relationships between them and wider Victorian attitudes of adults in Wilmington. He observed: "The Irish laborers would stagger home drunk on Saturday nights through our streets, hugging the maple trees and talking to themselves, and that was ludicrous with a touch of horror. And they were Catholics, which put them still further out of our world." Unlike blacks, "they did not speak our language, even the servant girls who were all Irish, even though it was an English that they used. They had their own life, and it never occurred to us to think of that life as part of ours."

The Irish did not constitute the entire unskilled labor force in Canby's Wilmington. Joining blacks and some unlucky white Protestant Americans in the bottom social and economic strata were Greeks, who Canby associated with fruit stands; and Italians, associated with railroad construction work. Whatever the origins of this "slave world of laborers," Canby declared, "no one ever went up or down between Us and them." Unlike the white Protestant "plain people," who had assimilated the Victorian culture, "they never came back with new clothes and different manners. If they moved it was always in their own world, and if their children escaped, it was not in our town."[73] Yet political orators, teachers, and school books in Wilmington, as elsewhere in the United States, described America proudly as the land of opportunity for all.[74]

Canby's recollections about the relationship between race, ethnicity, and economic class correspond not only to Alcott's and Howells's but also to William Edward Burghart Du Bois's. Du Bois was born in February 1868 in Great Barrington, a small town in western Massachusetts where he grew to adolescence. The foremost black intellectual of his and perhaps of any generation in the United States, a fine professional sociologist and historian, he recorded in autobiographical volumes his early impressions of racial and class differences. In one memoir he wrote: "I cordially despised the poor Irish and South Germans, who slaved in the mills, and annexed the rich and well to do as my natural companions." In another volume, he declared:

None of the colored folk I knew were so poor, drunken and sloven as some of the lower-class Americans and Irish. . . . I did not then associate poverty or ignorance with color, but rather with lack of opportunity; or more often with lack of thrift. . . . The colored folk were not set aside in the sense that the Irish slums [were]. . . . I was struck in later years when I came back from the South to New England, to find that the "nigger" jokes of Tennessee were replaced at Harvard by tales of the "two Irishmen."

Du Bois provides an excellent example of how nonwhite or non-Protestant individuals, even if they assimilated most Victorian values, were treated as "foreign," causing various degrees of alienation from American society within these individuals. In Du Bois's case, not until adolescence did he recognize the existence of racial prejudice directed at him. "Then," he recalled, "slowly I realized that some folks, a few, even several, actually considered my brown skin a misfortune; once or twice I became painfully aware that some human beings even thought it was a crime." At first, Du Bois claimed, "I was not for a moment daunted . . . , rather I was spurred to tireless effort. If they beat me at anything, I was grimly determined to make them sweat for it!"[75] By 1920, however, Du Bois was referring in published work to whites as "fools" and "devils" and stating that "I hate them well."[76]

❣|❣|❣

Scholars who have tried to trace the economic influence of a "spirit of capitalism" have offered theories which can help explain the meaning of descriptions such as those provided by Alcott, Howells, Canby, and Du Bois of Victorian domestic values. A modern industrial society, they agree, required the type of character developed in these mostly small-town and rural homes: dependably self-controlled, hardworking, independent, pious, confident, frugal, and willing to postpone gratification.[77] Victorian attitudes toward marriage, children, gender roles, race, community life, religion, work, and death may seem deficient from most late twentieth-century perspectives, but they helped create a culture sufficiently integrated and satisfying to hold together a rapidly changing society, though with increasing internal tension.

The first mass attempts to reduce these stresses by initiating economic and political reform in the United States came from groups which felt themselves dispossessed: the workers in the Knights of Labor, and the white farmers and southern black and northern workers in the People's Party (Populists). However, the Woman Suffrage and Progressive movements, which arose mostly among late nineteenth-century progeny of Victorians, came closer to success.

Theodore Roosevelt (born 1858) provides a good example of the late Victorian politician who attempted through the Progressive movement to bring political and economic reality closer to Victorian values and thus to protect those values. Except for several idiosyncrasies traceable to his wealth, education, youthful illnesses, and exposure to post-Victorian influences, Roosevelt practically embodied the Victorian virtues. In achieving success, he wrote in 1900: "no brilliance of intellect, no perfection of bodily development, will count when weighted against that assemblage of virtues . . . which we group together under the name of character."[78] He defined his view of the inherent differences between men and women when he wrote of his father: "He was the best man I ever knew. . . . He really did combine the strength and courage and will and energy of the strongest man with the tenderness, cleanness and purity of a woman." The favorable connotation Roosevelt gave to this combination indicates some uneasiness, if not dissatisfaction, with rigid gender roles. However, Roosevelt showed no desire to surrender these altogether. Of his fiancée, Roosevelt declared in his diary that the "aim of my whole life" would be "to shield her and guard her from every trial. . . . How she, so pure and sweet and beautiful can think of marrying me I can not understand, but I praise and thank God it is so."[79]

Roosevelt served as the consummate leader of Progressives who sought to reform American society and politics during the period from the 1890s to World War I, while retaining the essential elements of Victorian culture.[80] The devout Roosevelt rallied his largely middle-class followers for a valiant struggle against the two major political parties in the presidential election of 1912, declaiming when nominated that "We stand at Armageddon and battle for the Lord!" Roosevelt expressed almost perfectly the Progressive urge to enforce righteousness:

> The longer I have lived the most strongly I have felt the harm done by the practice among so many men of keeping their consciences in separate compartments; sometimes a Sunday conscience and a weekday conscience . . . sometimes a conscience for their private affairs and a totally different conscience for their business relations.

William E. Leuchtenburg described the entrance of the United States into World War I, which Roosevelt demanded, as "The culmination of a long tradition of emphasis on sacrifice and decisive moral combat," and as "that final struggle where the righteous would do battle for the Lord."[81]

Roosevelt served as an influential spokesman for Victorian ideas about race. In a perceptive book about Roosevelt's racial thought, Thomas G.

Dyer concluded that "Although Roosevelt gained his expertise from the world's most eminent race theorists, it might be argued that because of his enormous popularity TR became the most important racial educator of all."[82]

Dyer described how "TR, like every youth who grew up in an atmosphere of Victorian privilege, was bombarded from early childhood with ideas which stressed the superiority of the white race and the inferiority of nonwhites."[83] Roosevelt's early racial beliefs received reinforcement and scientific sanction from the teachers with whom he studied at Harvard and Columbia universities. He came under the influence of geologist-historian Nathaniel S. Shaler at Harvard and of political scientist John W. Burgess at Columbia, two of the most prominent advocates among American scholars of Anglo-Saxon, Aryan, and Teutonic racial superiority.[84]

During the forty-year period after completing his formal education, especially from 1881 to 1895, Roosevelt wrote a prodigious amount of scholarly literature. Racial themes dominated this work, particularly Roosevelt's four volume historical epic *The Winning of the West*. White supremacy, in the form of Nordicism, Anglo-Saxonism, Aryanism, and Teutonism, was his preponderant explanation for the winning of the West by white Americans, particularly from Indians and Mexicans. Roosevelt suffered no moral qualms about the theft of Indian territory, despite widespread contemporary criticism of those actions. "The conquest and settlement by the whites on the Indian lands," he wrote, "was necessary to the greatness of the race and to the well-being of civilized mankind." He wrote, too, about "the absolute unfitness of the Mexicans then to govern themselves." "It was out of the question," he declared, to expect Americans in Texas to "submit to the mastery of the weaker race."[85]

By the early twentieth century, fashions in the expression of racial ideas had shifted, and Roosevelt exchanged the then somewhat discredited terms he had used before, such as "Anglo-Saxon," for frequent references to "the English-speaking race." As Dyer observed, however, Roosevelt's "celebration of the heritage, exploits, and destiny of the 'English-speaking race' continued unabated throughout his life and scarcely differed from his earlier lauding of Anglo-Saxons and Teutons."[86] Roosevelt had nothing but praise for Madison Grant's classic lament in 1916 for the noble Teuton, *The Passing of the Great Race*.[87]

As president of the United States (1901–1909), Roosevelt continued to seek advice from the chief advocates of Victorian racial concepts among American social and biological scientists. The scholars with whom President Roosevelt corresponded most frequently were sociologist Edward

A. Ross of the University of Wisconsin; paleontologist Henry Fairfield Osborn, director of the Museum of Natural History in New York City; and biologist Charles Benedict Davenport of Harvard.

Roosevelt gradually tempered the racial views he expressed, partly for political reasons and in part because continued observations and education moderated his beliefs. For example, while a New York State legislator in 1882, he wrote that most Irish-Catholic members of the legislature were "vicious, stupid-looking scoundrels with apparently not a redeeming trait" and a "stupid sodden vicious lot . . . equally deficient in brains and virtue." As he became more friendly with Irish-Catholics and discovered the group's power in New York State politics, he ceased to express these views.[88]

Throughout his career, Roosevelt never doubted that African-Americans belonged to a distinctly inferior race. Still, he believed that extraordinary blacks should receive almost equal political and economic opportunity, though not social equality. Roosevelt invited Booker T. Washington to visit and dine with him in the White House, largely because Washington was giving him valuable support in his fight to win control of the Republican Party from Mark Hanna. He acknowledged to a friend that "the very fact that I felt a moment's qualm because of his color made me ashamed of myself and made me hasten to send the invitation." So much criticism followed Washington's visit that Roosevelt conquered his shame and never again invited a black to dine at the White House.[89] At a time when African-Americans were being deprived of their civil rights and lynched in record numbers, Roosevelt announced that black crime and vice were "evils more potent for harm to the black race than all acts of oppression of white men put together." Roosevelt denounced the lynching of blacks on numerous occasions but never without denouncing at the same time black men who raped white women, although he knew that suspected murder, not rape, was the chief offense for which blacks were lynched.[90]

Among Victorian Americans, Roosevelt was a moderate on the subject of race. His career illustrates the harshness of even moderate Victorian racial ideas and policies and how severely these ideas and policies could affect "inferior races."

❦ | ❦ | ❦

Unquestionably, American Victorianism became more flexible between the 1870s and the early twentieth century. The extreme restraint and fussiness of Alcott and Howells's world declined among most of the middle class. It is a tribute to the resiliency of Victorian culture and to the satisfactions it provided its members that such shifts in consciousness occurred without threatening seriously its essence or predominance.[91]

Subsequently, the overweening confidence in Victorian culture—inculcated in young Du Bois, as well as in Canby—which gave Theodore Roosevelt faith that his policies carried out America's divine mission at home and abroad, eroded noticeably. It becomes increasingly clear that this "illusion," as Canby called his culture's sublime confidence, played a major role in the military and economic domination Victorian societies achieved throughout the world and in the power Victorians maintained in the United States.

By the late 1920s, the conceptual framework which supported Victorianism had been impaired, largely because of concerted attacks on it by intellectuals. They aimed their assault mostly at points where the culture contained serious contradictions or failed to provide much satisfaction for many Americans. The weakened culture also suffered attack by various associations of ethnic, sexual, political, and economic dissidents, who attempted to take power away from the dominant Victorian groups. Yet, every basic Victorian idea retained vitality, though in different degrees, at the end of the 1920s. The powerful assaults launched against Victorian culture during the twentieth century failed to replace most essential aspects of that culture with durable values, concepts, and institutions derived from the severe critiques. An account of the first strong nationwide rebellion against most important aspects of Victorianism—in the 1920s—helps clarify the meaning of this assault, the extent of its successes and failures, and the nature of major movements for Victorianism's defense, both then and subsequently in American history.

2

THE DEVELOPMENT OF
AN AMERICAN
INTELLIGENTSIA[1]

During the nineteenth century, a large majority of American academic and literary intellectuals served as protectors of Victorian mores and ideas. By the 1920s, however, most leading American intellectuals had announced their rebellion against virtually the same conventions and concepts. This rebellion was supported by the nation's foremost book publishers, literary and scholarly journals, and heads of philanthropic foundations.

The crucial factor in causing the intellectuals' rebellion was a shift in their values. This led them inevitably into conflict with Americans who continued to hold and were attempting to protect the conventional ethos. Behind the shift lay an expansion of the parameters of late nineteenth-century literary realism and naturalism and of Victorian science and social science. These twentieth-century trends were encouraged by the reinforcement of dissident ideas provided by increased numbers of intellectuals, an enlarged audience for such ideas, and much more money available for their creation and dissemination.

During the mid- and late nineteenth century, trustees of colleges and universities in the United States almost invariably selected as presidents men who shared the trustees' piety and orthodox political, social, moral, and religious beliefs. These presidents, in turn, chose faculty members who almost all understood that their most important duty consisted of improving the characters and guarding the minds and souls of impressionable undergraduate students. As part of this task, they provided access to the accumulated higher knowledge of their academic specialties, including that scientific knowledge which appeared to confirm conventional American beliefs.

Exceptions did not exist in significant numbers outside a few of the most research-oriented universities. Johns Hopkins, the first real university in the United States, despite a president (Daniel Coit Gilman) who believed that he "*must* consider certain moral and social considerations" in hiring professors, opened in 1876 with a faculty including a cadre of free-thinking and in some cases free-speaking young scholars. During the 1890s, similar corps of scholars developed at Columbia University and the University of Chicago. This development occurred despite the publicly expressed views of the presidents of those universities. Columbia's President Nicholas Murray Butler wrote in 1902 that a professor "owes something to ordinary standards of sanity and good breeding as well as to the truth." Chicago's President William Rainey Harper in 1901 announced his sympathy for the Russian czarist government's attacks on academic freedom. Harvard University, by the 1890s, also harbored a group of scholars whose primary commitment was to original thought within their academic discipline, even when their conclusions disturbed Victorian conventions.[2] Groups of dissidents, such as those at Johns Hopkins, Harvard, Columbia, and Chicago, however, remained precarious examples of exceptional situations.[3]

When James B. Angell, the president of the University of Michigan and a renowned exponent of high intellectual standards within his university's faculty, sought a historian for Michigan in 1885, he wrote to President Gilman of Johns Hopkins: "In the Chair of History . . . I should not wish a pessimist or an agnostic or a man disposed to obtrude criticism of Christian views of humanity or of Christian principles. I should not want a man who would not make his historical judgments and interpretations from a Christian standpoint." Gilman agreed. A year later, Gilman declared that American universities should be "steady promoters of Knowledge, Virtue, and Faith."[4]

Shortly after a critic accused him of advocating "disguised socialism" in 1895, the economist John Commons told his president at the University of Indiana that he had been offered a more remunerative position at Syracuse University. The president urged Commons to "take it at once." Commons considered it only fair to warn Syracuse's chancellor that he agreed with Henry George's concept of a "single tax" and believed in municipal ownership of utilities. The chancellor replied that Commons's personal opinions did not concern him unless he was an "obnoxious socialist." Commons considered the matter, decided that he was not obnoxious, and accepted the position. Less than three years later, Syracuse's trustees fired him because his "radical tendencies" caused potential donors to withhold funds from the university.[5]

The New York *Observer* polled the presidents of nine leading Eastern colleges in 1880—Yale, Princeton, Brown, Amherst, Rochester, Union, Williams, Hamilton, and Lafayette—inquiring whether they allowed their faculty to teach the evolutionists' theory that man had evolved from "irrational animals." The presidents unanimously answered "No!" in one form or another, a few of them erroneously. In a typical reply, President Samuel Gilman Brown of Hamilton stated: "The doctrine . . . has never to my knowledge been taught at Hamilton. I trust it never will be. . . ."[6]

By acting as the chief intellectual bulwark for contemporary American racist ideas until the early twentieth century, distinguished administrators and scholars in American colleges and universities helped justify popular beliefs about a genetically determined racial and ethnic hierarchy. Scientific evidence to bolster theories about this social and economic hierarchy at first came mostly from Europe, especially from England and Germany. These studies showed that Anglo-Saxons, Aryans, or Nordics belonged at the top of the racial ladder, with southern and eastern Europeans far below, and Asians and African-Americans at the bottom.

American biological and social scientists accepted and extended the European conclusions. American social Darwinists measured and evaluated alleged racial characteristics, despite Charles Darwin's refusal to commit himself to the concept of "superior" or "inferior" races.[7] American eugenicists were inspired by the British physical anthropologist, psychologist, geneticist, and statistician Sir Francis Galton, founder of eugenics as a "science." In *Hereditary Genius* (1869) and *Natural Inheritance* (1889) Galton proved statistically to his satisfaction that a distinct gradation of races existed.[8] Happily for American nineteenth-century and early twentieth-century scholars—and other contemporary American conservatives—this statistically derived racial scale coincided with their previous beliefs.

Some Americans found supporting scientific evidence for their racial theories also in the ideas of Louis Agassiz, professor of geology and zoology at Harvard from 1847 to 1873. Agassiz discerned parallels between the distribution of what he believed were pure human races and that of flora and fauna which the Creator (by what Agassiz referred to as "premeditated plan") intended for specific regions of his earth. Convinced that blacks derived from a species different from and inferior to whites, Agassiz declared that attempts to force the two species into the same society must end disastrously.

However, Agassiz evidently formed his opinions about African-Americans before he began scientific research on the subject. After immigrating to the United States from Switzerland, Agassiz saw a black person for the first time in December 1846. He wrote to his mother: "The feeling that they [blacks] inspired in me is contrary to all our ideas about the confraternity of the human type [genre]. . . . It is impossible for me to repress the feeling that they are not of the same blood as us."[9]

Aided and encouraged by scientific evidence such as that supplied by Agassiz, the social Darwinists, and the eugenicists, American social scientists produced a vast literature justifying the racial and ethnic—and therefore much of the social and economic—status quo. Historians' research led those who studied the topic in the late nineteenth and early twentieth centuries to conclude that slavery had been a rather benevolent institution which contributed to the civilizing of the unfortunate black race. Attempts to give blacks a semblance of equality after the Civil War had been ill-advised and therefore pathetic or tragic failures in practice, according to these historians.

James Ford Rhodes, for example, in his multivolume study of the Civil War and Reconstruction, complained that Radical Republican leaders had ignored evidence available as a result of Agassiz's research and publications. "What the whole country has learned through years of costly and bitter experience," Rhodes declared, "was known to this leader of scientific thought before we ventured on the policy of trying to make negroes intelligent by legislative acts." John W. Burgess, founder of Columbia University's School of Political Science, which included all areas of learning that later would be classified as social science, published a history of Reconstruction in 1902. He called Negro suffrage a "monstrous thing" based on the illusion that skin color bore no relation to intelligence or ethics. "A black skin," Burgess asserted, "means membership in a race of men which has never of itself succeeded to reason, has never, therefore, created any civilization of any kind."[10]

Edward A. Freeman, professor of history at Oxford University, whose ideas about Teutonic origins of Anglo-Saxon democratic institutions gave him considerable influence among historians in the United States, compared Russian regulations that restricted the activities of Jews with California laws aimed at Asians. "There is no religious persecution in either case," he wrote in 1882, "only the natural instinct of any decent nation to get rid of filthy strangers." On a lecture tour of the United States, Freeman asserted, without arousing protest from intellectuals in his host country, that "the best remedy for whatever is amiss in America would be if every Irishman should kill a negro and be hanged for it."[11]

The nation's most influential anthropologists in the late nineteenth century, including the illustrious John Wesley Powell, director of the federal government's Bureau of American Ethnology at the Smithsonian Institution, subscribed in their published work to the concept of Aryan, if not specifically to Anglo-Saxon, superiority. The physical anthropologist Robert Bennett Bean diligently measured the brains of 152 blacks and whites, paying particular attention to the size of frontal lobes, believed to be the site of higher intellectual activity. Bean found the brain size, and more significantly the frontal lobe size, of white subjects consistently larger than that of blacks.[12]

As a result of such evidence, even most of the humanitarian reformers among late nineteenth- and early twentieth-century social scientists in the United States agreed that white, Protestant Americans, an obviously superior race, deserved to rank highest in status. Sociologist Lester Frank Ward, an advocate of state intervention to promote democratic purposes, was genuinely sympathetic with the plight of blacks in the South. Nevertheless, Ward asserted that black women who submitted to rape by white men in the South were motivated subconsciously by a desire to improve their race. Black male rapists and members of the white lynch mobs that murdered them were "impelled . . . by the biological law of self-preservation."

Sociologist Edward A. Ross, who believed that the chief purpose of sociology should be the improvement of human relations, while addressing the American Academy of Political and Social Science in 1901, warned that a further influx of Asian immigrants might lead to the extinction of "true Americans." Sociologist Charles Horton Cooley, another opponent of laissez-faire economic individualism and of eugenics, wrote that with great effort and patience Americans might assimilate Slavs, Italians, and Jews—eventually—but never Negroes or Asians. Even economist John Commons held conventional racist views.[13]

From the mid-nineteenth century to the second decade of the twentieth century, conventional values were safeguarded also by successive elite literary groups, each whose members were Protestant and largely of English or, to a lesser degree, of other northern European ancestry. These groups decided what America's better-informed individuals would read because they controlled the nation's large publishing houses and most prestigious magazines.[14] A statement by one of their leaders, Richard Watson Gilder, editor of the *Century*, the foremost in prestige among the magazines which served American middle-class readers, expressed the moralistic attitude of the literary elite. Replying to an Englishman who declared that Americans were prudes, Gilder refused to apologize for his country or to demand a comparison with Victorian England. "It may be that this accusation is well-founded," he acknowledged. "If so, we can only say that this is the price we pay for being, on the whole, the decentest nation on the face of the globe."[15]

Theodore Dreiser discovered the "decent" nature of America's literary elite and book-buying public in 1900, when he published his first novel, *Sister Carrie*. Dreiser's story, largely a barely fictionalized account of events in his sister Emma's life but based also on experiences of his own, dealt with a woman who lived in sexual sin with two different men and then, in defiance of Victorian conventions which demanded punishment for such violations of moral righteousness, enjoyed a successful career as an actress, attaining both fame and wealth.

The book was published only because the naturalist novelist Frank Norris worked at the time as a manuscript reader and an editor at the publishing house Doubleday, Page and Co. Norris's exuberant enthusiasm for Dreiser's manuscript sufficed to obtain for the author a contract from Doubleday.

However, when the head of the firm, Frank Doubleday, returned from a European trip and read his firm's new acquisition, he refused to publish it. Doubleday, a morally upright and devout Protestant, called *Sister Carrie* "immoral." In addition, Doubleday did not believe that Americans would buy such an "evil" book. Doubleday offered to compensate Dreiser financially for his trouble and to sell him the book plates. Dreiser refused. Doubleday then offered to give him the plates. Dreiser again insisted that Doubleday honor his contract and threatened legal action if he did not.

On the advice of the firm's chief attorney, Doubleday, Page and Co. published *Sister Carrie*. Because of Dreiser's threats, Doubleday ordered a fairly large first printing of the book, with an attractive red cover, black lettering, and a reasonable price. The enthusiastic Norris received the task of directing promotion of *Sister Carrie*. Therefore, every major magazine and newspaper in the country received review copies and letters praising the book signed by Norris.

An overwhelming majority of reviews condemned the book as immoral and complained also about Dreiser's use of vulgar language. Dreiser remained optimistic. He told an interviewer from the *New York Times* in January 1901: "The critics have not really understood what I was trying to do. Here is a book that is close to life . . . , a picture of conditions done as simply and effectively as the English language will permit. . . . When it gets to the people they will understand, because it is a story of real life, of their lives." Early twentieth-century Americans showed the extent of their desire to read about an immoral real life by purchasing a total of 456 copies of *Sister Carrie* during the year after its publication. Another publishing house, which considered purchasing rights to the book from Doubleday in order to reprint *Sister Carrie* in 1902, discovered that bookstores did not want it; copies of the first edition remained unsold on their shelves. These events so discouraged Dreiser that he did not write another novel for ten years.[16]

Mark Twain, who possessed a fine knowledge of Victorian Americans' sense of decency and who had a large store of it himself, declined to publish during his lifetime his grimmest portrait of American life and conventional ideas, *The Mysterious Stranger*. In a chapter which Twain marked as the concluding one,[17] the stranger denounced both the quality of American life and the God who either permitted or planned such a miserable existence. The character who represented the author then reflected: "I knew and I realized that all he had said was true." Although the novel probably came closer than anything else he wrote to embodying his perceptions of Victorian America and to using his mature abilities as a satirist, Twain stipulated that *The Mysterious Stranger* should remain unpublished and be omitted from any future collection of his work.[18]

By 1916, a rebellion of literary intellectuals had largely overcome the influence of the Victorian literary elite. Publishers then competed for the right to publish Dreiser's novels, which won an increasing number of favorable reviews, largely from a new group of younger reviewers, and eventually, with *An American Tragedy* (1925), achieved high sales. Mark Twain's "ordeal" became a leading symbol during the 1920s of the harm done to creative Americans by the constraints imposed upon them by Victorian culture. At the same time, America's finest universities were transformed into centers for the dissemination of values and ideas which undermined continued confidence in Victorian values and ideas.[19]

These changes required broad acceptance by the intelligentsia of a value system similar to that which had impelled Dreiser when he wrote *Sister Carrie*, Thomas Henry Huxley when he wrote about biology, and Twain when he wrote *The Mysterious Stranger*. These shifts in values reached such wide dimensions during the 1920s that sharp conflicts between most American intellectuals and the inheritors of nineteenth-century American Victorian culture became inevitable.

By the 1920s, a cluster of deeply held values, which eventually proved damaging to popular confidence in the Victorian synthesis, loosely united the great majority of literary and academic intellectuals. This shared value system was neither a peculiarly American nor a twentieth-century development. Most of these values would have seemed familiar not only to Walt Whitman, William James, Howells, Dreiser, Huxley, or Twain but also to Aristotle, Socrates, and Galileo. During the 1920s, however, a situation unique in American history occurred because of the appearance of a greater number of individuals who considered themselves professional writers or scholars, many of whom adopted the highest distinctive values of intellectuals and who seemed to accept, if not to welcome, conflict with traditional conventions.

Their common values inclined most intellectuals to respond sympathetically to criticism of American civilization launched by fellow intellectuals, reinforcing these critical views even when they met disapproval elsewhere in the society. The shared values and the increased number of intellectuals led also to an unprecedented amount of cooperation in rebellious activity among members of various literary, academic, and artistic groups. Socrates, Galileo, Whitman, Commons, Huxley, and Dreiser had suffered from an absence of such powerful support for their potentially subversive ideas.

The words "true" or "truth" symbolized for most intellectuals in the 1920s their fundamental values and the basis of their criticism directed at American society. This is not to suggest that Agassiz, Powell, Ward, Burgess, Ross, Norris, Cooley, or Howells intentionally or habitually falsified important matters. However, the later intellectuals carried significantly forward the boundaries of "truth" established by late nineteenth-century scientists, social scientists, and literary realists and naturalists.

The heart of the conflict between the intelligentsia's values and those of the great majority of their intellectual predecessors—including Howells and Norris—lay in differing perceptions of their obligations to "truth." To almost all the leading intellectuals of the 1920s, "truth" implied a willingness to accept evidence and to study and describe activities and emotions which would have seemed unacceptable to Victorians of high character, including almost all Victorian intellectuals.

A definitive statement of the intelligentsia's values, applicable to the ideal objectives of most of the era's finest poets, novelists, physical and biological scientists, and academic humanists and social scientists, was delivered in a manifesto by the poet Ezra Pound, published first in 1913 and restated by him in somewhat different phrases for over two decades thereafter:

> If an artist falsifies his report as to the nature of man, as to his own nature, as to the nature of his ideal of the perfect, as to the nature of his ideal of this, that or the other, of god, if god exists, of the life force, of the nature of good or evil, if good and bad exist, of the force with which he believes or disbelieves this, that or the other, of the degree in which he suffers or is made glad; if the artist falsifies his reports on these matters or on any other matter in order that he may conform to the taste of his time, to the proprieties of a sovereign, to the conveniences of a preconceived code of ethics, then that artist lies. If he lies out of deliberate will to lie, if he lies out of carelessness, out of laziness, out of cowardice, out of any sort of negligence whatsoever, he nevertheless lies and he should be punished or despised in proportion to the seriousness of his offence.[20]

The artist, Pound insisted, should utilize all information or techniques that would help him interpret his subject accurately, no matter whom this interpretation might antagonize. A similar ethic guided social scientists during the 1920s as they described terrible deficiencies in the lives of "typical" middle-class and working-class Americans. Social scientists reported that satisfaction and happiness among some economically "primitive" peoples far exceeded that found among the American middle class or working class. A group among these social scientists demonstrated, to other social scientists at least, that Victorian racial and ethnic beliefs lacked scientific validity. They placed scholarly values above conventional proprieties in presenting the most pertinent information (mostly unfavorable about America and Americans) and the conclusions (largely negative about America) suggested by that evidence.

Physicists who engaged in the quest for a usable theory of atomic structure—formulated during the 1920s as quantum mechanics—regardless of whether the new theory proved complementary with classical Newtonian physics and the worldview it represented, displayed attitudes which corresponded in important respects to Pound's. So did those physicists and other scientists who agreed with Werner Heisenberg's uncertainty principle about position and velocity at the atomic level rather than with the certainties of classical physics, which had comforted conventional minds.[21]

Most scientific and literary intellectuals in the 1920s shared the most important values connected with their work. For example, Sinclair Lewis, Theodore Dreiser, and Herbert Croly, the editor of the leading advanced

Progressive magazine the *New Republic*, understood the similarities between their objectives and the scientific aims of Jacques Loeb, the nation's
most eminent biologist. Loeb, in turn, admired Dreiser's novels and stories
and found in them a view of life akin to his own.

Lewis wrote one of his finest and most popular novels, *Arrowsmith*, in
1924. The author received aid from Paul De Kruif, Loeb's young former
research assistant at the Rockefeller Institute. De Kruif lived with Lewis
for months while the author plied him with questions about his life as a
scientist, about Loeb, and about the Rockefeller Institute. De Kruif read
and criticized carefully much of Lewis's completed manuscript.[22]

Midway through the book, Martin Arrowsmith, a youthful but already
successful member of the medical staff at a clinic for wealthy patients,
was invited to join the McGurk Institute for medical research in New
York at the instigation of his former teacher, the great biologist Max
Gottlieb, who had read a promising scientific paper written by the young
man. Arrowsmith bore a remarkable resemblance to De Kruif; the
McGurk Institute hardly differed from Lewis's conception of the Rockefeller Institute, and Jacques Loeb served as one of the chief models for
Gottlieb. After some hesitation, Arrowsmith placed his scientific integrity
above his income and accepted the McGurk Institute's invitation.

Welcoming Arrowsmith to the great research center, Gottlieb offered
this advice:

> To be a scientist—it is not just a different job, so that a man should choose
> between being a scientist and being an explorer or a bond salesman or a
> physician or a king or a farmer. It is a tangle of very obscure emotions, like
> mysticism, or wanting to write poetry; it makes its victim all different from
> the good normal man. The normal man, he does not care much what he
> does except that he should eat and sleep and make love. But the scientist
> is intensely religious—he is so religious that he will not accept quarter-
> truths, because they are an insult to his faith.
>
> Always remember that not all the men who work at science are scientists.
> So few! The rest—secretaries, press-agents, camp followers! To be a sci-
> entist is like being a Goethe: it is born in you. Sometimes I t'ink you have
> a liddle of it born in you. If you haf, there is only one t'ing—no, there is
> two t'ings you must do: work twice as hard as you can, and keep people
> from using you. I will try to protect you from Success. It is all I can do.[23]

In a sober moment of self-analysis, Lewis attempted in 1927 to expound
his deepest values, all but invisible, he feared, to those who knew him as
an alcoholic prankster: "All his [Lewis's] respect for learning," he declared,
"for integrity, for accuracy, and for the possibilities of human achievement

are to be found not in the rather hectic and exaggerative man as his intimates see him, but in his portrait of Professor Max Gottlieb in *Arrowsmith*."

Ernest Hemingway demonstrated his awareness that a similarity existed between the values of scientific and literary intellectuals when he advised F. Scott Fitzgerald about the role of an author's painful personal experience in writing fiction: "Use it—don't cheat. . . . Be as faithful to it as a scientist. . . ."[24]

As in practically all human endeavor, ideals varied from practice—not only Lewis and Pound but even Loeb, his friend Franz Boas, and Boas's student Margaret Meade sometimes slipped in practice. However, in general, in their work, by the 1920s American intellectuals accepted the primacy of the ideals expressed by Pound, Hemingway, and Lewis's Gottlieb.

Lewis, whose apostasy to Gottlieb's creed increased with his alcoholism and in rough correlation to the gradual loss of his writing skills, maintained the high ideal he professed as long as he could. During the 1920s, when Lewis enjoyed nearly full command of his artistic powers, the sociological research which preceded work on his novels rivaled that of the best professional sociologists. His finest novels of the period—*Main Street*, *Babbitt*, *Arrowsmith*, *Dodsworth* and *Elmer Gantry*—represent attempts to portray accurately and critically various important aspects of American civilization.[25]

Events and characters in the most celebrated novels, stories, and plays written during the 1920s—by Hemingway, Fitzgerald, Dreiser, Lewis, William Faulkner, and Eugene O'Neill—differed widely from what Victorians had considered appropriate for publication. For example, the casual sexual promiscuity of Lady Brett Ashley in Hemingway's *The Sun Also Rises* (1926), the desertion from the fighting during World War I by the chief character in Hemingway's *A Farewell to Arms* (1929), and the profanity in both books provoked hundreds of Americans to write letters to the publisher of the novels, Charles Scribner's Sons, protesting such immorality. However, Hemingway's novels enjoyed excellent sales. Also, the response to this criticism by Hemingway's (and Fitzgerald's) editor at Scribner's, Maxwell Perkins, contrasted sharply with the attitude of all the major nineteenth- and early twentieth-century American publishers, including Scribner's. Perkins received bags of mail objecting to publication of *The Sun Also Rises*. In a typical reply, Perkins wrote to one angry correspondent:

> Publishing is not, of course, dependent on the individual taste of the publisher. He is under an obligation to his profession which binds him to bring

out a work which in the judgment of the literary world is significant in its literary qualities and is a pertinent criticism of the civilization of the time.

Three years later, before his firm published *A Farewell to Arms*, Charles Scribner II approved payment to Hemingway of the largest sum *Scribner's* magazine ever had paid for serialization rights. *A Farewell to Arms* contained more profanity and accounts of sexual behavior than had *The Sun Also Rises*. However, Perkins, who understood that Hemingway believed these were necessary parts of his book and that many books with profanity and sex now were commercially successful, suggested only that the author consider deleting three words which the editor could not force himself to say aloud.[26]

Hemingway, describing the writing process which had produced *The Sun Also Rises* and *A Farewell to Arms*, illustrated the kinship between his artistic and intellectual ideas and values and those expressed by Pound:

> I found the greatest difficulty, aside from knowing truly what you really felt, rather than what you were supposed to feel, and had been taught to feel, was to put down what really happened . . . , the sequence of motion and fact which made the emotion and which would be as valid in a year or in ten years or, with luck and if you stated it purely enough, always. . . . [27]

The concept of "truth," as it was understood by members of the American intelligentsia, differed from the truths which the great majority of Victorian authors, editors, heads of publishing firms, college presidents, and teachers had spoken, written, and published. The American intelligentsia during the 1920s agreed that authors should know what they really believed and felt, making use of all available evidence, and that writers must report their full beliefs faithfully. Such a group posed a powerful threat to conventional ideas, including those about a racial hierarchy and gender roles.

3

A STRUCTURE TO SUPPORT INTELLECTUAL DISSENT

A confluence of interrelated events during the 1920s magnified the force of the assault by intellectuals on American Victorianism. Without those events, the intelligentsia's attacks would have been less effective and the defense against them less forlorn.

These related events created a structure which supported the growth of an intellectual subculture in America and, therefore, assisted the development of the intelligentsia and of its ideas. Four events were particularly consequential.

1. The number of people engaged in virtually every form of intellectual effort multiplied. Consequently, the number of potential recruits to the intelligentsia increased dramatically too.

2. Funds to subsidize intellectual activity and training grew rapidly, and those who controlled the flow of that money tended to approve and, in important cases, to encourage intellectual dissent. Thus, the intelligentsia received aid in turning potential recruits into members.

3. New ideas in the social, physical, and biological sciences and in literature and other arts stimulated intellectual creativity, attracted new participants to these fields, increased the money made available for intel-

lectuals, and provided new evidence and techniques to further intellectual dissent.

4. Leaders arose in every important area of intellectual achievement to mediate between intellectuals and major sources of funds for their assistance. In most cases, these leaders aided the recruitment of intellectuals; they helped channel money to those individuals, institutions, and types of intellectual work they considered most promising. In this fashion, they played an important role in determining which new ideas would develop most rapidly, and in fulfilling these functions, they often assisted the intelligentsia's attacks on Victorianism.[1]

❧ | ❧ | ❧

The proportion of the population of the United States between eighteen and twenty-one years of age enrolled in institutions of higher education increased from 4 percent in 1900 to 12.42 percent in 1930. Enrollment of graduate students rose from a total of 6,000 in 1900 to 47,000 in 1930.[2] American universities in the 1920s responded to this sudden quickening of the long-term increase in graduate and undergraduate enrollments by appointing new teachers at roughly the same rate as the increase in the number of students.[3]

A trend toward professionalization in nearly every field made academic degrees or professional credentials almost essential for advancement, if not employment. This shift occurred most noticeably in the sciences. American industrial corporations expanded enormously the size of their research staffs during this period, and the number of industrial research laboratories grew from about three hundred in 1920 to more than a thousand in 1927. These laboratories required mostly college-trained specialists and sought especially those with advanced university degrees. However, the same trend could be found in business, law, medicine, education, and even farming.[4] The ambitions of middle-class parents, who observed correctly that higher education would improve their children's occupational opportunities in most desirable vocations, also contributed to the growth of college populations. Students' awareness that these opportunities would increase still further if they obtained higher degrees increased the proportion involved in graduate academic or professional training.[5]

Most of the literary intellectuals in the era preceding World War I and an even higher proportion of those active in the 1920s had worked on college publications. An extremely large percentage of those who later enjoyed exceptional success within the intellectual subculture studied as undergraduates or graduate students at a small number of prestigious universities. This fact holds true also for the black literary intellectuals of the Negro or Harlem Renaissance.[6]

❣|❣|❣

The freeing of hundreds of young college and university instructors and advanced graduate students for research and creative thinking from the routines (which formerly would have been theirs) of elementary undergraduate teaching and administrative duties proved extremely important. Each year during the 1920s, scores of young academic scientists, social scientists, and, to a lesser extent, specialists in the humanities and the arts, who otherwise would have been overwhelmed by the heavy tasks involved in teaching the large introductory courses characteristic of early academic training, received foundation fellowships previously unavailable. These grants enabled the young scholars and artists to master their own fields, to learn the relevant concepts in closely related areas, and to use this knowledge to develop their own ideas and techniques.

These fellowships, which released the recipients from other obligations for one, two, and sometimes three or four years during the period just before or after completion of their doctoral dissertations or early in their literary or other artistic careers, encouraged original thought at fertile periods in the lives of intellectuals and artists. Their creativity, in turn, affected the general intellectual climate in the United States. For example, J. Robert Oppenheimer, commenting on the special qualities in the later teaching of young theoretical physicists who, like himself, had been enabled by foundation fellowships to spend years studying quantum mechanics during its development in European universities, declared: "Some of the excitement and wonder of the discoverer was in their teaching."[7]

Oppenheimer's comment could have been made with equal truth about young scholars permitted by foundation fellowships to work free of distraction on urban and rural sociology and anthropological studies of American Indians, South Sea islanders, Africans, or Mexican villagers. Oppenheimer's observation applied also to teachers among the young novelists, poets, painters, architects, and musical composers, whom the Guggenheim Foundation, especially, supported at critical points in their careers. The exhilarating process of exploration and discovery within rapidly developing and changing fields was an experience that had been available before only on a small scale to individuals from wealthy families or to the few recipients of fellowships from foundations or of grants taken from the income provided to universities by their endowment funds.

Until the 1920s, American philanthropic foundations supported little individual research or literary and artistic creativity. The National Research Council, subsidized largely by the Rockefeller Foundation, began the change in emphasis with a program of postdoctoral fellowships for scientists launched in 1919. Rockefeller Foundation officials had been considering creation of a research institute for the physical sciences analogous to the Rockefeller Institute for Medical Research. The shifting relationships between academic and foundation leaders found significant expression when spokesmen for the scientific professional associations persuaded the foundation's policymakers instead to back the National Research Council, within which the academic scientific leaders could exercise great influence.[8]

The Rockefeller Foundation's International Education Board began awarding similar fellowships in 1923, and in that same year, the foundation's General Education Board started awarding multimillion-dollar grants to specific university science departments and institutes. The Rockefeller Foundation itself provided some research funds for projects too large or unusual for its offspring agencies. Large amounts of money were donated both to individuals and to intermediary organizations to aid various types of academic research by the Laura Spelman Rockefeller Memorial Fund, established in 1918 by John D. Rockefeller, Sr., in memory of his wife. During the next ten years, before its consolidation with the Rockefeller Foundation in 1928, the Laura Spelman Fund distributed about $74 million. Gifts from the fund enabled both the Social Science Research Council (SSRC) and the American Council of Learned Societies (ACLS) to establish programs during the 1920s of grants for research or study in the social sciences and the humanities. The SSRC and ACLS received funds also from the General Education Board and the Rockefeller Foundation for these purposes. The Institute for Government Research—predecessor to the Brookings Institution—and the National Bureau of Economic Research also sponsored individual research beginning in the 1920s, using substantial financial aid from the Rockefeller Foundation.

The John Simon Guggenheim Foundation, commencing in 1925, supported creative work by talented individuals in almost every area of scholarly or artistic endeavor. In 1926, thirty-eight individuals received grants from the Guggenheim Foundation (giving most recipients a year of freedom to work at whatever they chose). The number of Guggenheim Foundation fellowships awarded rose annually. A number of other organizations, inspired by these programs, or perhaps moved by the same influences, began aid to research on a smaller scale during the 1920s: the Charles A. Coffin Foundation, the American School of Classical Studies, the Music Fund, the American Schools of Oriental Research, and the

American Institute of Architects. Large philanthropic foundations already in existence, such as the Carnegie Corporation, the Carnegie Institution of Washington, and the Russell Sage Foundation, reoriented their policies in varying degree toward assisting individual research.[9]

Literary intellectuals benefited not only from fellowships granted by the Guggenheim Foundation, the ACLS, and such smaller organizations as the American School of Classical Studies, but also from events within American colleges and universities. During the 1920s, numerous universities established positions for writers or poets in residence, and new lecture circuits, based in large part on fees from colleges, helped support authors. Expanded subsidization of scholarly and literary journals by colleges and universities provided outlets for publication by little-known authors, contributing to opportunities for recognition by the reading public and by publishers, thereby increasing some writers' future incomes.[10]

"Little magazines" outside the protective academic environment ("little" referring to number of copies sold, not size, and certainly not to the importance of the authors published) flourished even more during the 1920s than in the prewar era. The great majority of America's finest novelists, poets, short-story writers and essayists during the 1920s obtained exposure to readers by publishing their writing first in these magazines. American journals (such as the *Little Review*, *Poetry*, the *Dial*, the *Liberator* (until 1924), the *Smart Set* (until 1923, when the editors left to form the *American Mercury*) and short-lived publications established by writers in exile (including *Broom* (1921–1924), started in Rome and then moved to Berlin; Pound's *Exile*, edited in Paris (1927–1928); *This Quarter*, also Paris-based; *Secession* (1922–1924), published first in Vienna and then in Berlin; and Ford Madox Ford's Paris journal *Transatlantic Review* (1924–1925), which during its brief life published writing by Hemingway, Gertrude Stein, Pound, e.e. cummings, and William Carlos Williams, among others) gave contemporary writers the feeling that they were part of great experimental and rebellious movements involving large numbers of extremely talented people—as indeed they were.[11]

Another innovation for literary intellectuals, the financial equivalent to the steep rise in foundation grants to academic intellectuals, was the expanded system of publishing houses' advances to authors of funds against future royalties. The most able, young writers benefited especially from advance payments from relatively new publishers eager to contract for their work. At that point in time, the best young writers almost invariably were rebels against Victorianism. Among such new publishers, Alfred A. Knopf, Horace Liveright, Albert and Charles Boni, B. W. Huebsch (who with Harold K. Ginzburg founded the Viking Press in 1925), Bennet

Cerf's Random House, (started in 1925), and Simon and Schuster (begun by Richard Simon, who left Liveright to do so, and Max L. Schuster in 1923) emerged as the most successful. Knopf, Liveright, the Bonis, and Huebsch, at that time the largest of these new publishers, not only sought fresh authors but also welcomed dissident thought in the manuscripts they published.[12]

In part because of pressure on sales exerted by these fledgling publishers (caused largely by the exciting writers they uncovered), certain better-established publishing houses broadened considerably their conceptions of the style and type of literature fit for their presses. They also loosened their purse strings to meet their ambitious competition. Charles Scribner's Sons and Harcourt Brace led the way in this sacrifice of gentility when necessary to obtain contracts for books by promising authors. As part of that effort, Scribner's promoted Maxwell Perkins to serve as chief editor and allowed him to revolutionize the firm by bringing in such authors as Fitzgerald, Hemingway, Thomas Wolfe, Ring Lardner, and Erskine Caldwell. Before Perkins received this leeway, Scribner's had earned a reputation as "the most genteel and the most tradition encrusted of all the publishing houses." Literary critic Malcolm Cowley recalled that when Perkins began work at Scribner's, the firm's atmosphere resembled "Queen Victoria's parlor." Because of Perkins's sweeping changes, Cowley declared, Scribner's "took a sudden leap from the age of innocence into the midst of the lost generation."[13]

Established magazines, including those with the largest circulation (like the women's magazine the *Ladies' Home Journal* and the family magazine the *Saturday Evening Post*), vied for stories by writers who considered themselves young radicals. F. Scott Fitzgerald's fee for short stories in such magazines rose to $4,000 by the late 1920s, and contributions by Theodore Dreiser and Sinclair Lewis, for example, commanded almost as much. A literary historian, describing this metamorphosis, relates:

> By 1919 the Journal's vulnerability lay in its old-fashioned, Victorian image of the American family. The wives in its stories were invariably demure and uncomplaining, the husbands aggressive and virile, and the children obedient and well-mannered.... [Consequently], the November 1919 issue of the *Ladies' Home Journal*, which signaled [editor Edward] Bok's retirement, carried only four inconspicuous advertisements selling cosmetics....
>
> By 1919, two important developments had taken place in American life ... the behavior of teen-agers was no longer that described in popular magazine fiction. Moreover American youth was asserting itself as a new eco-

nomic market.... If a magazine like the *Saturday Evening Post* could somehow identify itself with these new values and attitudes, it could supplant the *Ladies' Home Journal* [sales over two million copies per issue] as the world's biggest magazine.[14]

George Horace Lorimer, appointed editor of the *Post* early in the 1920s, immediately recognized the potential for increasing sales, advertising, and response to advertising when he read for the first time a story by F. Scott Fitzgerald. He took a calculated risk and decided to publish tales about girls who drank, smoked, swore, wore tight and rather skimpy bathing suits, engaged in and enjoyed sexual adventures, and talked impudently to their parents. The audience for such stories almost certainly would purchase cosmetics. Lorimer's speculation paid off. Advertisements illustrating how other girls could enjoy similar popularity blossomed in the columns and pages adjoining these stories. Then advertisements advising mothers on how to look younger and enjoy life in the fashion of their daughters appeared. Circulation rose. Soon other magazines aiming at the same market—such as the *Ladies' Home Journal*, the *Woman's Home Companion*, *Liberty*, the *Metropolitan* and the *Delineator*—tried to emulate this success. Fine writers, such as Sherwood Anderson, formerly considered both obscene and subversive now received invitations to submit manuscripts to mass-circulation magazines. Dreiser became a regular contributor to the *Post*, and that magazine even ran a series of Dreiser's articles from the Soviet Union sympathetic to the Communist government. Dreiser also published numerous short stories in the once staid women's magazines.[15]

Malcolm Cowley exaggerated only slightly when he asserted that if Greenwich Village was dying as an outpost of life-styles inimical to Victorianism, it was because

> wherever one turned, Greenwich Village ideas were making their way; even the *Saturday Evening Post* was feeling their influence.... It was dying because too many people insisted on living there. It was dying because women smoked cigarettes on the streets of the Bronx, drank gin cocktails in Omaha and had perfectly swell parties in Seattle and Middletown—in other words because American business and the whole of middle-class America had been going Greenwich Village.

Cowley declared that by the late 1920s, Smith College girls in New York were modeling themselves after the promiscuous Lady Brett in Hemingway's *The Sun Also Rises*,[16] and Lady Brett was nearly the antithesis of a Victorian woman of character.

❦❘❦❘❦

Anthropologists, led by students of Franz Boas, refined the concept of culture in the 1920s and applied it to new topics and geographical areas. The two most widely read books in this literature were written by Boas's student Margaret Mead. Both books described the development of children in technologically primitive South Pacific cultures and compared the maturation of these children with that of children in middle-class American families. Mead's pioneering studies found the two primitive cultures superior to middle-class American culture in the vital area of female and male child rearing.

In her dissertation, published as *Coming of Age in Samoa* (1928), Mead presented evidence that Samoan children lived happier lives than American children and felt more useful to and more a part of their society. She claimed that Samoans suffered virtually no adolescent tempests or neuroses. Their early pleasurable sexual experiences led to friendlier and stabler marriages. Fundamental to this evidently superior Samoan child rearing was a family structure in which many people shared in the nurturing of children, a system almost diametrically opposed to the tight-knit Victorian family unit, which retained its role as the American middle-class ideal in the 1920s. Thus, Mead not only pointed to an apparent deficiency in the child-rearing practices Americans had inherited from Victorian culture but also described a model which suggested improvements that could change the entire society.[17]

As *Coming of Age in Samoa* moved onto the best-seller lists in 1928 and remained there, Mead traveled to New Guinea to expand her research into alternative modes of raising children. Concentrating this time on male socialization, Mead showed that boys in New Guinea benefited from close association with their fathers. This relationship protected these boys from the belief—then common within the American middle class—that certain jobs, such as child rearing, and educational and artistic pursuits were unsuitable for males. American boys tended to associate such tasks with women. Unlike the United States, where middle-class fathers often were practically strangers to their children, successful men in New Guinea helped their sons absorb skills and, with them, self-assurance, thus facilitating their assimilation into satisfying adult roles.[18]

Many other anthropologists wrote indictments similar to Mead's of American middle-class families and of work in America. Ruth Benedict and Edward Sapir, also Boas's students, produced the most damaging of these. Benedict completed her fieldwork among the Zuni pueblo Indians of New Mexico in 1923, though she did not publish her full account and conclusions in *Patterns of Culture* until 1934. However, a series of articles and addresses to professional organizations beginning in 1928 acquainted scholars with her message before the end of the 1920s.[19]

Benedict made use of Boas's research among the Kwakiutl of Vancouver Island and that of Mead's husband, Reo F. Fortune, on Dobu Island near New Guinea. She described the fiercely competitive economic and social behavior of the Kwakiutl and the Dobu as caricatures of some of the least lovely characteristics of American middle-class behavior. Benedict plainly preferred the cultural patterns she had observed among the communal and artistic Zuni. Sapir's supreme critique "Culture, Genuine and Spurious," published by the *American Journal of Sociology* in 1924, spread among other social scientists the arguments already familiar to anthropologists. Those American Indian tribes whose cultural cohesion had not been destroyed by white intruders, Sapir declared in this article, usually remained "inherently balanced, self-satisfactory . . . , the expression of a richly varied and yet somehow unified and consistent attitude toward life." He went on to compare these "genuine" Indian cultures to the "spurious" American civilization, with its spiritually unrewarding work for most people ("a desert patch of economic effort in the whole of life") and its education "that too often bore no relationship to the rest of students' lives."[20]

An aura of despair hung over a large portion of works derived from the most innovative sociological research undertaken during the 1920s. The chief theme of studies conducted at the University of Chicago's Department of Sociology—the first real sociology program—became the social disorganization rampant in the city. Rapid change of many kinds, the Chicago sociologists discovered, weakened traditional social controls, broke down feelings of community and group solidarity, and fragmented society. Crime, divorce, mental illness, social deviancy, and race and ethnic conflict—evidence of social disintegration—were subjected to intensive investigation. Poverty, graphically described in the monographs emanating from this research, accompanied the fragmentation as either cause or effect within ethnic and racial ghettos and among individuals described by the sociologists as "marginal."[21] A similar pattern in rural areas was discovered in research conducted by the Institute for Research in the Social Sciences, founded by sociologist Howard W. Odum at the University of North Carolina during the 1920s.[22]

This unhappy vision, which also served as a denunciation of American Victorianism, pervaded the single most influential book by social scientists published during the 1920s: Robert and Helen Lynd's *Middletown*. The clearest statement of the book's purpose appeared in its foreword, written by anthropologist Clark Wissler. The volume, he explained, was a pioneer effort "to study ourselves as through the eye of an outsider" by dealing with "a sample American community as an anthropologist does a primitive tribe."[23] The Lynds subtitled their book "A Study in American Culture," intending the work to be a general statement about American civilization. However, it served also as the first broad study of a single American community.

The Lynds' sample city, Muncie, Indiana, seemed like a stopping point along the way to Dante's inferno. The great majority of inhabitants, defined by the authors as "The Working Class"—over 70 percent of Middletown's population—earned on average less per family than the U.S. Bureau of Labor Statistics estimated as necessary for mere survival. Furthermore, interviews with businessmen and workers proved that the latter had good reason to fear periodic unemployment and the probable permanent loss of their jobs as soon as their physical capabilities began to decrease in their forties.

Among many symptoms of a society unable to satisfy its members' needs allegedly was a higher divorce rate. This had increased from nine divorces for each hundred marriage licenses issued (not all used, of course) in 1889 to forty-two for each hundred in 1924, and the rate appeared to be still rising. Among the possible causes of this massacre of marriages, the Lynds found a near total absence of what they termed "companionship" between husbands and wives of all classes. Interviewed privately, however, married men and women in Middletown demonstrated a desperate desire for this companionship. Yet, not a single woman of either business or working class mentioned spending more time with her husband among the things she would like to do if given an extra hour in the day.[24] Conversations with businessmen also disclosed deep dissatisfaction.[25] New stresses, added expectations, and lack of understanding or training in meeting them left the Lynds' sample of Americans perplexed and unhappy. University of Chicago sociologists termed this type of situation "culture lag," though they failed to inform Americans who resembled the unfortunate inhabitants of Middletown about what they might do immediately—beyond seeking a divorce—to alleviate their misery.

Probably the most significant achievement of the academic intellectuals between 1912 and 1930 was their crucial role in the nearly complete repudiation of every scientific rationale for racism. Early in the twentieth century, only a few humanitarians and scholarly skeptics doubted the premise that a hierarchy of races existed in the United States, with "Nordics" on top, recent immigrants from southern and eastern Europe far down but above migrants from Mexico and Asia, and, at the very bottom, blacks. By the late 1920s, the prevailing opinion among intellectuals had been almost entirely altered. The change was not early enough or widely enough disseminated, however, to prevent passage of immigration restriction acts in 1921 and 1924 or to affect the course of judicial opinions concerning blacks until after the 1920s.

Again Boas and his students led the way toward undermining Victorian verities.[26] Boas himself measured head forms and took other bodily measurements of recent immigrants and their children at a rate of up to 1,200 individuals a week and then reported "very striking and wholly unexpected results." In the American environment, the evidence showed conclusively that "far reaching changes" took place, demonstrating an unsuspected "great plasticity of human types." Boas's student Melville Herskovits came to a similar conclusion after measurements of black migrants to the North. Other students and protégés of Boas destroyed one of the major weapons used by those who tried to make a case for black inferiority—the results of the United States Army's and other intelligence tests. Supported by foundation fellowships—especially from the Social Science Research Council—which Boas helped them obtain, Mead, Herskovits, social psychologist Otto Klineburg, and others demonstrated that the intelligence test scores of blacks correlated closely with their length of residence in northern cities. Blacks who had lived for long periods in the North scored higher than southern whites.[27] By the late 1920s, a large number of influential social scientists had testified publicly to drastic changes in their opinions about the role of race in determining intelligence. As a consequence, textbooks and lectures were revised, journals reoriented, and books and articles announcing the correction of the authors' ideas were published.[28]

As a result of the all but unanimous rejection of racism by the scholars most involved in the study of race, the ideas of Boas and his disciples became the conventional wisdom of intellectuals, insinuated by them throughout American society, especially through educational institutions and the higher courts. The success of their efforts was shown when a careful survey of scientists carried out in 1929 revealed that a mere 4 percent still believed in the genetic inferiority of blacks. Only 19 percent even agreed that blacks *seemed* inferior. About half denied not only the existence of racial differences but also even the possibility of important differences based on race. This was tantamount to rejecting altogether the significance of race.[29] Thus, among these Americans with great influence over public opinion, one of the basic concepts that had given distinction and power to Victorianism virtually disappeared as a respectable idea.

During the 1920s, the largest, liveliest, and perhaps the most talented group of novelists, poets, playwrights, and literary critics to that point in United States history skillfully exposed the same faults in American civilization emphasized by the academic intellectuals. Such influential novels as Sinclair Lewis's *Main Street* and *Babbitt*, Dreiser's *An American Tragedy*, and Fitzgerald's *The Great Gatsby* contained social criticism which hardly differed from that of *Middletown* or *Coming of Age in Samoa*. The novelists denounced American materialism, pressure for conformity, bigotry, shattered family life, sexual repression, fragmented society, and, in general, the inability of American civilization to fill its members' needs or even to teach them what these were. Most of these themes could also be found in some of the period's best poetry—such as T. S. Eliot's *The Waste Land* and Ezra Pound's *Huge Selwyn Mauberly*—and plays—including Eugene O'Neil's *Marco Millions, Desire Under the Elms*, and *Strange Interlude*.

In this literature and in other novels, stories, poems, and plays by these authors, readers encountered a pessimism about the possibility of improving what the writers disliked in American civilization; nor did the writers find any higher being at work in the chaos they described.[30] In these respects, also, the attitudes of most literary intellectuals during the 1920s resembled those which pervaded *Middletown* and *Coming of Age in Samoa*. Their works differed sharply from those of the genteel Victorian authors. Moreover in the 1920s, publishers, journal editors, and producers of plays sought the work of the critical intellectuals for prestige as well as for profits. Denunciations of books, stories, articles, and plays made by the few remaining genteel literary critics or the banning of this literature in Boston or elsewhere because of obscenity only insured more energetic praise from critics like H. L. Mencken and seemed to guarantee high sales.

New ideas in science also attracted talented thinkers and funds, stimulated creativity, and disturbed the inheritors of nineteenth-century Victorianism. As knowledge of quantum mechanics spread among scientists—from theoretical physicists to experimentalists, physical chemists, biologists, and electrical engineers—elements in quantum theory that appeared to contradict the concept of an orderly and comprehensible universe became widely known. Explanations of probability, the uncertainty principle, and the duality or correspondence of wave and particle theories of atomic processes had, by the late 1920s, appeared not only in science textbooks but also in popular magazines and newspapers.[31] At the same time, vastly improved telescopes multiplied the size of the observable universe—perhaps, the planet earth might be only an insignificant part of an infinite universe containing galaxies without end.[32]

❧|❧|❧

New leadership within the more dynamic philanthropic foundations and academic disciplines bore much of the responsibility for the increasing tendency during the 1920s to support the most promising research centers, individual researchers, and ideas, regardless of the effects on established social conventions, morality, or intellectual concepts. This tendency resembled that of the new book and magazine publishers and of the recently appointed editors and heads of older publishing houses and literary magazines to search for authors with fresh themes and styles rather than to publish work, as Victorian publishers had, that protected conventional morality, social relationships, and ideas.

The foundation officials most responsible for the new policy were Wickliffe Rose of the Rockefeller Foundation's Sanitary Commission, International Health Commission, General Education Board, and International Education Board; Beardsley Ruml of the Laura Spelman Rockefeller Memorial Fund; and Henry Allen Moe of the John Simon Guggenheim Memorial Foundation. Each held views similar to the leading scholars with whom they frequently dealt. Although not distinguished scholars themselves, they had begun their careers as promising academics before deciding to place primary emphasis on their great administrative talents. As a result of their academic experience, however, they shared most basic intellectual views of their foremost scholarly contemporaries.[33]

Rose exerted a more profound and lasting influence on American education than any other foundation leader. The pattern of his educational and scientific activities can be traced back at least to his leadership of the Rockefeller Sanitary Commission, established in 1909 to drastically reduce hookworm disease in the South.

Rose had served as professor of history, philosophy, and mathematics for thirteen years at Peabody College in Nashville, Tennessee, and for several years as dean of that college. In 1907, he accepted a position as field director of the Peabody Fund for southern education. In that post, Rose established hundreds of "demonstration schools" in the South. Two years later, in May 1909, his uncle and godfather, Wallace Buttrick, head of the Rockefeller Foundation's General Education Board, attempted to persuade Rose to serve as chief administrator of the newly authorized Sanitary Commission. After much anguish over whether he could assume any new responsibilities and over his lack of medical training, Rose finally accepted the post in December 1909.[34]

Rose's remarkable achievements as the sole full-time administrator of the commission led to his selection as a member of the Rockefeller Foundation's first Board of Trustees when the foundation was incorporated in 1913. Rose suggested in his first report of the Sanitary Commission in 1910 the possible extension of the hookworm campaign to sixty-eight areas throughout the world with a high incidence of hookworm disease. Before accepting his position with the commission, Rose had extracted a promise that his duties would eventually include attempts to combat diseases other than hookworm. When Rose suggested a worldwide fight against epidemics, starting with hookworm, Rockefeller Foundation officials already had decided that his plans would receive approval.[35]

Rose presented his proposal at the first meeting of the Rockefeller Foundation's Board of Directors on May 23, 1913. Simon Flexner, the pathologist and bacteriologist who directed the Rockefeller Institute for Medical Research and who served with Rose as one of the foundation's first nine directors, had been advising Rose about medical—including public-health—matters since Rose's acceptance of the Sanitary Commission post. In 1899, Flexner had served as chairman of a special commission that had studied and eventually had identified the causes of dysentery in the Philippines. In 1900, the U.S. Secretary of the Treasury had appointed him chairman of the Plague Commission, which in 1901 had determined that bubonic plague in San Francisco's Chinatown greatly endangered the city and, therefore, the whole United States. After Rose's proposal to his fellow directors, Flexner wrote Rose offering assistance, including "letters sent abroad in advance of your going."

Walter Hines Page, a director of the Sanitary Commission had written to a friend on January 26, 1913 (four months before Rose's proposal to the Rockefeller Foundation directors):

> The most efficient workmanlike piece of organization that my mortal eyes have ever seen is Rose's hookworm work. . . . Congress seems likely to charter the big Rockefeller Foundation which will at once make five millions available for chasing the hookworm off the face of the earth. Rose will spread himself over Honduras, etc., etc., and China and India! That does literally beat the devil; for if the hookworm isn't the devil, what is?[36]

Between 1913 and 1915, Rose served as head of both the Sanitary Commission and the new International Health Board (IHB). He expanded the IHB's scope to combatting yellow fever, typhus, and malaria, as well as hookworm.[37]

Rose proved to be a creative administrator. Although the son of a fundamentalist Protestant minister, Rose displayed in his work none of the religious fervor shown by John D. Rockefeller, Sr., John D. Rockefeller, Jr., occasionally by his co-trustee of the Sanitary Commission Frederick T. Gates, or by the Sanitary Commission's scientific director Charles Wardell Stiles. Stiles, a federal government zoologist, was chosen for his position largely because he had proposed the campaign against hookworm. He went so far as to prepare a "hookworm catechism," containing use of the phrases "Thou shalt" and "Thou shalt not."[38]

Rose chose his scientific and administrative assistants on the basis of their demonstrated superior scientific and administrative qualifications. Writing to Simon Flexner on Sanitary Commission stationery late in 1913 Rose declared:

> For this service [the newly authorized IHB] we want the very best of men we can get. In addition to their having the best medical training and being able to command the respect of the medical profession, they must be men of personality and large administrative ability. I hope in time to bring together in this service a number of physicians which will stand for the very best in the field of preventive medicine.

Never did Rose mention in connection with the Sanitary Commission or the IHB the type of moral qualifications that still concerned many college and university presidents, as well as John D. Rockefeller, Sr.[39]

The system Rose found most successful in fighting disease throughout the world involved first identifying research centers within the nations afflicted with an epidemic where the understanding of that disease and of its treatment was most advanced. Then, those centers were expanded and improved with the assistance of financial contributions and advice from Rose and his assistants. Physicians and paramedical workers from areas especially affected by the disease received salaries for coming to these hospitals and medical schools to participate in research, classes, and other means of teaching them the latest techniques and medications for treatment. When these medical specialists returned to their homes, they received encouragement to train others, as well as to continue their own work, in the form of money, medicine, and medical equipment. In this fashion, Rose and the foundations he directed helped bring under control diseases that had decimated populations for centuries.

As Rose ascended toward the top among administrators within the Rockefeller Foundation—becoming head of its War Relief Commission and finally president of its General Education Board (GEB) and International Education Board (IEB)—he remained strong in his belief that the most rapid way to develop any area of knowledge was to strengthen and enlarge the world's foremost research and teaching centers in that field. Specialists and students brought to these centers afterward would radiate around the world, carrying the most advanced ideas with them.

While directing medical programs, Rose had decided that the future welfare of mankind depended most upon advances in the physical and biological sciences. This conclusion was based upon an amalgamation of his own experience and the ideas that were popular among the academic scientific leaders with whom Rose came into contact during World War I, when he helped direct cooperation between the Rockefeller Foundation and the National Research Council (NRC). Rose echoed those scientific leaders and summarized a chief reason for the success of the Sanitary Commission and the International Health Board when he recorded in his private notebook early in the 1920s: "This is an age of science. All important activities from the breeding of bees to the administration of an empire call for an understanding of the spirit and techniques of modern science."

As a result of Rose's success as an administrator, his fellow Rockefeller Foundation trustees placed him in a position to implement his ideas. Because the GEB's charter limited it to activities within the United States, the trustees created the IEB, at Rose's request, and made Rose president of that as well. They also gave the IEB funds sufficient to increase significantly the quality and quantity of work in the major foreign scientific centers and to provide assistance to excellent young scientists who wished to study or participate in research at the centers aided by the GEB and IEB.

Money from the IEB flowed to Europe's strongest research institutes and departments of science, especially after Rose's five-month tour beginning in November 1923 of over 200 research centers in 19 countries. Rose returned with the conviction that the primary emphasis of the IEB should be to offer financial support to centers of research in theoretical physics. The basic problems of atomic structure seemed near solution, and IEB funds could contribute to a breakthrough. Meanwhile, the beneficiaries of Rose's generosity would accept IEB and NRC fellows, who would assimilate an understanding of the basic questions as well as the latest knowledge in atomic theory. Furthermore, Rose believed, the tasks posed by the atom were so large and complex that they required international cooperation—another of his goals.

Rose returned to the United States persuaded that he had found three centers of research in theoretical physics capable of serving as models for other institutes or university departments which sought GEB or IEB support. As a result of reports from his NRC and Rockefeller Foundation advisers and of information he received from the scientific centers themselves, Rose selected Niels Bohr's Institute for Theoretical Physics in Copenhagen, the Department of Physics at the University of Göttingen, and the Department of Physics at the University of Leiden as the first IEB "training centers" in Europe. As a condition for receiving IEB financial assistance, these centers, and others selected by Rose later, agreed to accept greater numbers of IEB and NRC fellows and to provide additional faculty and facilities for them.

To direct the flow of money and students and to keep him informed accurately, Rose chose Augustus Trowbridge, professor of physics at Princeton University, who took a leave from the university to work full-time for Rose. Trowbridge remained in Europe, headquartered in Paris, sending Rose lengthy reports that played a large role in determining where IEB funds for equipment, construction, and additional faculty would go.

In order to stimulate basic research in the United States, especially theoretical research, Rose halted the GEB's policy of contributing to general endowment funds of American universities, contributions which had reached $60 million when he assumed the board's presidency. Instead, Rose inaugurated a program to strengthen the research and graduate teaching capabilities of the nation's strongest university science departments by contributing funds directly to these departments.

Between 1923 and 1928 (when Rose retired), the GEB committed about $19 million to science departments, mostly to hire additional faculty in theoretical areas. Almost all of these grants required recipients to obtain matching funds from private donors, their universities, or other philanthropic organizations. These policies placed use of the funds largely outside the jurisdiction of university officials.

American centers for research and training in theoretical physics comparable in quality to those at Copenhagen, Göttingen, or Leiden did not exist in the United States during the early 1920s. Even the next lower level of European centers—at Zürich, Münich, Berlin, Paris, and Cambridge—had no counterparts in America. However, due in large part to the complementary programs of the GEB, IEB, and NRC, by the late 1920s five American physics departments had created theoretical physics faculties on a par with at least the second level of European centers. Six other theoretical faculties stood not far behind these five. Virtually all the theorists who formed these faculties had studied at centers assisted by IEB and GEB funds with the aid of NRC and IEB fellowships.[40]

❦|❦|❦

Beardsley Ruml came closer than any of the other philanthropic leaders of the 1920s to exerting an influence on the social science and humanities analagous to Rose's on the physical sciences. Ruml earned his Ph.D. degree from the University of Chicago in 1917, doing research in the new mathematical field of psychological testing. As the wartime co-director of the government's Division of Trade Tests, he attracted the attention of business as well as foundation executives. When Raymond Fosdick and Abraham Flexner of the Rockefeller Foundation sought in 1921 the ablest and most available young man to assist in implementing the foundation's ambitious postwar plans, they made Ruml their first choice.

Ruml, then twenty-seven years of age, apparently stood on the verge of a successful business career; however, Fosdick persuaded him that the opportunities philanthropic work presented for service to mankind outweighed the smaller income he would receive. Ruml accepted the foundation's offer.

Within two years, Ruml received a promotion to director of the Laura Spelman Rockefeller Memorial. He decided to use the large amount of money available to the foundation to support a broad plan to aid research in the social sciences.

When Ruml and his foundation checkbook arrived on the scene, the disciplines he sought to aid were suffering withdrawal pangs as wartime programs and their temporary successors concluded. Assured of his support, the recently organized and financially destitute Social Science Research Council (SSRC) called a meeting of leading scholars in each of its representative fields at Dartmouth College in the summer of 1925. Ruml paid all expenses. A series of annual conferences followed, attended by two delegates to the council already selected by each professional association, by influential scholars invited by Ruml, and by representatives from several other foundations and of federal, state, and municipal research bureaus. Conversations at these meetings produced not only financial results but also agreement on research priorities and distribution of the funds promised—largely by Ruml. Throughout the 1920s, Ruml continued to act as chief and most certain financial angel for the SSRC.

Ruml's cooperation with leading social scientists—like Columbia University anthropologist Boas and University of Chicago political scientist Charles Merriam—made possible social-science research that contradicted established ideas in socially important areas of thought. Largely through projects proposed by Boas, the huge literature aimed at proving the inherent inferiority of blacks and of immigrants from southern and eastern Europe was discredited. SSRC funds supported a spread of American social-science research to the South Pacific, Africa, Mexico, and to comparative studies of American Indian cultures. These studies tended to demonstrate that the technologically primitive cultures were in many ways superior to conventional American middle-class culture. Studies of urban immigrant and migrant groups sponsored by the SSRC emphasized the disruptive force of the dominant American culture.[41]

❚|❚|❚

Like Ruml, Henry Allen Moe appeared headed for almost certain business success until foundation officials recruited him by appealing to his intellectual and humanitarian values. Moe, too, had assimilated these while doing graduate work at a great university. As a Rhodes Scholar at Oxford, Moe had studied law and medieval and Elizabethan English literature. Throughout his career as a foundation official, Moe continued to publish scholarly articles about English literature.

When Moe returned to the United States in 1923 at the age of twenty-eight, he received an offer to join a New York City law firm. As he prepared to accept, former United States senator Simon Guggenheim of Colorado—who had earned a fortune as head of the Guggenheim-family mining interests in the western United States—requested his assistance in drawing up plans for a projected major foundation. Moe postponed his legal career to participate in this project. Moe's partner in planning the new foundation, Frank Aydelotte, a professor of English at several universities before his appointment as president of Swarthmore College in 1921, joined him in months of intensive study. They collected data concerning practices of other foundations, determined amounts of money available from all sources for fellowships, and interviewed scores of scholars, artists, college presidents, professionals, and businessmen, seeking suggestions about intellectual and artistic areas which the Guggenheims' money might affect most fruitfully.

Moe drew up the final plans for the foundation, which Senator Guggenheim named after his son who had died of pneumonia, John Simon Guggenheim. After a luncheon meeting at which Senator Guggenheim and Moe discussed Moe's conception of the new foundation, the senator offered Moe the opportunity to direct the foundation. Moe later declared that he (like Ruml) had weighed the opportunity to affect the course of American intellectual and artistic life against the certainty of a larger income in business. The decision had required half a second of serious consideration, he recalled, and then he had replied, "Yes."

Moe described the donor of the funds he disbursed, in terms similar to those used about the senior and junior John Rockefellers by Rose and Ruml, as "always interested . . . , never obtrusive." These successful industrial magnates, having learned as their enterprises grew to delegate responsibilities among carefully chosen experts, applied the same principles to the foundations they established.

Moe established a tiered system of unpaid referees, juries, committees of selection, and an advisory board to read applications and letters of recommendation and to view works submitted by artist-applicants. At each level, these advisors culled from the host of applicants those most likely to use a grant for significant creative accomplishment. Among the artists, scientists, and social scientists that the Guggenheim Foundation supported for at least a year during its first ten years were composers Aaron Copeland, Gian Carlo Menotti, Roy Harris, and Walter Piston; poets Langston Hughes, Countee Cullen, W. H. Auden, Hart Crane, and e. e. cummings; novelists and literary critics Conrad Aiken, Louis Adamic, Stephen Vincent Benét, John Crowe Ransom, and Edmund Wilson; scores of historians; and scientists Linus Pauling, Arthur Compton, Norbert Weiner, and Hermann Joseph Muller.

Among the information the referees and committees considered were analyses of candidates by Moe himself. Moe's criteria for these evaluations were evident in some of his statements. He quoted with approval the declaration by one of his fellows that the concepts underlying great scientific achievements came from the minds of "a handful of men, scattered over a continent and a century—men who were willful, uncompromising, quarrelsome, arrogant, and creative." Called before a congressional committee investigating "security risks" in December 1952, Moe explained past decisions by the Guggenheim Foundation to grant fellowships to alleged radicals by asserting: "What I think you can say on the basis of history is that the great artists, and writers, and composers of all times have never been exactly cozy members of society . . . and in my view it is a good thing that they are not, too. They are the people that, when they are really good, carry the ball for civilization."

Moe did not search for unconventional thinkers to support. His interests lay more in the direction of his words "uncompromising," "creative," and "really good." A sizable proportion of such individuals may have held ideas contrary to accepted truths, but Moe never considered this one of his major concerns. His attitude in this respect can be discerned in the case of a scientist of whom Moe and his staff had never heard and who had requested a fellowship for unusual research in immunology. Inquiries revealed that the applicant possessed only one arm. "This gave me pause," Moe acknowledged. "Here was a man who did his research in a laboratory where a fellow certainly needs two arms, and could use three. Moreover one of the referees submitted by the applicant had written us that his ideas were old hat." Just to be sure a refusal was warranted, Moe requested a few of the scientist's papers and brought them to the Rockefeller Institute's experts in immunology. They reported that the man's research was far in advance of anything else then in progress. The selection committees accepted this opinion, and the applicant received a fellowship. About twenty years later, the research that the one-armed scientist had described in his application earned him a Nobel Prize. "That's how it goes," Moe declared, "We hooked that one and he did us proud, but I get nervous when I think of how close we came to losing him. We make mistakes."[42]

❦|❦|❦

The type of individuals whom Rose, Ruml, Moe, and the foundations directed by them assisted and the ideas which emanated from these individuals conformed to the ideals about intellectual activity expressed by Pound, Hemingway, and by Lewis's Gottlieb. They either ignored or actively opposed demands by the inheritors of Victorianism for limitations on intellectual and artistic exploration. In expressing the results of their investigations, they refused to comply with either conventional morality or accepted truths. As a result, some of them poked large holes in basic Victorian beliefs and values, leaving the foundation of Victorianism shaky and the defenders of Victorianism alarmed.

4

THE PROBLEM OF THE
TWENTIETH CENTURY

Late nineteenth-century Americans inherited the legacy of a caste system in which the lowest levels were determined by skin color. In descending order, Asians, American Indians, and African-Americans occupied the bottom layer. Victorians built their economic and social order upon this legacy, and in their hands, the color caste system became increasingly rigid, legally codified, and based upon elaborate rationalizations. These ideas concerning the "natural" superiority of whites—particularly of so-called "Nordics"—helped to justify not only the hardening of racial attitudes among Victorians toward American blacks but also imperial expansion into the lands of nonwhite peoples elsewhere.[1]

Americans had relegated blacks to a special place in their society by the middle of the seventeenth century. At that early stage of the colonists' history, white Americans had decided that nature intended blacks, whom they considered subhuman, to serve as slaves under the benevolent and nearly complete authority of white masters. Although a small proportion of blacks escaped slavery, they retained the stigma of their skin color, and none gained full equality with whites. During the late eighteenth and early nineteenth centuries, ideas of equality appeared close to including blacks, but that notion receded from popularity before reaching such an extreme. Even after emancipation, only marginal improvement in economic and social status took place for the overwhelming majority of African-Americans. The Victorian ethos was so pervasive that in places where a small black middle class developed—most noticeably in Charleston, Atlanta, Philadelphia, and New Orleans—these relatively educated and successful blacks themselves accepted most attitudes underlying the caste system. They placed a high value on light-colored skin and other supposedly non-Negroid characteristics and separated themselves as much as possible from ordinary blacks.[2]

After World War I, however, during a series of race wars in twenty-six towns and cities between April and October 1919, armed blacks defended themselves more aggressively than ever before. In Chicago, Knoxville, and Washington, D.C., especially, enraged blacks even took the offensive.[3] Other important evidence that blacks demanded to be taken seriously as human beings equal to whites included black nationalist movements, militant journalism, a literature self-consciously black, and enhanced pride in black music.

❧ | ❧ | ❧

Demographic changes played a critical role in creating conditions favorable to black attempts at improving their status in the 1920s. Until the late nineteenth century, over 90 percent of American blacks lived in the southern and border states. As the South industrialized, blacks moved gradually from rural to urban areas within that section in an effort to escape from the economic treadmill of sharecropping and farm labor and from the unrestrained violence, including lynching, directed at them in the southern countryside. Less than 15 percent of all Southerners and well under 10 percent of southern blacks resided in urban areas in 1890. Twenty-two percent of southern blacks lived in urban areas by 1910, over 25 percent in 1920, and 31.7 percent in 1930.

A stream of black migration to the North began late in the nineteenth century, fed by the adverse effects of cotton prices, which annually either fell or failed to rise nearly as much as the price of goods black farmers bought. This migration from both country and city in the South was stimulated also by heightened oppression against blacks by white Southerners, including a record number of lynchings and race riots in southern cities. Reports of jobs for blacks and less blatant prejudice in the North further encouraged migration.[4]

W. E. B. Du Bois, a skillful sociologist, then a professor at Atlanta University, described the South in the early twentieth century as "largely . . . an armed camp for intimidating black folk." Du Bois surveyed rural Georgia and in his classic *Souls of Black Folk*, published in 1903, reported that blacks were fearful and angry but not altogether cowed. Without realizing it at the time, Du Bois was describing a people ready to move. He reported as representative the statement of a black farm worker in Daugherty County near Albany, Georgia, who "muttered to me with the murmur of many ages . . . : 'White man sit down whole year; nigger work day and night and make crops; nigger hardly gits bread and meat; white man sittin' down gits all.' " Du Bois overheard a conversation in the store of an Albany merchant who was perplexed about why local blacks appeared "sulky, dissatisfied, and careless," while their parents had acted "happy and dumb and faithful." " 'Why you niggers have an easier time than I do,' said [the] puzzled Albany merchant to his black customer. 'Yes,' the black replied, 'an' so does you' hogs.' "[5]

The steady flow of black migrants north turned into a flood during and just after World War I, due largely to publicized shortages of unskilled and semi-skilled labor. The migration was propelled also by more rigid repression in the South—caused in large part by fear of black soldiers returning from the war—and it was encouraged by news circulating among blacks in the South verifying rumors of better treatment and greater economic and educational opportunities in northern cities. That information was transmitted to the South by thousands of letters from migrants to relatives and friends they had left behind, by articles in northern newspapers—especially the Chicago *Defender*, which reached much of the South and reprinted scores of the encouraging letters—by agents of northern corporations seeking cheap labor, and by railroads wooing passengers.[6]

Southern white employers tried to check this population outflow with tactics ranging from promises of improved conditions to intimidation, including kidnapping. But nothing worked. The commonest attitude among those blacks who planned to leave or had left was that periodic unemployment and freezing winter weather in the North was preferable to certain peonage and possible lynching in the South. A contemporary folk tale, repeated frequently with slight variations in northern ghettos, describes an unemployed black migrant, cold, wet, and hungry, appealing to God for advice.

"Go back to Mississippi," the Lord told him.

"You don't mean it Lord," the startled man replied, "you're jesting."

The Lord repeated, "Go back to Mississippi!"

Finally the man relented. "Very well, Lord, if you insist I'll go; but only if you'll go with me."

The Lord answered, "Only as far as Cincinnati."[7]

Most black migrants were young and, at first, predominantly male, a common pattern among immigrant groups. The Department of Labor established a Division of Negro Economics primarily to find the causes and probable duration of the black exodus. In its first published report, the division offered as a typical example of the process at work this account by a Southern rural black preacher:

> My father was born and brought up as a slave. He never knew anything else until after I was born. He was taught his place and was content to keep it. But when he brought me up he let some of the old customs slip by. But I know that there are certain things that I must do, and I do them, and it doesn't worry me. Yet in bringing up my own son, I let some more of the old customs slip by. He has been through the eighth grade; he reads easily. For a year I have been keeping him from going to Chicago; but he tells me that this is his last crop; that in the fall he's going. He says, "When a young white man talks rough to me, I can't talk rough to him. You can stand that; I can't. I have some education, and inside I has the feelins of a white man. I'm goin'."[8]

Census figures show that the black population decreased in every southern state except Florida, Arkansas, and Oklahoma during the 1920s, while every northern and western state except Maine, Vermont, and North Dakota gained black residents.[9]

Lacking capital to purchase land and to wait for a marketable crop, blacks who moved to the North settled almost entirely in urban areas, like most of the late nineteenth- and early twentieth-century European immigrant groups composed largely of former peasants. Furthermore, because of the earlier migration to southern cities, about one quarter of the black migrants had lived in urban areas. This portion, especially, gravitated to the major northern metropolitan centers. The black population of Chicago, for example, grew from 44,103 to 109,458 between 1910 and 1920—nearly 150 percent, seven times more rapidly than the larger white population increased. This discrepancy continued during the 1920s, as the number of blacks in Chicago rose to about 234,000 by 1930. The black population of New York City expanded 66 percent between 1910 and 1920—from 91,709 to 152,467—while the city's white population grew 17 percent; and the black population increased another 115 percent to 327,706 during the 1920s, while the number of whites in New York rose 20 percent.[10]

Blacks spread across the northern section of the uptown Manhattan district of Harlem, overcoming threats and resistance from white financial and real estate interests. Black-owned real-estate firms, led by the Afro-American Realty Company headed by Philip A. Payton, beginning in 1905 defied all attempts at intimidation and, encouraged by the black ministry and press, for a decade bought large numbers of apartment houses and evicted white tenants north of 130th Street. Payton, with assistance from Harlem undertaker J. C. Thomas, continued the struggle even after his company was forced into bankruptcy. Black churches also bought rows of Harlem apartments as part of the conscious effort to take over this architecturally superior area.[11]

Then during the 1920s, another 175,000 blacks migrated to New York City, most of whom settled in Harlem. By 1930, the black population of Harlem was 164,566. As blacks took over most of Harlem, NAACP official James Weldon Johnson wrote effusively in 1925:

> In the make-up of New York, Harlem is not merely a Negro colony or community, it is a city within a city, the greatest Negro city in the world. It is not a slum or a fringe, it is located in the heart of Manhattan and occupies one of the most beautiful and healthful sections of the city. It is not a "quarter" of dilapidated tenements, but is made up of new-law apartments and handsome dwellings, with well-paved and well-lighted streets. It has its own churches, social and civic centers, shops, theatres, and other places of amusement. And it contains more Negroes to the square mile than any other spot on earth. . . . There is nothing just like it in any other city in the country, for there is no preparation for it; no change in the character of the houses and streets; no change, indeed, in the appearance of the people, except their color. . . .[12]

Despite appearances such as those described by Johnson, the black takeover of Harlem did not improve the quality of living quarters for poor blacks appreciably. About 100,000 additional blacks crowded into Harlem during the 1920s. However, because of racism, the manifestations of which included restrictive real-estate covenants, even those blacks who prospered could not join white migrants from Harlem in moving to newly developed areas of Brooklyn, Queens, and the north Bronx. During the 1920s, therefore, the poor blacks who occupied most of Harlem knew what Johnson had called "handsome dwellings" as deteriorating buildings, subdivided into cubicles in which whole families dwelt, with ruinously high rents. As Johnson claimed, Harlem did contain "more Negroes to the square mile than any other spot on earth." However, increasingly, this situation began to resemble the crush and poverty in Calcutta and Bombay. In 1925, according to one investigation, two streets in Harlem probably had the most congested housing in the entire world. Investigations further revealed that while working-class whites in New York City paid 20 percent of their income for rent, a proportion considered appropriate by the Bureau of Labor Statistics, black families in Harlem spent between 40 and 45 percent of their lower earnings for rent.[13]

The combination of overcrowding and unsanitary housing, plus a population largely inexperienced in urban ways of life, led to widespread illness and to a high death rate. A study covering the years from 1923 to 1927 concluded that although Harlem residents were relatively young, their mortality rate exceeded that of the rest of the city by 42 percent. The proportions of mothers who died in childbirth and the infant mortality rate were twice as high in Harlem as in the rest of New York City. Deaths from tuberculosis were two-and-a-half to three times the city rate. Crime and violence of every kind also far exceeded that in other neighborhoods. Sociologist E. Franklin Frazier concluded after surveying the New York economic situation in the mid-1920s that the high rate of crime in Harlem almost surely was related to the adverse conditions. Frazier wrote that the city's business firms were divided between "those that employ Negroes in menial positions and those that employ no Negroes at all." These conditions were not very different from those in black neighborhoods within other major northern cities.[14]

❧|❧|❧

The state of northern urban blacks during the 1920s stimulated the activities of black intellectuals, artists, and social leaders. Many of these actions threatened the continued dominance of twentieth-century versions of the Victorian color caste system.

One of the most destructive of these activities to Victorian concepts arose from the sudden release of black speech, jazz, blues, and dances into white American society. Previously, those had been contained largely in black enclaves, especially in the rural South. By the 1920s, nightclubs and speakeasies in black areas of northern cities attracted white jazz fans who felt that "real" jazz could be heard only in its "natural" surroundings. In addition, novels, stories, and poems of black protest and musical shows featuring black social dances all proved alluring to white audiences. A high proportion of younger whites found black styles irresistible, often because they wanted to act and look up to date and to free themselves from restrictive Victorianism. Most of their elders lacked the audacity to open themselves to black styles, and they projected onto these their

deepest fears and most repressed wishes. Those black styles have continued to affect profoundly white music, dance, speech, dress, demeanor,
and literature.

Most white American adults of the 1920s had been persuaded at an
early age that Western symphonic music was the epitome of high culture,
superior to any other, especially to what sounded to them like savage black
"jungle music." Therefore, whites were disconcerted when they read statements during the 1920s from leading "classical" composers, conductors,
and music critics indicating that jazz would play a major role in forming
future musical forms. For example, when Russian composer Igor Stravinsky was interviewed during a visit to the United States in 1925, he
declared to a writer for the *American Mercury* that "The music of the future
will have to take it [jazz] into account. . . . In jazz you have something that
sneaked in on us from an out-on-the-corner cabaret. . . . We don't like to
admit it, but real music *has* such simple origins."[15]

Leopold Stokowski, conductor of the Philadelphia Orchestra, asserted
in 1924:

> Jazz has come to stay . . . and it is useless to fight against it. Already its
> vigor, its new vitality, is beginning to manifest itself.
> The Negro musicians of America are playing a great part in this change.
> . . . They are not hampered by traditions or conventions, with their new
> ideas, their constant experiments, they are causing new blood to flow in the
> veins of music. In America, I think, lies perhaps the greatest hope in the
> whole musical world.[16]

Maurice Ravel and other "classical" composers complimented jazz by
attempting to imitate it. Ravel spent part of a year during the 1920s in
Chicago listening especially to clarinetist Jimmy Noone's band and probably to Joe "King" Oliver's Creole Jazz Band, which included Louis Armstrong. Then Ravel used what he had learned from the Chicago jazzmen
in writing his next three compositions: *Bolero* and two piano concertos.[17]

However, according to Gunther Schuller—a classical composer, music
director, and a fine jazz historian and musicologist—Ravel, Darius Mil-
haud, Antonín Dvořák, and other modern composers all made the same
errors when they tried to use jazz in their compositions during the 1920s.
They mistook jazz instrumentation and its consequent resonance for its
main ingredients, ignoring jazz improvisation, rich inflection, and swing.
Schuller found such mistakes understandable: "These and similar over-
simplifications and misconceptions . . . are probably inevitable, for most
new art forms attract popular attention through their most external
aspects."[18]

Other white commentators on jazz during the 1920s were less generous than those who, like Stravinsky, were trying to create a modern music. As jazz swept into New York City in 1918, it was greeted by the publication of an article in *Current Opinion* magazine which began: "One touch of jazz makes savages of us all." A similar theme dominated an account entitled "Jazz" in the *Living Age* magazine (July 1920). The author declared that "My soul loathes it [jazz]." When obliged to listen to jazz, he did so with "serene toleration." He accomplished this feat by closing his eyes. The music itself then produced fascinating images in his mind: "There surges up before the inner eye a tropical African glade at night, the queer trees all lit by the light from a leaping fire below . . . a circle of cannibal forms, a great black pot . . . with the fire built up around it. . . ."[19]

The *New Republic* in September 1921 published an article by the widely respected English music critic Clive Bell, which announced that "Jazz is dead." In his "obituary" article, Bell declared that jazz had been a young people's music, "Like short skirts, it suits thin girlish legs, but has a slightly humiliating effect on gray hairs." Bell objected most strongly to the artistic pretensions of those who had perpetrated this "childish" music on whites: "Niggers can be admired artists without any gift more singular than high spirits: so why drag in the intellect?" What had turned so many "intelligent and sensitive people" against jazz, Bell concluded, "is the encouragement it has given to thousands of the stupid and vulgar to fancy that they can understand art and to hundreds of the conceited to imagine that they can create it." Four months later, in January 1922, the *Literary Digest* summarized the opinions of New York music and theater critics and found that they joined Bell in applauding the "demise of that form of music that came nearest to reviving some of the effects of the jumping maniacs of the Middle Ages."[20]

Nevertheless, jazz survived. So did white criticism of it. In the summer of 1924, the editors of one of New York's leading music magazines, the *Étude*, devoted most of two monthly issues to the responses to a survey of a cross section of illustrious Americans—most with some connection to the music world—seeking their opinions about jazz. The editors assured readers in their opening paragraph that "We do most emphatically *not endorse* jazz merely by discussing it." Respondents included Mrs. H. H. Beach, identified as a "renowned American Composer-Pianist," who declared, "Taken in association with some of the . . . dancing and the sentiment of some of the verses on which many of the jazz songs are founded, it would be difficult to find a combination more vulgar or debasing." Frank Damrosch, composer and director of New York's Institute of Musical Art, proclaimed that "When jazz was adopted by the highly civilized white race, it tended to degenerate toward primitivity." America's most influential rabbi, Dr. Stephen Wise of New York, declared that "When America regains its soul, jazz will go, not before.... "[21]

In 1926, as the audience for jazz and the blues continued to widen, the *Literary Digest* sampled opinions about the music expressed in English newspapers and magazines. The *Digest* found that "A veritable volcano of protest against that Afro-American product, jazz music, has flamed into action." As examples of that protest, the *Digest* cited statements to the *Times* of London and to the *New York Times* by one of the best-known English music critics, Ernest Newman. Newman told a reporter for the London *Times* that "The brains of the whole lot of jazz composers put together would not fill the lining of Johann Strauss's hat. Jazz itself is the last word in brainlessness and boredom." He also informed a correspondent for the *New York Times* that "jazzests"

> make a great point of their rhythmic innovations and the freedom of their rhythms. If they had any idea of what rhythm meant, they would know that in comparison with rhythms of any composers from the sixteenth century onward their own rhythms are merely as the singsong of a nursery rhyme to the changing subtleties of a page of Shakespeare.[22]

Newman's comments, which now seem ludicrous, become more understandable when considered within the context of the time in which they were made. The idea that a black music with distinctly African origins possessed cultural merit at least comparable with European "classical" music was unacceptable to Victorians in England or the United States during the 1920s. Furthermore, few white Europeans or Americans were accustomed yet to African rhythmic usages, which differed significantly from European concepts. Even specialists in the field of African ethnomusicology remained mystified until the mid-twentieth century by West African rhythms. As Schuller pointed out in 1968: "In respect to rhythm, African music is unquestionably the world's most complex music."[23] British specialist in African musicology A. M. Jones, in his two volume *Studies in African Music*, stated in 1959: "When we Europeans imagine we are beating strict time, the Africans will merely smile at the 'roughness' of our beating."[24]

Few Westerners understood the extent to which jazz and the blues were derived from African musical and oral traditions;[25] nor did the critics of jazz possess any knowledge about the severely competitive informal apprenticeship system through which black and white jazz musicians passed. All but the best candidates were eliminated by this system. Hundreds of taped oral-history interviews reveal that the creation of topflight jazz musicians followed patterns which resembled in fundamental respects the training received by other types of exceptionally fine artists.[26]

Beginning almost at birth, future black jazzmen heard music related to jazz during a large portion of every day. At practically every social or religious function—in the fields, where work songs, hollers, and spirituals were sung; in churches, where gospel music was played and sermons were sung as much as spoken; in homes, where jazz rhythms were often beat out on a kitchen table or where a guitarist playing and singing served as the chief form of early evening recreation in the rural areas where most Southern blacks grew up; and in their urban neighborhoods, where jazz bands were used to celebrate everything from weddings to funerals—music filled the air. This musical environment resembled West Africa, where ubiquitous drumming and singing continued all day.

The typical black jazzman of the 1920s reported taking part in the formation of a band as a preadolescent boy, often before the age of ten. The most talented youthful black musicians in an area or school gathered to play at local dances, fish fries, and picnics. The youngest musicians used banjos made out of tin cans or cigar boxes strung with fishing cord, washboards, metal pans, whistles, bells, wooden blocks, and anything else available that could be used as an instrument.

The especially talented boys made some money from donations and some from the sale of food and beer. As they saved money or received hand-me-downs from sympathetic listeners, they added more adult instruments. After years of competition at local affairs, the young musicians recognized as most skillful coalesced around a leader and sought work in the nearest city. There they learned the nuances of the regional style, usually by copying the recognized masters. Again, the most proficient musicians in these youthful bands were winnowed out, this time by requests to join as backup players the city's successful commercial bands. These positions became permanent if they passed the tests of their playing. Most recalled that they finally obtained their first professional jazz instruction from members of the bands which had hired them or from other master jazzmen who had heard them play and accepted them as students. Those who had been raised in the city sometimes had obtained formal classical musical training at home or school early in this process. They received recognition as masters themselves when their improvisations were regarded as advances in the music.

Almost every white jazz musician respected within that profession during the 1920s acknowledged that he had learned to play by listening to black bands and singers. One of the white jazzmen most highly regarded by black musicians, Texas trombonist Jack Teagarten, claimed that black spirituals influenced his playing more than anything else. He said that he had attended every black camp meeting and revival that he could while a youngster in Vernon and San Angelo, Texas, and in Oklahoma City early in the twentieth century. Also, he began imitating black music on a trombone at age ten. Clarinetist Mezz Mezzrow, another white jazz musician respected by blacks—who included him in important recording sessions—recalled that he had imbibed black music as a boy while an inmate of Pontiac Reformatory near Chicago. He entered that institution with some skill at playing reed instruments and while there participated in a jazz band with black boys. In the reformatory, he declared,

> I got me a solid dose of the colored man's gift for keeping the life and spirit in him while he tells of his troubles in music. I heard the blues for the first time... day and night. By the time that I reached home I knew that I was going to spend all the rest of my life sticking close to Negroes. I was going to learn their music and play it for the rest of my days. I was going to be a musician, a Negro musician. . . . [27]

Blues singers passed through a pattern of development similar in most important respects to that of the jazzmen.

Critics of jazz evidently had no comprehension of the meaning that playing music had for good jazz artists. They expected to earn some semblance of a living from their work. But even more important, that work provided them with an opportunity to express their individual dignity as well as their creativity and other musical capabilities. No orchestra conductor, arranger, or composer could tell the best of these musicians how to play the songs they agreed to play. In this respect, they resembled the finest scientists, philosophers, and novelists of their time. They voiced their understanding of truth through their music, in cooperation with instruments that they respected and often loved. [28]

❦|❦|❦

A so-called renaissance of African-American writers and artists—concentrated in New York and referred to as the Harlem Renaissance—often was associated with the release of jazz and the blues into American society. By the mid- to late 1920s, jazz musicians, too, were concentrated in New York. The major jazz recording companies—Columbia, Paramount, and Okeh—had their headquarters there, as did the radio networks. More nightclubs and theaters in New York hired jazz musicians than in any other city, and the audience for jazz there was the largest in the world. So the jazzmen migrated to New York City. A computer study of over 800 jazz musicians revealed that from 1927 to 1929 more black jazz musicians were playing in New York at any given time than in Chicago, New Orleans, Kansas City, and St. Louis put together. Furthermore, these musicians—in bands such as those of Fletcher Henderson, Duke Ellington, Chick Webb, Luis Russell, and Clarence Williams; as well as scores of excellent free lancers, including Fats Waller, King Oliver (whose playing in New York during this period has been underestimated),[29] "Cootie" Williams, Benny Carter, James P. Johnson, Henry "Red" Allen, Zutty Singleton, "Willie the Lion" Smith, Cozy Cole, and for part of the period, Louis Armstrong and Jelly Roll Morton—constituted the largest group of fine jazz musicians ever collected to that time in one city. These musicians formed the bands which accompanied blues singers like Ma Rainey, Bessie Smith, and Ethel Waters when they recorded or sang in clubs or theaters in New York.[30]

Nathan Huggins, the most perceptive author of a book-length study of the Harlem Renaissance, commented, "Harlem intellectuals promoted Negro art, but one thing is very curious, except for Langston Hughes none of them took jazz—the new music—seriously." Huggins found it "very ironic that a [black] generation that was searching for a New Negro and his distinctive cultural expression would have passed up the only really creative thing that was going on." As for expositions on their art by jazz musicians themselves: "They were too busy creating a cultural renaissance to think about what they were doing."[31]

❡ | ❡ | ❡

As Huggins observed, Langston Hughes was an exception among Harlem Renaissance writers. Increasingly during the 1920s, his poetry and stories drew their inspiration from his desire to create a distinctively black literary style. As part of that effort, Hughes more and more made use of black urban street speech, blues forms, and jazz rhythms and themes. In what amounted to his own manifesto about black art, Hughes responded to a published denial by a black writer in 1926 that such an art existed with an essay printed in the *Nation* entitled, "The Negro Artist and the Racial Mountain." His views came very close to those of jazz musicians and blues singers:

> Let the blare of Negro jazz bands and the bellowing voice of Bessie Smith singing Blues penetrate the closed ears of the colored near-intellectuals until

they listen and perhaps understand. . . . We younger Negro artists who create now intend to express our individual dark-skinned selves without fear or shame. If white people are pleased we are glad. If they are not, it doesn't matter. We know we are beautiful. And ugly too. The tom-tom cries and the tom-tom laughs. If colored people are pleased we are glad. If they are not, their displeasure doesn't matter either. We build our temples for tomorrow, strong as we know how, and we stand on top of the mountain, free within ourselves.[32]

A few months after writing this essay in the fall of 1926, Hughes completed and sent to his publisher, Alfred A. Knopf, a book of poems, almost half in blues form, entitled *Fine Clothes to the Jew*. Hughes took his title from one of the poems:

> When hard luck overtakes you
> Nothin' for you to do
> Gather up yo' fine clothes
> An' sell 'em to the Jew.

In most of these poems, Hughes allowed his black characters to speak for themselves, thus enhancing his ability to create lyrics inspired by black street language and urban blues:

"HOMESICK BLUES"

> Homesick blues, Lawd,
> 'S a terrible thing to have.
> Homesick blues is
> A terrible thing to have,
> To keep from cryin'
> I opens ma mouth an' laughs.

"MIDWINTER BLUES"

> Don' know's I'd mind his goin'
> But he left me when de coal was low.
> Don' know's I'd mind his goin'
> But he left when de coal was low.
> Now, if a man loves a woman
> That ain't no time to go.

"BAD MAN"

> I beats ma wife an'
> I beats ma side gal too.

Beats ma wife an'
Beats ma side gal too
Don't know why I do it but
It keeps me from feelin' blue

I'm so bad I
Don't even want to be good.
So bad, bad, bad, I
Don't even want to be good.
I'm goin' to be devil an'
I wouldn't go to heaben if I could.

"GAL'S CRY FOR A DYING
LOVER"

Black an' ugly
But he sho do treat me kind
I'm black an' ugly
But he sho do treat me kind
High-in-heaben Jesus
Please don't take this man o' mine.[33]

❧ | ❧ | ❧

The Victorian color caste system was challenged most comprehensively during the 1920s by Marcus Garvey and W. E. B. Du Bois. Despite their sound ideas and vigorous efforts, neither man accomplished much to raise the position of American blacks—nor could they. White racism remained too formidable, and it had left blacks without the experience, knowledge, or financial capital necessary to make successful use of these leaders' programs. Nevertheless, Garvey and Du Bois did arouse blacks to action, and they left a valuable heritage of their experience and concepts to future generations.[34]

Du Bois's ideas, particularly in the areas of black culture and education, covered a wider range than Garvey's.[35] However, the plans developed by the two men overlapped substantially. Most historians have treated Garvey and Du Bois as rivals, however this perception should not obscure the essential similarity of their objectives. Both Garvey and Du Bois recognized that similarity. Garvey attempted on at least two occasions to obtain assistance for his efforts from Du Bois.

The ideas which dominated the actions of these men during the 1920s focused on Pan-Africanism, thus encompassing blacks throughout the world. They included cooperation among blacks in business, education, and in cultural and political matters. Both Garvey and Du Bois accepted a large degree of separatism so that blacks could direct and obtain the benefits from their own enterprises, free from white control.

Garvey's Universal Negro Improvement Association (UNIA) gained the largest support of any organized black political or economic organization ever formed in the United States. The actual dues-paying membership very likely never rose above 15,000 to 20,000 at its peak in 1924; but the number who listened to Garvey's speeches, read the UNIA's newspaper the *Negro World*, subscribed to the stock offerings of Garvey's Black Star Line, or actively supported Garvey and the UNIA in some other fashion apparently amounted to hundreds of thousands and perhaps millions. The real number may never be estimated with any degree of accuracy since most of Garvey's records and those of the UNIA and the Black Star Line have been destroyed or lost.[36]

Garvey came to the United States in 1916 from Jamaica, where he had started the Jamaican UNIA on August 1, 1914. In Kingston, Garvey had assimilated concepts of international *negritude* from an early mentor, Dr. J. Robert Love, a radical black newspaper publisher and physician to the poor. Love had acquired this system of beliefs during ten years of residence as an army doctor in Haiti, where that philosophy would later dominate ethnological studies. "Most of my education in race consciousness is from Dr. Love," Garvey declared toward the end of his career.[37]

However, Garvey seemed little more than one of a thousand black agitators speaking on Harlem sidewalks and in Harlem's meeting halls and churches until May 1919. Then he announced plans to found a black-owned and -operated shipping line which would carry cargoes and passengers between the United States, Africa, the West Indies, and Central America. Still, most knowledgeable blacks remained skeptical—black-owned shipping lines had been announced before, often by swindlers. The skeptics surrendered most of their doubts, though, in October 1919, when Garvey announced the Black Star Line's purchase of an oceangoing ship, the S.S. *Yarmouth*.[38]

Garvey made the *Yarmouth* available to thousands of sightseers and sold hundreds of tickets for one dollar each to those who wished to tour the ship. His stock sales representatives traveled throughout the country, and Garvey spoke in New York, Chicago, and Philadelphia, urging the purchase of BSL stock at five dollars a share. Circulars passed out in the streets and at meetings proclaimed that "Now is the time for the Negro to invest in the Black Star Line so that in the future he may exert the same influence on the world as the white man does today." Garvey also made promises of financial rewards that bordered on fraud: "The Black

Star Line will turn over large profits and dividends to stockholders. . . . "[39]
In a published letter dated July 9, 1919, from Garvey to "Fellowmen of
the Negro Race," Garvey declared that "A five-dollar investment in the
Black Star Line today may be worth one hundred dollars six months from
now."[40]

The *Yarmouth* left on its first voyage late in 1919 carrying cement,
gasoline drums, and passengers to Jamaica and the Panama Canal Zone.
The trip netted a loss for the BSL. As soon as the *Yarmouth* returned,
Garvey ordered it to leave again with a cargo of whiskey for Cuba. However, repairs were needed on the vessel, which had been built in 1887.
Therefore, after the *Yarmouth*'s second voyage, the BSL continued to
operate at a large net loss.[41]

Garvey authorized the purchase of two more vessels early in 1920—the
Shadeyside, a small ship built in 1873 and bought for $35,000; and the S.S.
Kanawha, a 370-ton yacht. The *Shadeyside* made a few money-losing ex-
cursion trips up the Hudson River in the summer of 1920 and then sank
the next winter during a storm. The BSL made no attempt to salvage the
vessel. The *Kanawha* also tried to sail up the Hudson but made it only as
far as 206th Street before a boiler blew out. About a month later, the
Kanawha attempted a trip to the Caribbean, but all the boilers blew near
Delaware. The yacht finally was abandoned in a Cuban port. Late in
1921, the BSL sold the *Yarmouth* for $1,625 after it had cost the line
$194,803 (the purchase price and accumulated deficits). Meanwhile, a BSL
circular issued in May 1921 asked black Americans to "Invest your money
in the Most Colossal, Most Prosperous Negro Industry [the BSL] of All
Times."[42]

Garvey and his closest associates realized during 1921 that the federal
government had collected sufficient evidence of fraud to bring serious
charges against them. Thereafter, funds which might have been used to
repair or purchase ships went into their legal defense instead. As a consequence, operations of the BSL were suspended in April 1922.[43]

Unfortunately, Garvey knew next to nothing about ships, maritime
trade, or ship repairs. He took bad advice when it agreed with his political,
legal, and financial plans, and he rejected good advice from his closest,
best-informed counselors when it did not agree with those plans. His
business projects, particularly the Black Star Line, suffered the usual fate
of companies run by managers who are inexperienced and backed by
insufficient capital.[44]

Garvey's organizing efforts accomplished much more than did his business ventures, though his deficiencies as a businessman eventually undermined the whole UNIA. Garvey's decline began just when he seemed

about to create a lasting movement, which, as Du Bois stated, would "succeed in at least starting some of his schemes toward accomplishment." Garvey's career reached its high point during the UNIA's first annual international convention in August 1920. Delegates arrived in New York from chapters in every one of the forty-eight states and from nations with large black populations throughout the world. These delegates included several African tribal chiefs dressed in their tribal costumes, who attracted great attention in Harlem.[45]

During the convention, which started on August 1 and lasted until the end of the month, delegates, the black population of New York, readers of many black-owned newspapers, and representatives from some major metropolitan dailies (including the *New York Times*) were treated to a spectacular show. No black organization ever had presented—or planned—anything like it before.

Other business in Harlem came almost to a halt on August 2 when blacks filled Lenox Avenue's sidewalks to watch a gigantic UNIA parade, miles in length. Led by the precisely drilled and smartly uniformed paramilitary African Legion, whose members wore swords to remind onlookers of their potential functions, thousands of UNIA members from most parts of the world marched during the hot afternoon. The marchers included the UNIA's large woman's auxiliary, two hundred competent-looking Black Cross nurses, a platoon of policemen and one of firemen, twelve marching bands spaced at intervals throughout the parade, choirs, and a juvenile auxiliary. These marchers created the image that Garvey sought to project of a huge, disciplined, and permanent movement that could command respect from whites.

That image was reinforced that same night when about 25,000 blacks, including the convention delegates, packed Madison Square Garden to hear Garvey speak. The *New York Times* reported that thousands more blacks, unable to find space in the auditorium, nevertheless remained outside discussing the convention. When Garvey rose to speak, the crowd cheered and waved UNIA banners for at least five minutes while he tried to quiet them. Then Garvey announced: "We shall now organize the 400,000,000 Negroes of the world into a vast organization to plant the banner of freedom on the great continent of Africa." Other speakers that evening also demanded that Europeans leave Africa and threatened unified black action if whites failed to obey this order.

The delegates adopted a declaration of fundamental civil rights for blacks all over the world. At the same time, they demanded "complete control of our social institutions without interference by any alien race. . . . "

When the delegates adjourned late in August, Garvey announced that the convention had made the nations of the world aware that "the Negro of yesterday has disappeared from the scene of human activities and his place [has been] taken by a new Negro who stands erect, conscious of his manhood rights and fully determined to preserve them at all times."

Meanwhile, stockholders in the BSL demanded an accounting for their funds, and the office of the United States District Attorney for the Southern District of New York (New York City) investigated Garvey's use of the mails to sell BSL stock. In January 1922, Garvey and three associates were arrested. Three months later, a federal grand jury indicted them on twelve counts charging use of the mails to defraud. Garvey acknowledged that intentional fraud had been committed by officials of the BSL. But he asked his followers and stockholders, "What can Garvey do if men are employed to do their work and they prove to be dishonest and dishonorable . . . ?" A jury was not satisfied with this rationale, and Garvey was convicted in 1923. The United States Circuit Court of Appeals reaffirmed the verdict, the Supreme Court refused to hear the case, and Garvey entered Atlanta Penitentiary on February 8, 1925. President Calvin Coolidge commuted his sentence on November 18, 1927, and Garvey, who never had found time to fulfill his much earlier declaration that he would become a United States citizen, was immediately deported to Jamaica in accordance with immigration law.[46]

❧ | ❧ | ❧

Garvey had sought to ally himself with W. E. B. Du Bois, the leading American proponent of Pan-Africanism and of black cultural and economic nationalism. "The problem of the twentieth century," Du Bois had declared in 1903 in *Souls of Black Folk*, "is the problem of the color line—the relation of the darker to the lighter races of men in Asia and Africa, in America and the islands of the sea." Du Bois began suggesting in *Crisis* editorials in 1913 that the NAACP supplement its civil-rights program with projects intended to help blacks lift themselves economically. After World War I, his suggestions became more specific, his emphasis on black communal effort became stronger, and he began organizing such efforts himself.[47]

Garvey evidently recognized the advantage in some form of cooperation between Du Bois and himself and in April 1916, he traveled downtown to the offices of the *Crisis* in order to speak to Du Bois. Informed that the *Crisis* editor was out of town, Garvey wrote to him: "I called in order to have asked you if you could be so good as to take the 'chair' at my first public lecture on May 9." Du Bois replied, thanking Garvey; however, he would be out of town on May 9.[48]

On July 16, 1920, Garvey wrote to Du Bois informing him that at the forthcoming UNIA convention "The Negro people of America will elect a leader by the popular vote of the delegates from the forty-eight States of the Union. This leader . . . will be the accredited spokesman of the American Negro people. You are hereby asked to be good enough to allow us to place your name in nomination for the post." The position would have placed Du Bois nominally beneath only President-General Garvey in the UNIA's official American hierarchy. Du Bois thanked Garvey for the proffered nomination but declined. He offered to publish an account of Garvey's organizations and a biography and picture of him in the *Crisis* if he would provide factual information about his businesses and himself and a photograph.[49]

Meanwhile, Du Bois studied carefully Garvey's plans and business dealings. He declined to join the large number of black intellectuals and businessmen who denounced Garvey's economic projects. Not until he had analyzed the incomplete financial statement on the BSL that UNIA leaders and the U.S. District Attorney's office had forced Garvey to present to the 1920 UNIA international convention did Du Bois give his tentative appraisal of Garvey's business programs.

In two articles in the *Crisis*, published in December 1920 and January 1921, Du Bois praised what seemed to him Garvey's undoubted honesty and sincerity but criticized his lack of business sense and of any gift for business administration. Du Bois acknowledged that "Garvey is an extraordinary leader of men. Thousands of people believe in him. He is able to stir them with singular eloquence and the general run of his thought is of a high plane." Garvey's exceptional ability to get his programs started, Du Bois declared, gave him an enormous opportunity to aid all black people but presented him with an enormous obligation also.

Near the end of his second article on Garvey, Du Bois concluded:

Shorn of its bombast and exaggeration, the main lines of the Garvey plan are perfectly feasible. What he is trying to say and do is this: American Negroes can, by accumulating and ministering their own capital, organize industry, join the black centers of the south Atlantic by commercial enterprise and in this way ultimately redeem Africa as a fit and free home for black men. This is true. It is *feasible*. It is, in a sense, practical; [but] . . . it will call for every ounce of ability, knowledge, experience and devotion in the whole Negro race.

Garvey presently served as the beloved leader "of poor and bewildered people who have been cheated all of their lives. His failure would mean a blow to their faith, and a loss of their little savings, which it would take generations to undo."[50]

As Du Bois's articles about Garvey indicated, he long before had reached conclusions similar to Garvey's. Born and raised in Great Barrington in western Massachusetts, recipient of a Harvard Ph.D. and a fellowship that enabled him to do further advanced study in Germany, Du Bois knew his white adversaries well. Du Bois directed research on urban blacks in Philadelphia during the 1890s and on rural blacks while a professor at Atlanta University in the twentieth century. Such books as *Black Philadelphia* (1899) and *Souls of Black Folk* (1903) demonstrated that Du Bois understood American blacks. Du Bois left Atlanta to edit the *Crisis* for the NAACP in 1910. He replied to a charge made in 1914 by his strongest supporter among white NAACP officials, board chairman Joel E. Spingarn, that he often acted obstinately by admitting that some of his actions might *seem* obstinate. He contended, however, that he differed from white NAACP officers over long-range plans for the organization. This made conflict at many points inevitable:

> But deeper than all this [Du Bois continued,] the pathos of an organization like ours has not begun to strike you. I sometimes listen to you quite speechless, when you urge easily co-operation and understanding. . . . No organization like ours ever succeeded in America; either it became a group of white philanthropists "helping" the Negro . . . ; or it became a group of colored folk freezing out their white co-workers by insolences and distrust. Everything tends to this break along the color line. You do not realize this because there is no shadow of the thing in your soul. But you are not "American." [Spingarn was of Jewish descent]. . . . Now what I have been trying to do is to try to work out a plan for colored and white people to work together on the same level of authority and co-operation. It is difficult. But if it fails, the failure will not be due to obstinacy or intractability—it will be due to the color line.
>
> Our problem, therefore, is to front this fact squarely. . . . In America colored and white people cannot work in the same [organization] and at the same tasks except one is in authority over the other. . . . If the head is colored, the whites gradually leave. I have seen the experiment made a dozen times. If the head is white, the colored people gradually drop out of the inner circle of authority and initiative. . . . To avoid this dilemma I've tried to see if we could not have two branches of the same work, one [the NAACP Board] with a white head and one [the *Crisis*] with a colored; working in harmony and sympathy for one end.

Du Bois then pointed out that the authority he requested was granted to whites of ability and integrity without question. "The colored man gets no such chance. He is seldom given authority or freedom. . . . So far has this gone that even in the black world such authority is feared and given over to white folk." The situation could be changed only "by trusting black men with power." Du Bois clearly meant power separate from whites. This situation was projected by Du Bois over all of American society. One can understand Du Bois's sympathy with Garvey and his fear of the consequences if the UNIA failed.[51]

During World War I, Du Bois decided to give white Americans another chance to show that they could overcome their prejudice if blacks demonstrated strong loyalty to the nation. He urged blacks to cooperate in the war effort and agreed to enlist in the army himself. Du Bois was infuriated when he learned about the pattern of discrimination against black troops who had volunteered to die for the United States. He charged that according to black soldiers, "American white officers fought more valiantly against Negroes within our own ranks than they did against the Germans." The postwar race riots and lynchings and the formation of a new Ku Klux Klan completed his alienation.[52]

Du Bois gave vent to his anger in a book of essays, poems, and stories entitled *Darkwater: Voices from Within the Veil*, published in 1920. The book made Garvey's distrust of whites seem quite temperate. In his poem "The Riddle of the Sphinx," published in that volume, Du Bois denounced

> The white world's vermin and filth:
>   all the dirt of London
>   all the scum of New York
>   Valiant spoilers of women
>   And conquerors of unarmed men
>   Shameless breeders of bastards
>   Drunk with the greed of gold
>   Baiting their blood-stained hooks
>   With cant for the souls of the simple;
>   Bearing the white man's burden
>   Of liquor and lust and lies! . . .
>   I hate them, Oh!
>   I hate them well
>   I hate them Christ!
>   As I hate hell!
>   If I were God
>   I'd sound their knell
>   This day!

Who raised the fools to their glory,
But black men of Egypt and Ind,
Ethiopia's sons of the evening,
Indians and yellow Chinese . . . ,
And they that raised the boasters
Shall drag them down again,—
Down with the theft of their thieving
And murder and mocking of men;
Down with their barter of women
And laying and lying of creeds;
Down with their cheating of childhood
And drunken orgies of war,—
    down
      down
        deep down,
Till the Devil's strength be shorn. . . . [53]

In *Darkwater*, Du Bois declared that colored Americans demanded the return of all Africa to Africans and the immediate establishment of a free African nation to be created by granting independence to the former German colonies on that continent. Unless Europe and America changed their past policies, Du Bois asserted, " . . . there is one thing for the trained man of darker blood to do and that is definitely and as openly as possible to organize his world for war. . . . " The colored man must act. "He represents the vast majority of mankind. To surrender would be far worse than physical death." This essay in *Darkwater* grants some insight into Du Bois's ultimate plans for the Pan-African Conference he helped organize during the Paris Peace Conference in 1919. [54]

Du Bois's concepts of black cultural distinctiveness and black economic cooperation remain useful for black Americans. During the 1920s, however, both Du Bois and Garvey served largely as prophets, though potentially dangerous ones to Victorian ideas and social arrangements.

5

THE DILEMMA OF AMERICAN FEMINISTS

The largely white middle-class leaders of the early woman's rights movement derived most of their ideas from their experiences as Victorian women. The most influential of these leaders, Elizabeth Cady Stanton, had to overcome strong opposition to her participation in the movement from both her husband (Henry B. Stanton, an antislavery lecturer) and her father. Henry objected to her writing and speeches on behalf of woman suffrage. Her father, a judge and a member of Congress, disinherited her when she began lecturing about woman's rights until just before his death. Stanton complained in September 1855 that "All in me of which my father would have felt a proper pride had I been a man, is deeply mortifying to him because I am a woman." She protested also that "Henry sides with my friends. . . . They are not willing that I should write even on the woman question. But I will both write and speak."[1]

Susan B. Anthony, recruited to the movement and trained as a feminist by Stanton, was the only early leader who never married. When Anthony failed to write to her during a period in late 1855, Stanton, busy caring for a home and five young children, inquired, "Where are you Susan and what are you doing. Are you dead or married?"[2]

Anthony objected when a fellow woman's rights leader, Lucy Stone, found herself unable to prepare adequately for an important debate because of household duties. Writing about Stone to their common friend, feminist Antoinette Brown, who had seven children herself, Anthony asked, "What man would dream of going before the public on such an occasion . . . tired and worn from such a multitude of engrossing chores?"[3]

After women delegates to the London World's Anti-Slavery Convention of 1840 were denied the right to seats on the convention floor and, therefore, to speak or vote, Stanton and Lucretia Mott, founder of the first Female Anti-Slavery Society, conceived the idea of a woman's rights convention. Thus, from the origins of its first major event, the woman's rights movement borrowed its methods from the antislavery movement.[4]

When Mott visited friends in July 1848 near Seneca Falls, New York, where the Stantons lived, Stanton, Mott, and her friends agreed to issue a call for a woman's rights convention immediately. They wrote an announcement which appeared in the following day's issue of the *Seneca County Courier*. The Seneca Falls woman's rights convention—the first woman's rights convention in the world—met five days later, on July 19 and 20. About three hundred people, including forty men, attended. The women were so unaccustomed to directing such meetings that they chose a man—Mott's husband—to preside.[5]

When Stanton arose to address the convention, she declared that she would have found it difficult to speak, "having never before spoken in public," had she not believed

> that the time had come for the question of woman's wrongs to be laid before the public, did I not believe that woman herself must do this work; for woman alone can understand the height, the depth, and the breadth of her degradation.[6]

The meeting adopted a Declaration of Sentiments, written by Stanton and modeled upon the Declaration of Independence, that included a feminist agenda applying to family life, work, education, religion, laws, and politics. After reading it, Henry Stanton informed his wife that he would not attend the convention if it were introduced there and, moreover, would leave town while the convention lasted—which he did.[7]

American females, as well as males, were far from ready for the convention's proposals, even though they were cloaked under a proper Victorian description, Declaration of Sentiments. Antoinette Brown described for Lucy Stone in 1848 the response in Oberlin, Ohio, when she spoke about woman's rights: "Sometimes [they] believe I am joking, sometimes stare at me with amazement and sometimes seem to start back with a kind of horror. Men and women are about equal [in their reactions]."[8]

Gradually, woman's rights advocates, except for radicals like Stanton and Anthony, were persuaded to reduce the movement's immediate objectives to one—woman suffrage. Stanton and Anthony proclaimed in 1868 that the vote would not affect women's chief discontents: "her social and particularly her marital bondage." When Stanton and Anthony started a weekly feminist newspaper, which began publication January 8, 1868, they announced in the January 22, 1868, issue that "not only the ballot but bread and babies" would be discussed. They entitled their paper the *Revolution*. As late as December 1899, Stanton complained to Anthony that "At present our association has so narrowed its platform for reasons of policy and propriety that our conventions [for example, Seneca Falls] have ceased to point the way."[9] Nevertheless, they agreed that suffrage would help women gain other objectives.

In 1869, Stanton and Anthony organized the National Woman Suffrage Association (NWSA). Angry with the Republican Party for refusing to grant the vote to women in the Fourteenth and Fifteenth amendments, which enfranchised blacks, they demanded a Sixteenth Amendment which would apply to women. They urged feminists to leave other reform movements in order to devote themselves to working for the NWSA. A leading historian of woman suffrage, Ellen Carol Du Bois, called the creation of Stanton's and Anthony's association "the greatest achievement of feminists in the post [civil] war period."[10] The NWSA continued Stanton's and Anthony's earlier policy of viewing the vote as just one of many objectives for women, though the most immediate task.

When a Senate committee held hearings on the proposed Sixteenth Amendment in 1878, only one woman, Madeline V. Dahlgren, wife of Admiral John A. Dahlgren, offered a statement in opposition. However, her argument prevailed. She gave a standard Victorian defense of the status quo—one that would become familiar again during twentieth-century debates about an Equal Rights Amendment:

> We cannot see our cherished privileges endangered, and have granted us only in exchange the so-called equal rights. We need more, and we claim, through our physical weakness . . . that protection which we need for the proper discharge of those sacred and inalienable functions and rights conferred upon us by God. To these *the vote* . . . would be adverse.[11]

Between 1870 and 1890, the number of women college graduates grew steadily, as did the number of women professionals. The number of

women teachers, librarians, nurses, and women in manufacturing and
clerical jobs multiplied manyfold. Women's clubs proliferated. Demographic shifts toward a more urban population, an enlarged middle class,
and smaller families gave women more time for outside interests. Changes
in the training of females helped foment greater dissatisfaction with wom-
en's traditional activities. Consequently, the number of recruits to the
woman's suffrage movement increased steadily.[12]

In 1890, the National Woman Suffrage Association merged with the
American Woman Suffrage Association (formed by Lucy Stone and
Henry Ward Beecher to support the Reconstruction amendments and to
encourage the Republican Party to keep its promise that women would
be enfranchised). The new organization, the National American Woman
Suffrage Association (NAWSA) increased its membership rapidly, and it
remained the largest woman's suffrage organization until women were
granted the vote.[13]

In *The Ideas of the Woman Suffrage Movement, 1890–1920*, Aileen S. Kraditor estimated that membership in the NAWSA increased from 13,150
in 1893 to over 75,000 in 1910, to 100,000 in 1915, and to 2,000,000
in 1917, when passage of the Nineteenth Amendment to the U.S.
Constitution appeared assured.[14] Between the passage in 1896 of
state constitutional amendments giving women the vote in Utah and
Idaho and the NAWSA's victory in Washington in 1910, no state granted woman suffrage. Between 1870 and 1910, states held seventeen
referenda on woman suffrage, with the suffragists victorious in only
two. The federal amendment virtually disappeared from Congress's
agenda between 1896 and 1913 while the NAWSA concentrated on
the states.[15]

❧|❧|❧

In 1912, two young women who had devoted several years to working
for the militant wing of the British suffrage movement, Alice Paul and
Lucy Burns, asked to serve on the NAWSA Congressional Committee.
Paul, who had been chosen to lead demonstrations in Britain by Emmeline
Pankhurst—leader of that militant wing with her two daughters—went
to jail for her activities, engaged in hunger strikes, and was subjected to
forcible feeding. Burns, too, had taken part in the Pankhursts' commando
operations and had suffered even more arrests and imprisonments than
Paul.[16] Late in 1912, after intercession on their behalf by Jane Addams,
Paul and Burns received appointments to the NAWSA's moribund
Congressional Committee. Paul, who agreed to raise all funds for the

committee, was made the committee's chairperson, and Burns was appointed vice chair.[17]

A large group of mostly young women chose Paul as their role model and joined her in working for the Congressional Committee and its successor organizations—the Congressional Union and the National Woman's Party (NWP). Concentration on a federal amendment and a willingness to use militant methods to achieve that end distinguished this generation of "new suffragists." Unlike the NAWSA, which urged votes for women to protect the home and family and to make society more moral, the "new suffragists" returned to the tradition of Stanton and Anthony in demanding the vote as their natural right. Also, their inspiration came not from the NAWSA's conservative policies but from the much more aggressive British suffrage movement. These largely college-educated, career-oriented, aggressive activists chose to express their identities principally through winning the fight for woman suffrage.[18]

In reviving the federal amendment, Paul and her followers acted moderately compared to the British militants. They destroyed no property and broke no laws. However, the anger they aroused and the violent treatment they received resembled the British reaction to the Pankhursts' organization's actions.[19]

Paul understood when she took over the Congressional Committee that the fate of the federal amendment lay largely in the hands of the newly elected president, Woodrow Wilson. As a result of her experience in Britain, Paul believed that dramatic publicity about woman suffrage would serve as the most powerful lever in forcing Wilson and other politicians first to recognize the importance of the issue and then to support a federal amendment.[20] Therefore, the first activity arranged by the reorganized Congressional Committee was a parade—organized largely by Burns—of about eight thousand woman-suffrage supporters on March 3, 1913, the day before Wilson's inauguration. Large crowds and hundreds of newspaper reporters would be in Washington to witness the inauguration ceremonies. Over half a million people gathered along the parade route on March 3.

The publicity generated by the parade exceeded Paul's expectations. Despite the fact that Paul bombarded the District of Columbia's police superintendent with demands for adequate police protection, the marchers, who included many senators and congressmen with their wives, were assaulted by mobs. Most of the march ended quickly, and it took a U.S. Cavalry unit to restore order so that some marchers could complete the parade route. A special Senate investigating committee convened on March 6 to hear four days of testimony about the riot. The inquiry heard Senator

Miles Poindexter of Washington testify that he had taken the badge numbers of twenty-two police officers who had refused pleas to help the
marchers. Blame for the riot was placed upon the police, especially on
the police superintendent, who resigned.[21]

Because some of those to whom the Congressional Committee sent
requests for funds made their donations to the NAWSA, Paul and Burns
requested and received permission in April 1913 to form an affiliate organization, the Congressional Union. Less than a year later, the Congressional Union and the NAWSA separated, ostensibly because of
disagreement over the Congressional Union's policy of holding the national
party in power responsible for failure to pass a woman's suffrage
amendment.[22]

Carrie Chapman Catt, who assumed the presidency of the NAWSA
for the second time in September 1915 had viewed such a division
as inevitable even before it occurred. In mid-February 1914, she told
NAWSA's President Anna Howard Shaw that she expected the suffrage
movement to divide in two, "that the militants and the militant sympa-
thizers would gather in one group while those of us who really want
suffrage and not advertising would gather into another." The disagreement
went deeper than a dispute over methods. During a speech in June 1914,
Catt expressed what her biographer, Jacqueline Van Voris, described as
her "basic conviction": "It is no longer a question of right for women to
have a vote, it is the question of duty, duty of motherhood, to take care
of the race."[23]

After their organizations separated, Catt and Paul, both astute politicians, played complementary roles. Both recognized the advantages of
doing what they and their organizations did best. Catt evidently understood that if Paul's group used militant methods to win sympathy and
publicity for the cause, her group could assume the part of the reasonable
and traditional women to whom politicians, particularly Woodrow Wilson, could submit gracefully.[24]

This division of labor worked well. Members of the organization led
by Paul and Burns evolved into the National Woman's Party in 1916.
This group used its First Amendment rights to freedom of speech and to
peaceful assembly in order to petition the government for a redress of
grievances and picketed the White House. District of Columbia commissioner Louis Brownlow stated that "Mr. Wilson did not want them [the
suffragists] arrested, and I did not want to arrest them." Nevertheless,
police arrested the pickets for obstructing traffic on Pennsylvania Avenue
from their positions on the sidewalk adjoining the White House gate and
for loitering. Judges sentenced them to terms in prison, where they en-

dured such atrocious conditions as beatings, solitary confinement, and diets of bread and water. Many went on hunger strikes and were fed forcibly. Some of those who protested strongly—including Alice Paul— were transferred to psychiatric wards. Also, Washington mobs, including servicemen, assaulted the NWP pickets. These events were reported by the nation's newspapers, debated in Congress, and brought to the attention of Woodrow Wilson.[25]

During 1916–1917, Wilson, who held a position that women should remain in the home when he entered the White House, became a leading advocate of woman suffrage. Frequently, he announced his new position in speeches and letters to NAWSA members, thus avoiding the appearance of surrender to the NWP.[26]

Wilson persuaded senators to provide the votes crucial to the passage of the Nineteenth Amendment, which passed by a two-thirds majority on June 4, 1919. He was directly responsible also for convincing Tennessee legislators to cast the voters which ratified the amendment as a part of the Constitution on August 18, 1920.[27]

After the Nineteenth Amendment took effect, NWP member Charlotte Perkins Gilman, then America's leading feminist ideologue, gave voice in a poem to the high expectations of all but the radical feminists among the weary suffragists. The poem proclaimed, in part:

> Gone are the ages that have led us bound
>   Beneath a master, now we stand as he,
> Free for world-service unto all humankind,
> Free of the dragging chains that used to bind,
>   No longer pets or slaves are we, for lo!
> Women are free at last in all the land.[28]

❦|❦|❦

Those who held high hopes for the results of woman suffrage soon suffered bitter disappointment. Women quickly divided like men between the major political parties. Women's votes accomplished very little. Female activists disagreed more implacably than ever about the best policy for women. Also, women made only slight gains in politics. Social historian Jill Conway observed:

> There is no escaping the fact that in the very decade of the twenties when the franchise was secured . . . the vast majority of women began to find social activism unattractive and to return to an ethic of domesticity as romantic and suffocating as any code of the high Victorian era.[29]

Females barely held on to most of their earlier gains in the professions and in education during the 1920s; and in some cases, lost ground. The proportion of physicians who were women fell from about 6 percent in 1920 to 4.4 percent in 1930. The number and proportion of women dentists, architects, chemists, and industrial drafters also fell during the 1920s. The 1930 census returns showed a total of twenty-nine women civil engineers, eighteen women mechanical engineers, four women mining engineers, and two women electrical engineers in the whole country. Women attorneys accounted for only 2 percent of the total in 1930. During the 1920s, the percentage of women among undergraduate college students decreased—so did the proportion of women among graduate students and those earning Ph.D. degrees.[30]

Twenty-seven women ran for Congress in November 1922. But only one was elected, and she went to Congress to fill the brief, unexpired term of her father. When only a handful of women won election to state legislatures in 1922, a national wire service asked Alice Paul for her reaction. The following story appeared in a great many of the nation's newspapers:

> "Women don't deserve anything better!" savagely cried Alice Paul.... "Women won't vote for women. Women won't patronize women in business. Women won't go to women doctors. Women won't take their cases to women lawyers.... The disgraceful situation in which women find themselves today is their own fault.... They remain a subject class because they have no sense of solidarity. They will never advance until they refuse to be a subject class...."[31]

The proportion of women college and university teachers rose slightly during the 1920s to 32.5 percent of the total. However, these women generally worked in the less-prestigious schools and, even in women's colleges, congregated in the lower, untenured ranks of instructors and assistant instructors.[32]

Barnard College dean Virginia C. Gildersleeve, who had directed the woman's college of Columbia University since 1911, complained that during the 1920s, female students handicapped themselves with their own "blasé indifference, self-indulgence, and irresponsibility." Sociologist Jessie Bernard recalled about her generation that "By the 1920's the éclat of the earlier years had spent itself, and all of a sudden . . . the excitement which had characterized the first generation[s] of college women ebbed."[33]

Highly respected historian Ella Lonn conducted a survey in 1923 of women faculty members in seventy research-oriented universities. She found that these women generally held positions in the lower ranks. In her analysis of the reasons for this situation, Lonn declared that "few women [are] willing to pay the price [and to] drive themselves in research. We must grant in all candor that this is one of our weaknesses." Women, Lonn asserted, must demonstrate a "willingness to train hard, and to conduct more high calibre research on *worth-while* subjects—to TOIL! I fear that I must admit that as a class we do not set ourselves so stubbornly to a task as a man. . . . "[34]

National advertisers, assisted by sophisticated market research during the 1920s, provided evidence that the overwhelming majority of American women continued to view their role in society as distinctly different from that of men. Advertisers perceived that while women desired increased personal satisfaction and independence, they wanted these within their traditional role.

An advertisement for Modess sanitary napkins entitled "Don't Weaken Mother," typified ads run during the 1920s for that product. Above the caption "Modernizing Mother" appeared an illustration of a mother and daughter engaged in calisthenics. The advertising copy read:

> Millions of mothers whose girlhoods were repressed are being trained by their daughters to be young again—to know freedom—to grasp the idea that drudgery and useless labor are a sinful waste of life.
> Modess is one of the many recent inventions which do away with drudgery and discomfort. . . .

The three soaps which enjoyed the largest sales used similar advertising themes. Typical copy for Lux asked,

> Need a Woman's Hands say "I have no maid" . . . ?
> 236 leading beauty shops answer:
> With all our experience, we are unable to distinguish between the hands of a woman who never washes dishes and those of a housewife who uses *Lux in the dishpan*.

Lifebuoy asserted: "What every woman knows—when children keep well [because they are washed with antiseptic Lifebuoy]—mothers stay young." Palmolive's headline declared: "Proud to say 'This is Mother'—

> The reward that comes to many mothers—unconscious tribute from the younger generation to the woman who has retained her youth. That youth can be retained, as experts know and urge, is proved on all sides today. It "is being done" by women everywhere. Start now with the simple skin care

printed at the right. The result in youthful charm and skin cleanliness will
amaze you.

Piggly Wiggly Stores, over three thousand of which could be found in
more than eight hundred American cities and towns, claimed that shopping at its stores was more exciting than ordinary food shopping:

> Women of today want to choose for themselves. When they shop for foods
> they want no clerks trying to urge and persuade them.
>   Within easy reach the choice foods of the world are waiting to be looked
> over at Piggly Wiggly. Beyond the turnstile, a land of adventure.

Automobile advertisements also enticed women with promises of greater
satisfaction within their conventional roles. An ad for the new Ford Tudor
Sedan, which appeared in January 1929, claimed that the car would "give
men the means by which they can do more work and better work...,"
and would "help women in the equally important business of running a
home." Cadillac, meanwhile, advertised only to men, even in the woman's
magazine *Good Housekeeping*. Ads for Cadillac Fleetwoods promised
power—and not only in performance:

> The purchaser may avail himself at any time of the counsel of professional
> motor-coach designers who [will] aid him precisely as the architect and
> interior decorator advise him in the construction, decoration and furnishing
> of his home.[35]

Several leaders of women's business and professional groups denounced
advertisements aimed at women during the 1920s. Rosa Falls Bres, president of the Women Lawyers' Association, complained in 1927 that the
ads "brand women as a class apart—inferior."[36]

However, those who struggled during the 1920s to expand equal rights
for women did receive encouragement from certain changes in women's
occupational patterns. During the period from 1870 to 1920, the types of
jobs held by women shifted drastically. The proportion of working women
employed in manufacturing fell steadily, and these women increasingly
worked in different manufacturing industries. The proportion of female
manufacturing workers employed in the garment industry, for example, fell, while the proportion in the less-exhausting cigarette and food-
packaging industries rose.

Meanwhile, the number of women working as secretaries, stenog-
raphers, typists, and office clerks multiplied by ten. Women virtually

took over the occupations of librarian, nurse, elementary school teacher, and telephone operator. About 20 percent of all librarians had been women in 1870; over 90 percent were women in 1930. The proportion of women salesclerks in retail stores increased from 3 percent of the total in 1870 to 40 percent in 1930. By 1920, more women were employed in white-collar jobs than in manufacturing.[37] These shifts meant that fewer women workers required protective legislation, while a larger proportion wanted salaries and opportunities for promotion equal to those of men.

♀|♀|♀

Leaders of the National Woman's Party decided in 1920–1921 to work for an Equal Rights Amendment (ERA) to the U.S. Constitution in order to obtain greater equality of opportunity for women. Their campaign revealed a schism between the NWP's radical feminists, who insisted that the natural rights of American citizens applied to women, and those women who continued to cherish the Victorian concept of a distinct female character. The NWP stressed the disabilities that special laws and customs imposed on women. Their opponents emphasized the need for these laws and customs to protect the inherent delicacy of women and their ability to fulfill their primary roles as wives and mothers.

The majority of former woman suffragists believed that the Nineteenth Amendment by itself would enhance dramatically women's position in American society. NWP leaders, however, insisted that women must press on toward completing the agenda approved by the Seneca Falls convention of 1848. They agreed with Stanton and Anthony's statement that the ballot was "not even half a loaf, it is only a crust—a crumb" and did not affect social discrimination against women.[38]

Most NWP leaders in 1920 wanted to begin fighting for an ERA immediately. However, some of the leaders who had suffered most in prison during the drive for the suffrage amendment, including Alice Paul, felt that they needed an indefinite period to recuperate. Lucy Burns, who more than anyone else had helped Paul lead the struggle for suffrage, declared that she felt exhausted: "I don't want to do any more. I think that we have done all this for women, and we have sacrificed everything we possessed for them, and . . . let them fight for it now. I am not going to fight . . . anymore." Paul suffered from "extreme fatigue" and doubted that she could continue the battle. She wrote to a friend in January 1921 that she would leave further efforts "to the women who will have to go on with the work if the organization continues. . . ."[39]

The editors of the NWP's journal, the *Suffragist* (later renamed *Equal*

Rights), seemed uncertain about the future. In a front-page editorial in September 1920, they declared that the party had "accomplished the purpose for which it was founded. It will meet in national convention within the next three months, and it will then determine whether to disband or to adopt a . . . program of work for the future advancement of women."[40]

The convention met in Washington, D.C., on February 16, 1921. Among the nearly eight hundred delegates, alternates, and invited guests from other organizations were future leaders of the opposition to the ERA. They included Mary Anderson, a former garment and shoe worker who directed the Labor Department's Women's Bureau; Florence Kelley, who had dominated the Consumers' League since 1899; former social worker Julia Lathrop of the Department of Labor's Children's Bureau; and Ethel Smith, chairman of the Legislative Committee of the Woman's Trade Union League.[41] However, at the convention only Kelley spoke on behalf of protective legislation concerning women's work conditions and hours. Three months earlier, Kelley had written in favor of recommendations that, she declared, would enable women "to perform more perfectly their especial share in the experience of the race, giving, saving and cherishing life." The other eventual opponents of an ERA were either intimidated by the large majority at the convention who supported equal rights or not yet aware of the inevitable conflict between equality and protection.[42]

The lengthiest debate took place over a resolution introduced by Crystal Eastman (a radical on almost every major matter, including woman's rights). Eastman called for legislation enabling women to retain control over their own property, women's rights to all types of education and occupations, and birth control and salaries for those women who chose to be mothers. Eastman's program lost, largely because it was too specific and, therefore, would arouse opposition to its separate sections. Nevertheless, it won one-third of the final vote.[43]

The resolution that gained majority approval called for eventual equal rights and more immediate removal of women's "legal disabilities." It gave the NWP's Executive Committee authority to decide how to implement that resolution.[44]

❦ | ❦ | ❦

Alice Paul resigned as chairman of the NWP Executive Committee in 1921 in order to obtain a doctoral degree in law. If she were to lead an attempt to do away with women's legal disabilities, Paul reasoned, she needed to learn as much as possible about those laws.[45]

Nevertheless, the Executive Committee, in response to the instructions provided by the January 1921 NWP convention, began preparing equal-rights amendments for both the federal and state constitutions. At the committee's request, Paul wrote and introduced the first version of a federal equal-rights amendment. She presented this to a convention of the NWP which met in Seneca Falls, New York, in 1923 on the seventy-fifth anniversary of the original Seneca Falls convention. In addition to meeting at Seneca Falls, the NWP obtained added symbolic legitimacy for its federal amendment by calling it the Lucretia Mott Amendment. The proposed amendment stated that "Men and women shall have equal rights throughout the United States and every place subject to its jurisdiction. Congress shall have the power to enforce this article by appropriate legislation."[46]

The NWP attempted to legitimize their amendment further by arranging for its introduction in the House of Representatives by Republican Congressman Daniel R. Anthony of Kansas, nephew of Susan B. Anthony. In the Senate, the measure was introduced by Charles C. Curtis of Kansas, about to be elected Republican floor leader, and later, a vice president of the United States. Curtis presented the amendment on December 10, 1923; Anthony, on December 13.[47]

A sign that other women's organizations might soon join the NWP in support of the ERA came from the Annual Convention of the American Association of University Women (AAUW) in April 1924. Convention delegates read a report opposing the amendment prepared by Mary Van Kleeck, director of the Russell Sage Foundation's Department of Industrial Studies. During World War I, Van Kleeck, a social worker, had served on the Committee on Women in Industry of the Council of National Defense. She had brought Mary Anderson to Washington, D.C., to assist her when she was selected to head the Ordinance Department's Women's Division. Van Kleeck recommended that action to remedy women's legal disabilities should be taken in the states by the women most affected by these disabilities. Those women should decide whether state protective legislation remained necessary.

M. Carey Thomas, president emeritus of Bryn Mawr College, then addressed the AAUW convention on whether or not the organization should continue to oppose the ERA. Thomas, the nation's foremost woman educator since 1894 when she was selected as president of Bryn Mawr, was the first president of a woman's college to add graduate study to the institution's program. Previously, she had been undecided about the ERA.

Thomas's report took up virtually every argument advanced against an

ERA and disposed of each with well-chosen evidence and cogent logic. "Unequal pay for equal work is the rule and not the exception in the United States," Thomas reminded the AAUW convention. She declared,

> Sex discrimination is intricately interwoven throughout the whole fabric of social, intellectual and financial life in the United States. . . . It is strangely unsympathetic for opponents of such an equal rights amendment to suggest removing these thousands of inequalities and injustices by slow and painful piece work in 48 state legislatures while women are being born, living their lives and dying without the rights for which they have been waiting since the time of the cave men.

Thomas concluded that she found it disappointing that ERA opponents considered the amendment exclusively from the angle of its effects on protective legislation for female industrial workers. These opponents "ignored the needs of equal rights of all other women . . . " including AAUW members, most of whom were teachers.

Thomas wisely did not ask association members to suddenly discard their concern for states rights and for protective legislation. Instead, she requested only that the organization's official opposition to an ERA be withdrawn while the association considered a new policy. The association's Committee on Legislative Policies introduced a resolution calling for continued opposition to the ERA. Thomas then moved that a substitute motion be adopted based on the recommendation in her report. Her motion passed the convention by a 299 to 117 vote.[48]

Following this apparently auspicious event, an editorial in *Equal Rights* listed those women's groups which still officially opposed the ERA and declared:

> In these organizations, as with the Association of University Women, there has been premature resistance to a new idea. But this resistance will be undermined and crumble in all of these organizations. . . . Which will be the next organization to follow the lead taken by the Association of University Women?[49]

Even though protective legislation applied only in rare instances to business and professional women, almost every specialized association of such women refused to support the ERA. Among these were the Medical Women's National Association, the National Association of Women Lawyers, the Federation of Business and Professional Women's Clubs, the American Federation of Teachers, the Association of American [Women] Dentists, the American Society of Women Certified Public Accountants, and the National Women's Real Estate Association. Most members of these groups did not feel strongly about protective legislation, except when that applied to them—then there was unanimous opposition; nor was their dislike for the ERA strong enough for them to send representatives to congressional hearings on the measure. However, the discomfort of their members with the changes in perceptions of women that might accompany an ERA and a disinclination to act solely in their own interests caused all these associations to continue their opposition through the 1920s.[50]

When male political leaders in industrial states began calling for and winning passage of protective legislation that covered business and professional women, however, these women reconsidered the ERA. For example, when Governor Franklin D. Roosevelt of New York asked the state legislature in 1929 to approve legislation limiting hours that business women could work, the Federation of Business and Professional Women's Clubs formed a Legislative Council to fight against the measure. Nevertheless, it passed and was signed into law by Roosevelt in 1931. The state federation then decided to support the ERA. In 1939, the Federation of Business and Professional Women's Clubs became the first major national women's organization to join the NWP in advocating the ERA.[51]

❧|❧|❧

Not until the hearings on their measure before the House Judiciary Committee on February 4 and 5, 1925, did NWP members discover the extent and vehemence of their opposition among other women's organizations. After those hearings, congressmen also understood that virtually all women's organizations strongly opposed the ERA. The hopes aroused in the NWP by the vote at the AAUW convention were not realized until the 1940s when almost all other women's groups shifted their positions.

The House Judiciary Committee hearings opened with statements by NWP leaders, the only proponents of the ERA to appear. Attorney Maud Younger, NWP congressional chairperson spoke first:

> In coming before you today, in this first hearing ever held in behalf of the equal rights amendment before Congress, we recall that it was 60 years ago that Congress was first asked to act on this measure, when the fourteenth amendment was under consideration.

At that time, Stanton, Anthony, and other woman's rights leaders had requested that Congress remove all discriminations because of sex as well as race. Only those with regard to race were removed. "It rests with the men of this day and generation to do justice to the women of this country," Younger declared.

Other NWP members described the legal disabilities that handicapped women. In some states, women's property fell under the control of their husbands after marriage. In others, a father could appoint a guardian who would take charge of the family's children after he died. Numerous states did not provide for the father's support of illegitimate children whom he acknowledged. In several states, wives could not enter business without the consent of their husbands or the courts. In Texas, Governor-elect "Ma" Ferguson was obliged to petition a court asking that her legal disabilities be removed so that she could legally enter into contracts as governor. A decree granted Mrs. Ferguson began: "Consent of her husband having been granted. . . . " Women were denied the right to sit on juries in more than half the states.

A double standard of morality existed in many state divorce laws. A wife guilty of one act of marital unfaithfulness could be divorced for it. A husband could not. He had to desert his wife and live in infidelity before she could divorce him. In almost every state, (only eight had community property laws), all property acquired during a marriage belonged to the husband. In some states, earnings of a wife became her husband's, and if a child died, the father inherited its entire estate. Under the 1924 immigration law, a man who married a foreigner could bring in his wife regardless of national quotas. A wife's foreign husband was subject to the quota.

NWP speakers described also the negative effects on certain women workers of state protective legislation. Even the enlightened state of Ohio excluded women from sixteen supposedly hazardous occupations, including street crossing guard, taxi driver, bellhop, gas or electric meter reader, shoe shiner, freight or baggage handler, and truck driver. In other states, women were excluded from the most remunerative work—such as that involved in waiting on tables as dinner waitresses—by hour laws for women. These laws kept women from positions as evening ticket salespeople and as conductors on buses or subway lines. Thousands of women had been thrown out of work in ice cream parlors, candy stores, drug stores, newsstands, department stores, pharmacies, and printing companies by laws forbidding evening work for women. In some states where women retained their evening jobs, they could not earn overtime pay.[52]

❧ | ❧ | ❧

A representative of the National League of Women Voters—organized by Carrie Chapman Catt as the successor to the NAWSA—began the presentation of opposition arguments before the House Judiciary Committee by stating:

> We draw, gentlemen, a distinction between *equality* of legal and social status and *identity* of legal and social status. It appears that this amendment tends toward a conception of the status of women which at least would tend in the direction of an identical status. . . . Our conception of the relation of the sexes is a conception of a complementary relation in which women shall be free from any . . . limitations which prevent them from . . . performing for the community and civilization their characteristic functions as women.[53]

Fear that the ERA would somehow cause women to give up their separate but equal status and their traditional character and roles for those of men pervaded the remaining testimony by ERA opponents. To some degree, these fears were justified. The ERA would enable those women who wished to do so to surrender their "characteristic functions as women" in favor of those "characteristic functions of men" that they wished to assume.

National League of Women Voters representatives gave several examples of the types of practical questions that they feared would be answered by the ERA:

> What would be the effect of identical legal status upon a woman's right to support from her husband; what of her . . . alimony. . . . And what of widow's pensions? . . . What about . . . the age of majority . . . the age of marriage? To bring in a rather remote application, but still rather conceivable, what about conscription?[54]

Actually, well-to-do women already were paying alimony to poorer former husbands when the Judiciary Committee hearings were held. The other questions have been answered subsequently by Congress and the courts on the basis of equal treatment of males and females. Title VII of the Civil Rights Act of 1964 answered many of these questions. Title IX of the Civil Rights Act of 1972 settled other questions, such as those about the ability and right of women to compete in strenuous collegiate sports. Although conscription ended in 1973, several women's organizations worked successfully to open nontraditional positions in the armed forces for women. These organizations included the National Organization for Women (NOW), the Women's Equity Action League (WEAL), the ACLU's Women's Rights Project, the Center for Women Policy Studies, the Lobby for Women's Policy Concerns, the National Council of Jewish Women, and the Girl Scouts, operating under the umbrella organization the National Coalition for Women in Defense, established in 1977. These organizations won important court decisions for women in the military services. As a result, women now hold high military ranks and serve, for example, on long-range nuclear submarines.[55] For those women in the 1920s, however, who still possessed most of their Victorian heritage, questions such as those asked by the League of Women Voters in the 1925 hearings were frightening.

Mary Anderson, speaking as director of the Department of Labor's Women's Bureau, opposed the ERA because of the effect she maintained it would have on protective legislation for women. Very soon after her opening arguments, Anderson found herself involved in an exchange with Congressman Hatton W. Sumners of Texas:

MR. SUMNERS: But this constitutional amendment does not propose that there shall be equality in each of the States, as States, but proposes there shall be equality in the whole United States—dealing with the United States as a whole, without regard to the States. . . .

MISS ANDERSON: That would mean, of course, to legislate for men and women alike.

MR. SUMNERS: Yes.

MISS ANDERSON: It would mean, of course, Congress could legislate, for example, an 8-hour day for men and women throughout the United States.

MR. SUMNERS: If that would be possible.

MISS ANDERSON: I think that it would be very desirable, but I doubt whether it could be done.

MR. SUMNERS: Then would you desire a constitutional amendment which would make it possible?

MISS ANDERSON: I doubt whether that could be done at all.

Later in her testimony, however, Anderson acknowledged that every basic industry in the country already operated under eight-hour-a-day regulations. She pointed out, though, that few women worked in those industries yet.[56]

Women's organizations that opposed the ERA in brief appearances before the House Judiciary Committee, because they claimed that the amendment threatened protective legislation, included the General Federation of Women's Clubs, the National Women's Trade Union League, the National Consumers' League, the Young Women's Christian Association, the National Council of Catholic Women, the American Home Economics

Association, and the Woman's Christian Temperance Union, most of which maintained that they represented large numbers of women voters.[57]

Several organizations diverged from the protective-legislation argument. A written statement from Thomas F. Cadwalader, chairman of the Executive Committee of the Sentinels of the Republic and the only male who offered testimony to the House committee, asked,

> Would a woman obtain by virtue of the amendment the right to enlist in the Army or Navy on the same terms as men? It is difficult to see why not. But as to jury service, it is almost preposterous to lay down an unbending rule. Some States have women on the panels now. Others do not. . . . Nobody has ever seriously suggested that their civil rights before the law were jeopardized by excluding them from jury service. . . .
>
> Every consideration . . . of right, of wisdom, and of the merest expediency, alike, requires the Congress not to propose to the states this or any such amendment.

Mrs. Frank C. Scanlon, president of the Massachusetts Congressional, Trade and Civic League told the committee that the amendment threatened "a great deal that is very sacred. . . . The home is endangered by this sort of legislation." The vice president of the National Council of Jewish Women expressed hope that Congress would not attempt "to pass leveling laws which nature and time have not been able to achieve."

Mrs. Edward B. Cameron, president of the Women's Constitutional League of Virginia, stated: "We believe this amendment to be of communistic origin . . . to abolish the home and to establish the new social order recommended by Karl Marx and Frederick Engels. . . . " Finally, Margaret C. (Mrs. B. L.) Robinson, president of the Massachusetts Public Interest League, which claimed members in thirty-six states, declared that her organization was "unalterably opposed" to the ERA because it proposed by government action to decree that men and women shall be equal. "To deny and ignore the fundamental differences between men and women . . . is both unscientific and inhuman."[58]

After hearing this outpouring of opposition to the ERA by women, the Judiciary Committee decided not to refer the measure to the House of Representatives.

Hearings on the ERA before a subcommittee of the U.S. Senate Committee on the Judiciary in 1929 produced arguments essentially similar to those expressed in 1925 before the House Judiciary Committee. The prospect of these conflicting arguments by women produced the following exchange during the NWP's testimony:

SENATOR WATERMAN: Don't you think that the poor men have their troubles
                    trying to find out just what the ladies want?
SENATOR STEIWER: If you don't think so, you will discover that is a fact
                    in about an hour from now.[59]

Fear of the ERA evidently had increased outside of the women's business
and professional organizations. For example, Margaret C. (Mrs. B. L.)
Robinson now declared:

> Official statements and publications of leading advocates of this amendment
> demonstrate that they intend nothing less than to thrust all women into
> ruthless, compulsory, unnatural, and entirely untenable competition with
> men . . . in all the professions and occupations throughout the social fabric.[60]

Florence Kelley, who in 1925 had testified effectively but very briefly
about the benefits to women of protective legislation, decided in 1929 that
stronger words were needed. In 1920, Kelley had attempted to win NWP
support for anti-lynching legislation and voting-rights legislation for
blacks. Now she asked the Senate subcommittee of a committee on which
several members were Southerners: "Does this amendment mean there
will be wholly and absolutely equal rights between the black and the
white?"

Kelley told the senators that she had benefited from an unusual education in the results of congressional attempts to impose equality by
legislation:

> No one of us can know what the amendment is going to do. My father
> [known as Congressman "Pig Iron" Kelley of Pennsylvania] was 30 years
> in Congress. He voted for the Reconstruction Amendments. Many times
> he expressed his permanent amazement at the unforeseen consequences of
> the amendments.

"We [the National Consumers' League] believe," Kelley continued,
"that this amendment will confer . . . equal rights of black women with
black men and of white women with white men. . . . " Kelley did not
mention equality of black men with white women; however, that implication was not likely to have escaped the senators' attention.[61]

❧|❧|❧

The image of themselves as women held by NWP members resembled
Louisa May Alcott's sculptured fantasy of the ideal woman in *An Old-*

Fashioned Girl. Alcott had been converted to the woman's rights movement partly by the resolutions approved at the 1848 Seneca Falls convention.[62] The potential rebellion symbolized by the sculptured woman—and by the sculptor, and by characters such as Rose in *Rose in Bloom*—described by Alcott was obviously underway in the 1920s. During that decade, however, anxiety about the result of shifting gender roles kept the great majority of organized women from joining the revolt against Victorian concepts of women. By the late 1940s, however, the ERA was supported by most women's organizations, the major political parties, the AFL-CIO, and some of the women who previously had been strong advocates of protective legislation—including Eleanor Roosevelt. In 1959, the last major women's organization to oppose ERA, the League of Women Voters, joined the measure's backers.[63]

Propelled especially by the efforts of NOW (founded in 1966), the ERA passed both houses of Congress by large margins in 1972. Eventually, it fell three states short of the three-fourths needed for ratification. A large majority of the adult American population still approves of the amendment. Whether this means that Victorian views of women have been largely rejected by American males and females, however, remains problematical.[64]

6

TOWARD A NEW ECONOMIC
AND POLITICAL ORDER

The coalition which supported Senator Robert La Follette's campaign for president in 1924 constituted the closest equivalent in American history to the European labor, farmer-labor, socialist, and social democratic political parties. La Follette's backers included almost every large labor union in the United States, the Socialist Party, virtually every city central union and state labor federation, almost all state farmer-labor organizations, the largely agrarian and socialist state nonpartisan leagues, and almost every politically active intellectual in the country. Most of the participants in that 1924 coalition, including La Follette, thought of the campaign as the first step toward forcing an eventual realignment of political parties in the United States along lines of divergent economic interests. This realignment would lead, they expected, to a fundamental redistribution of economic power and to the diminution, if not the end, of corporate domination of America. If successful, it would have led also toward the separation of economic policy from Victorian virtues. No such independent effort of comparable magnitude had been made in the United States before, nor has one since.[1]

La Follette's coalition failed, almost as badly as Garvey's black nationalism or the National Woman's Party's attempt to win passage of the Equal

Rights Amendment during the 1920s. Historians usually have viewed the Progressive effort from the perspective of its failure. More attention should be paid to the coalition's origins and to the reasons why the Republican Party concentrated on attacking La Follette and virtually ignored the Democratic candidate for president in 1924. The Republicans' campaign against La Follette required a huge amount of money and used every conceivable method to defeat his candidacy, including charges that La Follette posed a communist threat to the nation.

❦|❦|❦

Events in Great Britain, especially, after World War I captured the attention of American labor-union leaders and intellectuals. Leaders of the major unions identified easily with their English, Scottish, Welsh, and Irish counterparts. Bonds of ethnic ancestry, personal friendship, and similar attitudes toward the role of trade unions united these officials. American labor leaders, therefore, followed events in England carefully after British leaders decided to give their influence and financial support to a separate Labour Party, which most of them did gradually between 1900 and 1906. The events which had swung the conservative heads of the British unions toward supporting an independent labour party bore a close resemblance to the series of reverses after World War I which disturbed the American leaders from their customary independent political positions.

The leaders of the large British trade unions had clung to their influential position within the Liberal Party until unfavorable court decisions and successful attacks by business groups on union membership caused them to experiment with direct political action. They started hesitantly with a "Labour Representation Committee" in 1900 and, encouraged by the results, committed successively larger amounts of money, men, and energy to the effort. As a foundation of its campaign in 1918, the British Labour Party issued a manifesto announcing its postwar program, *Labour and the New Social Order*. That document was written by Sidney Webb, head of the Fabian Society (a society composed largely of intellectuals), which had been nudging English workers toward socialism since the 1880s. The policies defined rather vaguely in the manifesto were mildly socialistic, though to the right of the objectives already attained in America by the North Dakota Nonpartisan League. Leading labor and intellectual journals in the United States reprinted the entire text of the Labour platform, which seemed to them applicable to conditions in the United States. The magazine that exerted the greatest influence among politically active intellectuals, the *New Republic*, published *Labour and the New Social Order* as a supplement, along with a plea to American unions for cooperation in the formation of a new party based on the British program.[2]

The Labour Party further encouraged its American admirers by polling over 25 percent of the total vote in 1918, thus winning recognition in Great Britain as one of the nation's major parties. While Americans prepared to choose their presidential candidates in 1924, the Labour Party became the chief component in the combination which formed a new British government. When the American party conventions met, the Labour Party already had placed its recognized leader, J. Ramsay MacDonald, in the office of prime minister. MacDonald's ascent in twenty-four years from chief officer (unpaid) and organizer of the "Labour Representation Committee" to prime minister of the British government electrified large portions of the American labor movement.[3]

❦|❦|❦

In the third meeting of the Conference for Progressive Political Action (CPPA) held in St. Louis on February 11 and 12, 1924, dominated by the railroad unions, the United Mine Workers, other large independent unions, farmer-labor parties, Progressives, and the Socialists, the conferees shifted toward the position that a separate political entry should receive labor's support in 1924. A motion, adopted almost unanimously, praising the perseverance and triumph of the British Labour Party signaled a strengthened disposition on the part of the labor leaders to follow the British example.[4]

The resolution approved in St. Louis declared that the Labour Party's success provided "conclusive evidence that workers in any country having universal or general suffrage may come into peaceful control of their government whenever they have the intelligence and will to do so." The CPPA resolved also to call a convention of nationwide Progressive forces on July 4 in Cleveland "for the purpose of taking action on nomination of candidates for the offices of president and vice-president of the United States." The motion fell short of a direct call for a third major party, but this cautious start seemed auspicious to all but a few CPPA members. It practically guaranteed a separate political coalition, unless a miraculous transformation occurred in either the Democratic or the Republican parties. The few who remained dissatisfied, however, consisted largely of experienced Socialist Party and farmer-labor politicians and a number of left-wing union officials who understood the organizational efforts and time necessary to mount a national campaign. Despite their misgivings, they saw no choice except continued cooperation.[5]

The thoughts and plans of the railroad unions can be inferred from the insistence of their top officials in June 1923 that Senator La Follette visit Europe that summer as a guest of the unions. The chief purpose of the trip was to bring La Follette into contact with European—especially English and Scandinavian—labor, farmer-labor, and Social Democratic party leaders. Warren S. Stone, grand chief of the Brotherhood of Locomotive Engineers, who by common consent acted as chairman at all meetings of railroad union leaders, wrote to La Follette about progress in creating an American farmer-labor political organization: "While I realize that you are anxious to get into the fight," Stone commented to the 68-year-old senator, "it might be advisable for you to conserve your forces for the following [presidential election] year. Meanwhile, I am figuring on you and Mrs. La Follette taking this trip to Europe." Union officers would conduct the tour. "All your expenses from the time you say you will go, until the time you arrive back home will be taken care of . . . and you will not be under obligation to anyone. . . . And really Senator, while I do not want to become a nuisance, I do not want to take 'no' for an answer. . . ." La Follette, Stone maintained, should consider the trip partially as token compensation for his many years of devotion to the interests of labor but also as one more favor he owed labor organizations: "I am making this demand upon your time for fifty-two days," Stone declared. As a result of the trip, Stone concluded "I believe you would be in a much better position to handle the questions that will arise next winter."[6]

La Follette accepted the offer, an action the scrupulously honest senator would have taken only if he considered it a legitimate campaign donation for the 1924 election. In keeping with that perception, upon arriving in Britain La Follette asked his friend Lincoln Steffens, by then an acknowledged radical living in London, for the names of European politicians and intellectuals with whom he should meet. Steffens supplied names of radical and labor leaders and instructions about how to get in touch with the influential officials and intellectuals in Britain's Labour Party. "I am glad you are come," Steffens added. "It was wise to do so. The trip should interest and stimulate your mind."[7] The senator returned from Europe and announced that he had indeed learned a great deal about the operation of cooperative economic enterprise that could be put to use in the United States. He reserved specific praise for successful examples he had observed in Great Britain and Denmark.[8]

❣|❣|❣

Only one of America's great unions conspicuously retained its commitment to nonpartisan political activity in early 1922. That holdout, though, was the largest union in the United States—the AFL. Samuel Gompers, president of the union during every year but one from its inception in 1886, had acted as the most formidable opponent of independent political action by labor since his first denunciation of proposals advocating that course in 1887. The AFL's experience with labor injunctions during the Wilson administration (after supporting Wilson's presidential candidacy in order to gain an end to such injunctions) verified Gompers's previous opinions.

Gompers had warned workers repeatedly that legislation could be repealed or overturned in the courts. Contracts negotiated directly with employers, however, remained valid for their life. When contracts expired, labor could depend on its rights to strike and boycott to force employers to grant further concessions.[9] Besides, Gompers trusted that union negotiators understood the real needs of the workers they represented and that they would fight to fulfill them. Politicians, on the other hand, with very few exceptions, he explained scornfully, valued their own careers above all else and would sacrifice the cause of workers whenever they considered such betrayal expedient. In speeches and editorials, he criticized the intellectuals who called upon workers to follow them into labor or socialist parties as parasites seeking power through the use of labor's sweat, votes, and money. The only lower form of human species to appear in Gompers's pronouncements were judges who issued injunctions against strikes and other activities necessary for union success in labor negotiations. His contempt for these enemies of labor and for the politicians who encouraged, requested, or condoned their actions usually was expressed in terms reserved by others for wartime traitors.

Gompers considered businessmen who fought unions as honest antagonists who naturally sought every possible advantage—just as labor did. Business firms inevitably combined for greater power and efficiency, as did labor unions. Gompers, like the Socialists, regarded the antitrust movement as useless from the start; at times, he seemed to view it as a trick used by intellectuals and politicians to avoid the real issues raised by labor unions. He expected large corporations or associations of corporations to eventually realize the benefits to themselves of accepting powerful labor unions as partners.[10] Meanwhile, the AFL negotiated for more satisfactory contracts and demanded protection from politicians they supported against any legislation which might weaken their position in negotiations. They also expected help from those politicians in eliminating obvious injustices, such as competition from child labor.

Yet in the summer of 1924, when the Executive Council of the AFL considered endorsing La Follette, Gompers left a hospital bed to urge full and unqualified participation in La Follette's campaign. Some other members of the council, though willing to express support for La Follette, as they had for William Jennings Bryan and Woodrow Wilson—objected to this departure from their long-established policy. Gompers's willingness to argue with his closest associates, such as Matthew Woll and William Green (his eventual successor as president), demonstrated his conversion to the idea that a point had been reached in the country's history which demanded a reconsideration of the AFL's traditional negative attitude toward participation in a national political coalition.

Between 1919 and 1922, a series of events persuaded the pragmatic chiefs of the railroad unions as well as most other labor- and farm-organization leaders (eventually including Gompers) that the rights and welfare of workers and farmers could best be protected by direct political action. In fact, when analyzing one type of infuriating case for their members, leaders of the AFL found themselves obliged to acknowledge that British unions had stopped the same kind of antilabor activity through political action by the Labour Party.

An incident of a kind which union officials had believed too optimistically could no longer occur in the United States took place in November 1919. Gompers had led the fight against injunctions issued against labor unions for violating the Sherman Antitrust Act of 1890 ever since Eugene V. Debs and other officers of the striking American Railway Union had received prison sentences in 1894 for conspiracy to obstruct interstate commerce during the Pullman strike. Subsequently, courts treated secondary boycotts and blacklisting of nonunion products as criminal offenses. Gompers hailed President Wilson's ambiguous compromise wording in the Clayton Antitrust Act of 1914 as labor's "Magna Carta." He may have persuaded himself that it actually guaranteed freedom for unions from federal injunctions.[11]

Responding to intense pressure from members whose wages had fallen seriously behind the rise in prices during and after World War I, President John L. Lewis of the United Mine Workers (UMW), one of the largest unions in the AFL, called a nationwide strike for higher wages, to begin on November 1, 1919. With winter approaching, Americans worried about inadequate reserves of coal, and patience probably was the commodity in shortest supply in the United States during the fall and winter of 1919–1920, the height of the Red Scare. While President Wilson lay seriously ill in the White House, Attorney General A. Mitchell Palmer sought votes in the Democratic presidential primaries from fearful voters, and he came into the 1920 Democratic convention with more pledged delegates than any other candidate possessed.

Palmer had been elected to Congress three times with decisive labor support. The AFL rated his congressional voting record as perfect. In addition, he had sponsored a number of important labor laws and investigations of labor conditions. Now Palmer, along with most members of the "labor bloc" in Congress, responded to public opinion, which was shifting against labor disturbances. He prepared a request for an injunction against the miners, and a federal judge stood ready to issue it. A delegation from the four large railroad brotherhoods visited Palmer and left frustrated. So did Gompers. The UMW leaders, Lewis and William Green, fared no better.

Palmer obtained the injunction, and the strike was crushed with few concessions by mine operators. Gompers, furious at the use of a weapon that he thought had been outlawed, denounced the injunction as an action "so autocratic as to stagger the human mind." Nevertheless, when another nationwide strike broke out five months later—this time a walkout by railroad workers who had suffered even more than the miners from declining real wages—Palmer again mobilized all federal power to subdue the strikers. He obtained another injunction, and when it was ignored, he arranged for the arrest of every strike leader.[12]

Further shocks awaited labor leaders when the Republicans took over the national government in 1921. The most serious one originated in the Supreme Court in the form of a majority decision written in 1922 by former Republican President William Howard Taft, appointed chief justice in 1921 by President Warren Harding. In the case of *Coronado Coal Company v. United Mine Workers*, which arose from violence that took place after the company violated—in fact canceled—its contract with the union, the Supreme Court ruled for the first time in the history of the United States that a union was liable for damages caused by individual members acting on their own. Most of this damage had occurred during fights between miners and private detectives protecting strike breakers. Taft's decision warned that, henceforth, all unions and other unincorporated associations, including farm organizations, would be held fully responsible for the actions of their members, regardless of whether they were acting under orders from the organization or spontaneously (as in the case of the mine workers). Even before this far-reaching ruling was handed down, the AFL Executive Council warned that the imminent verdict might well cause divisive passions in America as serious as those unleashed by the *Dred Scott* decision in 1857.[13]

Taft's ruling stunned union leaders, not only because of its latent paralyzing consequences but also because he based it fundamentally on English common law, best exemplified, he declared, in the British *Taff-Vale* decision of 1900—as well as on the Sherman Act. Taft even relied on quotations from the English judge who had written the *Taff-Vale* verdict.

As a result of the *Taff-Vale* decision, however, political activity had followed that changed the whole complexion of British law as it applied to trade unions. A historian of the British Labour Party wrote: "The case caused great agitation in the trade union world: for if the funds of the unions were to be liable for damages caused by their members during strikes, they would not dare to undertake strike action for fear of financial ruin." The primary result, he declared, was that "The prospects of the Labour Representation Committee at once enormously improved." Membership in the committee multiplied, and the new accessions included several of Britain's largest, wealthiest, and formerly most conservative unions. Within two years of the decision, so many labor candidates succeeded in winning election to Parliament that the Labour Representation Committee changed its name to the Labour Party. The first item on that party's agenda was legislation successfully nullifying the *Taff-Vale* decision.[14]

The AFL Executive Council protested in its report to the union membership:

> It is singular that Chief Justice Taft does not complete the story, the remainder of which is that the *Taff-Vale* decision became a great political issue in England and was ultimately reversed, that the English Parliament as a direct result of the case passed the Trade Disputes Act which made such decisions forever impossible in the future. The *Taff-Vale* decision, which Mr. Chief Justice Taft quotes with approval . . . could not be rendered under English law today.

The council reprinted the entire Trades Dispute Act of 1906 and then showed how closely Taft had followed the reasoning of the *Taff-Vale* decision, which the act had repudiated and practically nullified. The argument ostensibly was aimed at Taft and other judges, but its implications could not have been lost on members of the AFL or on their officers.[15]

Within a period of three weeks, the Supreme Court in 1921 disposed of unions' customary picketing practices. Rendering a decision concerning an Illinois strike in which four to twelve pickets stood peacefully at each gate of the American Steel Foundries Co., Chief Justice Taft declared the word "picket" itself "sinister" and suggestive of "a militant purpose" (which it was in the context of the armed forces). He allowed unions only one picket to a gate. More than that, he found, were "unlawful and cannot be peaceable and may properly be enjoined." Then the court struck down an Arizona statute that forbade judges to issue injunctions against peaceful picketing, on virtually the same grounds. State courts used these Supreme Court decisions as precedents for verdicts damaging to unions.[16]

Federal officials and the judiciary took further action that angered union officials during a walkout by the seven railroad shop craft unions in 1922. After two wage reductions, the elimination of overtime pay for Sunday and holiday work, other modifications by the railroads in overtime work agreements, and futile negotiations about these matters, over 200,000 railroad shopmen around the country laid down their tools at 10 a.m. on July 1, 1922. The Railroad Labor Board, established by the Esch-Cummins Act of 1920, which had returned control over the roads to their private owners over the objections of the Railroad Brotherhood, approved the establishment of company unions to hire strikebreakers. When this failed to end the walkout, Attorney General Harry M. Daugherty obtained permission from President Harding and his Cabinet to seek an injunction on antitrust grounds to stop what he called at a Cabinet meeting a plot to take over the government by bringing American industry to a halt. The court order granted in response to Daugherty's plea—by a judge appointed by Harding on Daugherty's recommendation—was one of the broadest ever issued. It declared illegal under the Sherman Act every action imaginable that might tend to continue the strike by anyone connected with it.[17]

Earlier, the railroad unions had threatened to help form a national labor party unless Congress agreed to the Plumb Plan (drawn up by their attorney Glenn E. Plumb) to nationalize the railroads that the government had operated successfully during the war. Despite heroic efforts on the unions' behalf by La Follette, Congress had passed the Esch-Cummins Act instead. After the shopmen's strike, members of fifteen major railroad unions were thoroughly politicized, and their leaders moved into the forefront of the movement to create a farmer-labor political organization—though not necessarily a political party (about which most of them remained ambivalent)—and to select a farmer-labor presidential candidate in 1924.[18]

The AFL Executive Council, whose emotions already were inflamed by a wealth of other grievances, denounced the federal executive and judicial actions during the shopmen's strike as resulting in "the most infamous restraining order ever conceived or decreed by either a federal or state court." Congressional refusal to take action toward rectifying this situation indicated to the Executive Council "clearly that no hope of relief may be found in that check upon the judiciary which the American people have been led to believe was inherent in the power of Congress. . . ."[19]

Significantly, only one politician was invited to address the AFL's annual convention in 1922, the year of the union's greatest setbacks—Robert La Follette. At the end of an attack upon the Supreme Court, in which it literally accused the Court of attempting to institute slavery for workers, the Executive Council expressed its gratitude for the "masterful presentation to the convention by Senator La Follette of the attitudes of the courts toward labor. . . ."[20] At that point, the railroad unions and the state farmer-labor organizations already had decided on La Follette as their choice to lead an independent presidential campaign in 1924. Most leaders of the AFL, though quieter about their intentions, already were leaning toward that course.[21]

These court decisions, about which labor leaders complained bitterly, helped upset the previous balance of power between employers and unions. The AFL, which had won 61 percent of its strikes in 1917, claimed victory in only 37 percent of its strikes in 1920, and the percentage continued to fall. So did total union membership. Leo Wolman, whose statistics on this subject generally are accepted, derived a total of 5,110,800 members in all unions in the United States for 1919, dropping to 3,592,500 by 1923.[22] By then, the AFL Executive Council realized that nonpartisan politics no longer operated to the benefit of the AFL or of American workers as a whole, despite the record number of strong supporters of labor elected to Congress in 1922.

Gompers had visited England as recently as 1919. He understood, therefore, the alternative type of politics that could be used to put pressure on public officials, judges, and business executives. Probably years of habit as much as the caution of an elderly man made him hesitate to back a farmer-labor presidential candidate until 1924. And when Gompers hesitated, so did most of the AFL.[23]

❦│❦│❦

The long-standing traditions and beliefs which restrained the major unions from joining and thus directing the movement toward a third major party—rather than merely an independent presidential candidacy—were severely tested by the remarkable success of state farmer-labor organizations. These groups, which developed when agrarians and labor unions found nominees of the Republican and Democratic parties unacceptable, elected or helped to elect large numbers of candidates at every level of politics, especially in 1922. Two sets of elections in the Midwest, particularly, intrigued those considering the possibility in the early 1920s that the time might be right to establish a third political party.

In North Dakota, the largely agrarian Nonpartisan League, with help from virtually every labor union in the state, gained complete control of the state's political machinery in 1918.[24] Depending upon thorough and skillful organizing in every corner of the state and a professionally edited newspaper which gave each member accurate information and kept morale high, the Nonpartisan League took over the previously conservative Republican Party. The league enjoyed the advantage of leadership by a genius at political organization, Arthur C. Townley.

Republicans and Democrats who opposed the league gradually gathered in an Independent Voters' Association, leaving the league, essentially, a second major party. The league proceeded to elect the governor, huge majorities in both houses of the legislature, and about three quarters of state supreme-court justices. It obtained passage for all ten of the state constitutional amendments that league administrators believed were necessary to implement the organization's program. The league also elected both of North Dakota's congressmen.

Then the league secured passage of a program that went further than the North Dakota Socialist Party ever had dared even to suggest: a state-owned bank with rural branches; a state-owned and -operated grain-elevator system to manufacture and market farm products; a state industrial commission to start and manage other state enterprises; state insurance against various types of agricultural disasters, such as severe hail; and numerous state welfare plans, including workmen's compensation and public-works programs for the unemployed. The idea of farmer-labor cooperation toward these objectives won approval from Samuel Gompers, who previously had opposed both special-interest political parties and socialist legislation, which, to him, included workmen's compensation. Gompers sent an enthusiastic letter to be read at the convention at which North Dakota's State Federation of Labor discussed whether or not to ally itself with the league. Gompers pointed to the success of such alliances in other countries. These had been successful in establishing welfare states in Scandinavia (along with Germany, the source for a very high proportion of North Dakota's population). Gompers strongly advised consummation of the proposed alliance.

The league reorganized after its triumph in North Dakota and expanded into nearby states and two Canadian provinces with some success. Enemies waiting for them in these other areas, able to use violence and other means of blatant intimidation, justified their illegal actions by references to spreading Bolshevism. Thus, they prevented duplication of the North Dakota experience. Nevertheless, the league helped La Follette's followers widen their control over Wisconsin, joined in forming the strong Minnesota Farmer-Labor Party, and for a while exercised control over the legislatures of Idaho, Montana, and Washington. The severe agricultural depression of the early 1920s drove first the North Dakota farmers, then the league's enterprises, and finally the league itself into bankruptcy. However, the Nonpartisan League's North Dakota opponents, a combination of conservative elements in the Republican and Democratic parties, found it impossible to win back the state as long as they opposed the league's banks, grain elevators, and insurance plans. Only after they promised to manage these more efficiently did the major parties regain political control in North Dakota.[25]

Events in Minnesota affected the attitudes of those considering formation of a national farmer-labor party more compellingly than did the startling success of the North Dakota Nonpartisan League. Minnesota, a state with such large cities as Minneapolis and Duluth, important industrial firms, and strong labor organizations as well as agrarian interests, was more representative than North Dakota of the states that a new political party would have to capture. Also, in Minnesota the Nonpartisan League's technique of capturing an established party in primary elections failed almost completely. The major parties were well-organized and retained their vitality and popular officeholders. Therefore, the Minnesota rebels formed a separate party at a convention held in April 1922. This united the state Working People's Nonpartisan League—composed of the State Federation of Labor, Minnesota railroad brotherhoods, and a majority of the state's Socialists—with the Minnesota Farmers' Nonpartisan League. Actually, these groups had been working together unofficially since 1918. In Minnesota, as in North Dakota, those who were entranced with the results of farmer-labor cooperation observed the meshing of established local organizations; the nomination of almost full slates of state, county, and municipal candidates; control over journals which reached almost all supporters; and agreement, sometimes by compromise, on both specific and general objectives as well as on candidates.[26]

The Minnesota Farmer-Labor Party startled politicians who had scoffed at the prospects of third parties by electing both its candidates for the U.S. Senate—Henrik Shipstead and Magnus Johnson—in 1922 and 1923. Shipstead defeated Frank B. Kellogg, one of the ablest and most popular members of the Republican senatorial elite. Kellogg was appointed secretary of state by President Coolidge in February 1925. Johnson beat Minnesota governor Jacob Preus. The Minnesota party also elected three

U.S. congressmen, twenty-four state senators, and forty-six members of the state legislature. This success, unexpected outside Minnesota, demonstrated convincingly that strong farmer and worker organizations could merge their sometimes conflicting interests in a program that benefited both.[27]

❦ | ❦ | ❦

Among the advantages enjoyed during the early 1920s by advocates of a new national party was widespread evidence of unusual vulnerability within both the Republican and Democratic parties. The Republicans, who controlled the national government, took credit for business prosperity. However, they also received the blame for plummeting farm prices, failure of wages to advance appreciably against living costs, and judicial attacks on labor unions.[28] Moreover, beginning in March 1923 and continuing until after the presidential election, the nation was treated to the spectacle of investigations revealing evidence of sordid corruption within the highest echelons of the national administration.[29]

The Democratic Party suffered from even more serious problems than the Republicans in 1924. Divided almost evenly between wets and drys, supporters and opponents of the Ku Klux Klan, and between those who viewed joyfully and those who opposed fiercely the nomination of a Catholic, Governor Alfred E. Smith of New York, for president, the Democrats probably were lucky to survive the election in condition to return for another. Their symptoms were those of a party susceptible to severe challenge from a determined third entry, which could start the Democrats along the way toward the near oblivion of the Liberal Party in Great Britain.

Even before the nominating procedure at their 1924 convention began, the Democratic platform, which virtually ignored the modest requests of Gompers, had completed the party's alienation from the AFL.[30] Early in the 1920s, the railroad unions had supported the candidacy of William G. McAdoo, who had been more than fair to labor when he served as head of the Railroad Administration, which operated the nation's railroads during the war. Before the end of Wilson's administration, though, McAdoo had resigned from the Cabinet to repair his personal financial situation. He lost some labor support when he refused to endorse the Plumb Plan. Then McAdoo suddenly became an advocate of Prohibition and the candidate of the national Ku Klux Klan. When Edward L. Doheny testified—and McAdoo confirmed—that he had retained McAdoo to represent his oil interests and had paid him fees totalling $150,000 for his services as a negotiator concerning Mexican oil leases (with $900,000 more to come if he overcame Mexican law and prevented expropriation of Doheney's Mexican oil lands), railroad unions decided finally that they favored an independent candidate.[31]

The Democratic convention produced a series of ghastly deadlocks. These were terrible not only because of the intense heat that the delegates endured for long periods in New York's Madison Square Garden, but also because of the severe divisions they caused in the party. From June 24 to the afternoon of July 9, the delegates fought, despite the heat, about one matter after another. Twelve hundred New York City policemen assigned to the convention prevented violence, though their own patience was strained when the Texas delegation attempted to burn a KKK cross outside the arena. After a long and acrimonious debate on the subject, the convention voted against mentioning the Klan in its platform by a vote of $543\frac{3}{20}$ to $542\frac{7}{12}$.[32]

When William Jennings Bryan realized after nineteen roll-call votes that neither McAdoo nor Smith could win the nomination, he feared that the hot and tired delegates would turn to the Wall Street corporation attorney John W. Davis. Davis had represented the Coronado Coal Company against the United Mine Workers in that notorious case, and he served as attorney for J. P. Morgan and Co. At that point, Bryan took action reminiscent of his role in the 1912 convention. During a vehement speech, he shouted, "This convention must not nominate a Wall Street man. Mr. Davis is the lawyer of J. P. Morgan." Someone shouted back, "And who is Mr. McAdoo the lawyer for?" Compromise plans were shelved for a while.[33]

After 103 ballots, Davis, nevertheless, obtained the nomination—a practically worthless honor by then. The convention further harmed Davis by nominating Bryan's brother Charles for vice president, a much too obvious attempt to keep the older brother quiet and to obviate the presidential candidate's liabilities.[34]

❣|❣|❣

The movement for a farmer-labor alternative to the Republican and Democratic parties, which reached its climax in 1924, had been gathering support and momentum since the end of World War I. Even Woodrow Wilson spoke of the need for a third party in 1918 and predicted that he himself would move to the Left.[35] Scores of autonomous local and state labor and agrarian parties, as well as the nonpartisan leagues, participated in the elections of 1918 and 1919.

One of the strongest city labor parties, the Chicago Federation, took the initiative and called for a national labor-party conference in 1919.[36] The immediate results were extremely encouraging. The AFL did not respond, but at least half of its affiliated unions sent representatives. The United Mine Workers, in their 1919 convention, voted overwhelmingly to support a national labor party, though few of its officers attempted to implement that resolution. The numerous city and state farmer, labor, and farmer-labor groups seemed ready for melding. At the request of the Chicago local, the Illinois State Federation polled all its locals, and they voted ten to one in favor of a labor party. Official representatives from the Committee of 48, an organization of liberal and radical intellectuals and former Progressive Party leaders formed in January 1918 who sought to bring the many state and local agrarian and worker organizations into a new Progressive coalition, attended also. So did officers of the nonpartisan leagues. La Follette showed interest in a nomination, if he approved of the platform.

The Socialist Party, reluctant to entrust its national machinery to what its leaders perceived as a group of political amateurs, stood aloof. So did the experienced politicians in the Minnesota Farmer-Labor Party, who decided (like the Socialists) that this particular third-party movement lacked the maturity necessary for cohesion and the big union muscle needed for success. The leaders of the largest railroad unions remained committed to McAdoo, and the whole project made Gompers unhappy. The third-party movement hardly caused a ripple, therefore, in the 1920 national election.

Every important group that the fledgling Farmer-Labor Party had attempted unsuccessfully to bring together in 1920 agreed to coalesce in the CPPA behind La Follette in 1924. In addition, the individuals who offered to endorse him read like a Who's Who of politically active intellectuals and the more Left-leaning former Progressive leaders. The economists who supported La Follette included Paul H. Douglas (later a U.S. senator), Rexford G. Tugwell, John R. Commons, Thorstein Veblen, Alvin Hansen, and John Ise. W. E. B. Du Bois, James Weldon Johnson, William Pickens, and other NAACP leaders headed the most significant break among black leaders—and the first since Wilson's 1912 campaign—from the Republican Party. The former Progressives included Jane Addams, Florence Kelley, Harold L. Ickes, Frederick C. Howe, Oswald Garrison Villard, Amos E. Pinchot, George L. Record, Norman Hapgood, Donald Richberg, Herbert Croly, and Walter E. Weyl. Debs encouraged longtime Socialists to back La Follette. Theodore Dreiser announced his support for La Follette, as did other writers such as Joseph Wood Krutch, Lincoln

Steffens, Roger Baldwin, Charlotte Perkins Gilman, George Jean Nathan, Sinclair Lewis, Robert Herrick, Elmer Rice, Upton Sinclair, H. L. Mencken, and Carl Van Doren. Among politically active intellectuals of distinction, only Walter Lippmann refused to endorse La Follette.[37]

The impressive and potentially strong movement supporting La Follette's election proceeded rapidly toward self-destruction even before his nomination. The most serious error came early in 1924 when La Follette, endowed with great leverage as the favorite candidate of every part of the coalition—and, in fact, the only candidate upon whom each element could agree—decided not to press for commitments to a separate party. He sincerely believed that the strong showing he would make in the election would arouse what he referred to as an "irresistible" public demand for a third party.

Explaining his decision later, La Follette claimed that "permanent political parties have been born in this country after, and not before national campaigns, and they have come from the people, not from the proclamations of individual leaders." Also, La Follette was convinced that a large vote for him would prevent Coolidge from obtaining a majority of electoral votes and, therefore, would send the election of the next president to the House of Representatives, where a Progressive coalition would prevail. Establishment of a third party before the election, he believed, might cost too many Progressive congressmen their seats. By running on La Follette's ticket, they would lose some of the Republican or Democratic vote.[38] He maintained this position despite arguments with his close friend and former law partner, Gilbert E. Roe (who warned against all the major mistakes that were to occur during the campaign). Roe suggested that La Follette's self-deception was due in part to his long control over an established Republican party in Wisconsin. Only by nominating full state tickets and candidates for Congress in the majority of districts in which the old parties had nominated "Tories," declared Roe, would La Follette's coalition continue "after you and all the rest of us have passed out of the picture."[39]

At first, La Follette insisted upon supporting all Progressive congressional candidates. He surrendered this plan when he found out that the AFL and railroad brotherhoods opposed some candidates he favored.

La Follette's decision concerning the establishment of a separate party becomes more understandable when considered within the context both of his relationship with Gompers and the other leaders of the AFL and of his long-range expectations about the AFL. He and the Socialists expected the heads of the state and local labor parties and the Progressive leaders of some of the largest affiliated unions eventually to prevail within the AFL. La Follette believed that the AFL would not risk its unity by refusing to affiliate with a labor party backed by virtually every other major union, especially if that party showed signs of success. Meanwhile, La Follette decided that he must maintain peaceful, if not cordial, relations with Gompers and his Executive Council. Therefore, he allowed the AFL to dictate which congressional, state, and local candidates he would support. Roe analyzed the situation for La Follette accurately, but La Follette told his campaign manager, Congressman John M. Nelson of Wisconsin, that decisions regarding congressmen made without the AFL's approval would be "fatal" to his candidacy.[40]

The Socialists, the leaders of the Minnesota Farmer-Labor Party, and Sidney Hillman (later head of the Congress of Industrial Organizations' Political Action Committee) representing the clothing workers—all experienced and successful in managing political campaigns—objected to the hesitation about starting a third party. However, the seriously ailing Gompers continued to contemplate the matter into the summer of 1924. Most Railroad Brotherhood leaders also wavered, and a few entertained illusions about McAdoo's chances at the Democratic convention. Former Congressman Edward Keating, editor of the weekly railroad-workers' journal *Labor*, however, advised McAdoo to withdraw altogether.

The CPPA and the brotherhoods began preliminary organizational work for a national campaign early in 1924. Without an independent party, though, practically no fund-raising took place. No state or local candidates to supplement the national candidates' campaign were ever nominated. Democratic and Republican candidates supported by La Follette feared to reciprocate, anxious about reprisals by the party whose primary elections they had won.

La Follette's candidacy was endorsed by the CPPA convention which met in Cleveland on July 4 and 5, 1924. The convention avoided a formal nomination of La Follette, which would have implied the formation of a third party. The Socialists and the farmer-labor groups objected to this hesitancy. Experience told them that absence of state and local party candidates would hinder organizing and fund-raising for the national ticket. However, the labor unions and the Committee of 48 preferred to await both the AFL's support and evidence from the November election that the American people wanted an alternative to the two major parties. Formation of a third party would then be much easier, they believed. As part of the effort to endorse independent candidates, the convention voted to allow the CPPA National Committee to name a vice-presidential candidate. The committee, following La Follette's recommendation, selected

Senator Burton K. Wheeler of Montana, a former Democrat who recently had declared himself an Independent.[41]

❡|❡|❡

La Follette's platform, submitted by him and approved by the convention, was brief and simple. It appeared designed to deflect criticism that La Follette was a dangerously radical—if not a Bolshevik—candidate. The platform called for abolition of injunctions in labor disputes, a child-labor amendment to the Constitution, government construction of a St. Lawrence seaway, public works in times of economic depression, public ownership of the railroads and of water power, the right of Congress to overrule the Supreme Court, direct nomination and election of the president, and a popular referendum before Congress could declare war.[42]

Still, Gompers hesitated. His dilemma went beyond the question of whether to break with AFL traditions to include deeper qualms about the directions taken by Progressive politicians such as La Follette. Testifying before the House Labor Committee in 1916, Gompers had referred to federal unemployment insurance as "socialist," a very strong epithet to him. He declared that he preferred workers to suffer from economic adversity rather than "give up one jot of the freedom . . . to strive and struggle for emancipation through their own efforts." Until the end of his life, Gompers continued to worry less about the need for workers' old age, disability, or any other form of insurance than about what he called "the softening of the moral fibre of the people." Gompers's chief assistant, Matthew Woll, extolled the comparative moral advantages of voluntary aid to workers, even in 1930. This attachment of AFL leaders to aspects of the Victorian concept of character was not easily overcome.[43]

When Gompers finally decided in August 1924 that the AFL should join the Progressive coalition, he not only left his sick bed in Lenox Hill Hospital in New York to inform his union and the public of his decision but also gave his all-out backing to La Follette. "If it takes the last bit of [my] energy," he declared, "I have to put it in the campaign for La Follette."[44] Unfortunately for the new political coalition, Gompers's conversion came less than three months before the presidential election.

The inability of the CPPA to organize early and properly left La Follette without sufficient funds for travel or advertising. He delivered only twenty full-length speeches during the campaign, and the first of these took place on Labor Day. He began his first speaking tour much too late, on October 6, only a month before the election. He lacked the money necessary to travel west of Omaha or south of Baltimore. A planned trip to the West Coast, where California and possibly Washington were leaning toward La Follette, had to be canceled. Advance schedules, even when prepared, usually meant nothing. Toward the end of the campaign, he began charging admission to his rallies. Money collected at the entrance for a speech in one city enabled La Follette to travel to the next. He had expected the unions to provide the needed funds, but the AFL contributed only $25,000, and he probably received a total of about $50,000 from all of organized labor. According to their official acknowledgments, the Republicans collected over $4 million for the national ticket alone; the Democrats spent over $900,000; and the La Follette-Wheeler campaign, less than $222,000.[45]

Unable to conduct a wide speaking tour and with practically no support from daily newspapers (except for the twenty-five paper Scripps-Howard chain, owned by his friend E. W. Scripps[46]), La Follette could not adequately explain his chief message: that ordinary Americans must take control of their economy away from the large corporations and their political lackeys. He was obliged to select the topics of his speeches from among many scattered subjects. These included Republican corruption, the need for action against business monopolies, the plight of farmers, the crimes of railroads, imperialism, and Republican ties to international financiers.[47] With so little time and so few opportunities available, he declined to take the advice of Basil Manley, head of his Washington campaign office, to devote more time to tying the Republican Party to the scandals of the Harding administration and to symbols like Teapot Dome. Manley suggested that attacks on the reprehensible behavior of Republicans would force their speakers onto the defensive and away from their assaults on La Follette's alleged Communistic tendencies.[48]

Millions of farmers and workers—especially those likely to vote for La Follette, if they could be persuaded to vote at all (such as marginal farmers, low-paid workers, members of the most oppressed ethnic minorities)—never heard him speak or read his arguments. But they did learn from daily newspapers, popular magazines, and speeches by Republican orators that La Follette advocated Bolshevism and anarchy. These charges increased in intensity when polls taken by the *Literary Digest*, the Hearst newspaper organization, and other indicators of voters' intentions in October 1924 showed La Follette well ahead of Davis and gaining fast on Coolidge.[49] Widely circulated ads placed by wealthy individuals and corporations and articles in major magazines attempted to make a vote for La Follette seem like a ballot cast to put a Bolshevik in the White House.[50]

The vitriolic Republican vice-presidential nominee, Chicago banker

Charles G. Dawes, alone made 108 speeches during the campaign. In these, he repeatedly identified La Follette and his rather bland platform with socialism and communism. In one favorite cry, Dawes asked audiences, "Where do you stand? On the rock of the Constitution of the United States under the American flag and behind President Coolidge—or on the sinking sands of Socialism, with the red flag?"[51] Dawes concentrated also on La Follette's proposal to allow Congress to overturn Supreme Court decisions, which in Dawes's addresses somehow became La Follette's plan to subvert the whole Constitution.[52] Coolidge hardly campaigned, ostensibly because of his son's death in July. But he did emerge from the White House to declare that the real issue in 1924 was "whether America will allow itself to be degraded into a communistic or socialistic state or whether it will remain American."[53] Apparently this strategy worked. A poll taken after the election by a professional sociologist of 1,088 voters in the Midwest, 875 of whom were university students, disclosed that over half stated that the "most important" reason they had voted for Coolidge was La Follette's "subversive and dangerous" policies.[54]

The finest statistical analyses of the 1924 presidential vote indicate that La Follette's total barely suggested his potential electoral strength.[55] La Follette swept the votes of ethnic groups with a heritage of labor, farmer-labor, or Socialist political activity. He ran especially strongly among Catholics, first- and second-generation German-Americans, Scandinavian-Americans, and eastern-European-Jewish–Americans. However, in many areas, only slight efforts were made to insure that members of these groups voted.

Wherever an organization existed which could inform workers; wheat farmers; and German, Scandinavian, and eastern-European-Jewish ethnic groups about La Follette or remind Catholics of La Follette's unequivocal stand against the Klan—and could get these voters to the polls—La Follette did remarkably well. The Socialists delivered most of their voters; so did the statewide nonpartisan leagues and La Follette's Wisconsin organization. Even the Socialists, though, did not penetrate far into the ethnic enclaves of New York State controlled by Tammany and other precinct-level machines, except among some Catholic groups and Eastern European Jews. Many of these Jewish voters belonged not only to Hillman's Amalgamated Clothing Workers or to David Dubinsky's International Ladies' Garment Workers' Union, which supported La Follette, but to the Socialist Party as well. A high proportion read Abraham Cahan's *Jewish Daily Forward*, and Cahan backed La Follette in speeches and editorials.[56] In Chicago, La Follette ran well among the most highly unionized ethnic groups—Jews and Germans—which contained relatively high proportions of Socialists. In Chicago, he pulled a significant number of Czechoslo-vakian and Polish-American voters from their party roots.[57] A study of voting in Minnesota indicates a similar pattern there.[58]

The farmer-labor organizations, Socialists, and comparatively well-organized union political activity brought La Follette about as many votes as Davis in Michigan, and he ran well ahead of the Democratic candidate in the urban counties of Michigan and Illinois. He won four times as many votes as Davis in heavily industrialized Pittsburgh and piled up large margins over his Democratic opponent in such industrial areas as Rochester, Paterson, and Cleveland, where he received aid from long-standing labor and Socialist organizations. La Follette won more votes than Davis in every northwestern state between Michigan and the West Coast. In the South, his support came from the groups which had voted for Populist and Socialist candidates during the previous thirty years.[59]

The Democrats required their usual turnout of habitual Democratic voters arranged by such machine politicians as Tom Taggart of Indiana, Frank Hague of New Jersey, Tom Pendergast of Missouri, and Ed Flynn of New York, plus bitter opposition to La Follette from the Ku Klux Klan to defeat La Follette in those states. However, it took the Democrats' supremacy in the South, where they obtained 59.1 percent of all votes cast against La Follette's 5.5 percent (La Follette was unable to campaign in the South) to establish their national margin of 28.8 percent to La Follette's 16.5 percent.[60]

Why did the AFL and railroad unions desert the independent political movement so completely after this promising start? La Follette himself professed to be awed by the magnitude of the popular response to his candidacy. At first, he claimed, he had hoped that he might win seven or eight states and thus allow Congress to choose a president. On September 9, before the Republicans threw a sea of money, orators, and literature into the campaign and as he was running out of funds, La Follette addressed a meeting of more than a score of labor leaders, including heads of the AFL, the railroad brotherhoods, and the UMW. He told the gathering that he had worked with many of those present for years and expected to work in harmony and trust with them for "ten or twenty years to come." He would not want, therefore, "to jeopardize my reputation as a seasoned political observer. . . . I don't want you to feel that I am exaggerating, but today our movement is even with the candidacy of Coolidge." Conservative political analysts, he claimed, agreed.[61]

After the election, La Follette displayed no loss of enthusiasm. Organizational defects that would be corrected, he maintained, had prevented the Progressives from gaining more than a small percentage of the votes that should have been theirs. The next election, he predicted, would demonstrate this. National campaign chairman Congressman John Nelson proclaimed: "We have brought a new spirit, a new life stream into American politics. . . . The Progressive movement will go on unabated and ever more successful." Edward Keating, never far from the views of railroad union chiefs, apparently agreed. An editorial in *Labor*, published on November 8, 1924, titled "Prepare for the Next Battle: A Cause Supported by 5,000,000 Ballots is Not Lost," stated: "We have lost the first battle. Well, what of it? It is not the first time that right has lost and wrong has won." La Follette, the editor pointed out, had gained as many votes as the British Labour Party had polled after twenty-five years of intensive campaigning:

> Two years from now we must face the enemy again—that time in a Congressional election. We must prepare for that election and for the contests which will follow. . . . Our organization, which was so obviously weak in this campaign must be strengthened.[62]

On November 9, representatives of twenty railroad unions met in Cleveland to discuss future political plans. Warren Stone, presiding as usual, and L. E. Sheppard, head of the Conductors' Union, declared that during the campaign, Socialist politicians unsympathetic to labor unions had taken over the CPPA. Unless the railroad unions regained their preeminent place, they recommended leaving the CPPA. At that point, however, a majority of the railroad union leaders wanted to remain in a coalition similar to the one which had endorsed La Follette. The meeting also passed unanimously a resolution opposing immediate formation of a third party.[63]

However, the Socialists, and La Follette's allies among the farmer-labor organizations, independent unions, Progressives, and intellectuals—preferred to wait no longer. Continuing the election campaign's disunity, they insisted upon organizing an independent political party at a conference held early in 1925. When L. E. Sheppard introduced a resolution, seconded by other railroad union representatives, designed to continue a nonpartisan CPPA, opposition was so strong that no vote was taken. Faced with what amounted to an ultimatum, one of the necessary components in a third party on the Left—the railroad unions—politely withdrew. The remaining groups found agreement difficult, and most of them soon succumbed to discouragement.[64] Meanwhile, the railroad brotherhoods reached an accommodation with the Republican administration.[65]

Chance events also played a role in destroying altogether the coalition which had backed La Follette. Because of severe illness (from which he died in June 1925), La Follette hardly took any part in negotiations with the railroad unions or in the Chicago meeting of the CPPA. No substitute for La Follette had been groomed, though several were available. Some participants in La Follette's presidential campaign suggested that George W. Norris, for example, might well be a better campaign leader than La Follette. Norris, who had offered to support La Follette, broke with the Republican Party in 1928 and supported Al Smith, despite disagreement with Smith about issues he thought vital.[66]

Gompers died on December 3, 1924, soon after the election, and at that point, the future political role of the AFL could not have been predicted. Most veteran AFL leaders accepted James Duncan, one of the founders of the AFL and first vice president since 1894, as the logical successor, and Duncan himself claimed that position. Duncan had supported La Follette and the formation of a third party in 1924. At the Executive Council meeting that chose a temporary president, Duncan argued that he had served the AFL in its second highest position for thirty years, and that the first vice president customarily succeeded to the presidency in any labor union until members voted at the next convention. Had Duncan been granted the temporary position he requested, AFL political policies would have turned sharply from Gompers's ideas. Duncan had helped lead the Seattle general strike in 1919; he had worked for the Washington Farmer-Labor Party in 1920; and he had run for the U.S. Senate as a Farmer-Labor candidate in 1922, despite a request from Gompers that he withdraw.[67]

Opponents of AFL participation in independent political activity led by conservative Dan Tobin of the Teamsters, and Gompers's protégé Matthew Woll, fearful of the actions Duncan might take during a year in office, including arranging for his reelection, declared that the presidency should go instead to the representative of a major union. They successfully pressed the candidacy of William Green, secretary-treasurer of the UMW. As in most organizations, the incumbent won the next general election. Green's strong political ties to the Democratic Party decided the AFL's political affiliation for decades thereafter.[68]

In his comprehensive study of La Follette's candidacy, David Waterhouse concluded that the most important single reason for the collapse of La Follette's coalition was attachment to the system of two major parties and to the well-established system of rewards that they offered to their supporters.[69] Whether or not this attachment would have continued if the La Follette coalition had persisted through subsequent elections, especially if it had supported local and state candidates for office, is a question that historians can merely ponder.

The La Follette coalition did play a significant role as a bridge for various groups to the New Deal. As Allan J. Lichtman has declared: "Certainly there is much greater continuity between the electoral coalitions forged by La Follette and FDR than pluralist historians have suspected."[70] The New Deal carried forward La Follette's effort to separate economic policy from Victorian morality and to form a farmer–labor–ethnic-group alliance in order to do so.

7

THE GUARDIANS

The early twentieth-century assaults on Victorianism provoked a strong organized defense by fundamentalists, Prohibitionists, and various conservative and patriotic organizations. However, the huge nationwide Ku Klux Klan, with at least three million members, emerged as the most visible and powerful guardian of Victorianism during the 1920s.[1]

Unlike the vigilante groups which had used the name Ku Klux Klan after the Civil War and during the mid-twentieth-century battles against integration, the Klan of the 1920s did not focus on protecting white supremacy in the South. At the height of the Klan's power in 1924, Southerners formed only 16 percent of its total membership. Over 40 percent of early twentieth-century Klan members lived in the three midwestern states of Indiana, Ohio, and Illinois. The Klan enrolled more members in Connecticut than in Mississippi, more in Oregon than in Louisiana, and more in New Jersey than in Alabama. Klan membership in Indianapolis was almost twice that in South Carolina and Mississippi combined.[2]

Also, Klan members in the mid-1920s were not any more violent than other native, white, middle-class Protestant males. After the Klan organized nationally for maximum profit and political action in 1921, the organization expelled members and whole chapters charged with having taken part in vigilante activities.[3] However, inconclusive newspaper and government investigations into the activities of a small minority of early Klansmen during 1921 gave the organization a violent image.[4] The name Ku Klux Klan (adopted mainly because of the Klan's role in the immensely popular film, *The Birth of a Nation*), the Klan's secrecy, and the order's refusal to admit anyone except native white Protestant males contributed to this image, especially among blacks, Catholics, Jews, and champions of civil liberties.

The image of the Klan held by critics of the organization during the 1920s was affected too by the Klan's rhetoric. That rhetoric reflected still widely accepted Victorian ideas about a racial hierarchy and about the dangers to American society posed by Catholics, blacks, Jews, and Asians. These popular beliefs had assisted the passage of immigration-restriction acts and had helped to defeat the presidential bid of Al Smith. They already had led to nationwide segregation and to disenfranchisement of southern blacks. Therefore, almost nowhere that Klan-backed politicians won power did Klan racist rhetoric need to be transformed into legislation. Nowhere did Klansmen running for office need to advocate violence under any circumstance, even against blacks in the South.

The near absence of Klan violence against southern blacks was explained, in part, by a perceptive editorial in the Savannah, Georgia, *Tribune*, a black-owned newspaper which strongly supported Marcus Garvey's black nationalist Universal Negro Improvement Association and was outspoken about civil-rights violations. The *Tribune*'s editorial (whose conclusions were corroborated by other evidence), published July 13, 1922, stated:

> The evidence is that in the South the Ku Klux are not bothering with the Negroes. The naked truth is that when a band of lynchers sets out to kill a Negro they do not take the trouble to mask. They do not think it necessary to join a secret society, pay initiation fees and buy regalia when Negroes are the quarry.[5]

A Georgia mob did not find it necessary to don masks before lynching Leo Frank in 1915, the year that the early twentieth-century Klan met to organize outside Atlanta.

❦|❦|❦

The Klan's primary objectives consisted of guarding the major Victorian concepts and the interests these protected. The ideas of character, largely reserved for white Protestants, the home and family in which character was formed, and distinctly separate gender roles stood foremost among these concepts. A series of articles entitled "The Klansman's Criterion of Character," published weekly from March 1 to March 29, 1924, in the Klan's national newspaper *Searchlight*, illustrated what the Klan expected of its leaders as well as of its ordinary members.

Jesus provided the chief model for *Searchlight*'s definition of character: "He never compromised when dealing with the leaders of the Jews. He would not dissemble in order to induce men to follow him. He would not lie in order to save his own life." Jesus "was the unflinching, accomplishing, achieving Christ, because he was the purposeful, steadfast, determined Christ." Furthermore, Jesus accomplished his great mission on earth without the advantages enjoyed by members of the privileged business elites and the intelligentsia: "He controlled no centers of influence; He commanded neither learning nor wealth."

Searchlight implied that Klan members had undertaken the task of guarding, in the United States, Jesus' accomplishments:

> The Klan is engaged in a holy crusade against that which is corrupting and destroying the best in American life. The Klan is devoted to the holy mission of developing that which is right and clean and beneficent in our country. The Klan is active in its ministry of helpfulness and service. . . . Such enthusiastic devotion to right principles and the holy cause must characterize true Klansmen, if they are to be like Him whom they have accepted as their "Criterion of Character."[6]

The "Kloran" of the "Knights of the Ku Klux Klan," the order's ritual book used to conduct all meetings and initiations, declared on its cover the order's dedication to "Karacter, Honor, Duty."[7]

Every recent study that has examined the characteristics of Klan members—in urban and rural communities of California, Colorado, Georgia, Indiana, Ohio, Oregon, Tennessee, Texas, and Utah—has found that Klansmen constituted a cross section of the local native white Protestant male population, except for the very top and bottom socioeconomic levels of that population. Virtually every Klan candidate for state and local office appealed to this constituency—Klan and non-Klan—with promises to reduce or eliminate those results of character defects which threatened the home and family: violations of Prohibition especially, but also drug abuse, prostitution, gambling, political corruption, traffic violations, and Sunday blue-law offenses.[8]

As local Klan chapters, or Klaverns, prepared to sweep almost every political office in rural Fremont County, Colorado, the county's Klan leaders invited a national Klan lecturer, "Colonel" McKeever, to help bring out the Klan vote. Speaking to an overflow audience in the Canon City armory (1920 population of 4,551), the county's largest community, McKeever proclaimed a typical Klan message:

> The Klan stands for law enforcement; money and politics must cease to play a role [particularly in Prohibition enforcement] in our courts. The Klan stands for the American home; there is no sanctuary like a mother's heart, no altar like a mother's knee. The Klan stands for good men in office.[9]

The Klan attempted to combat all "forces of evil which attack the American home." Threatening the "purity of women," claimed an editorial in the *Fiery Cross*, Indiana's Klan newspaper, were businessmen who employed female secretaries: "Everyone knows of instances where businessmen insist on dating secretaries and imply that should they refuse, their jobs are in danger."[10]

$$\textbf{?|?|?}$$

William Joseph Simmons, founder and first Imperial Wizard of the early twentieth-century Ku Klux Klan, contracted on June 7, 1920, with Edward Young Clarke and Elizabeth Tyler of Atlanta to allow Clarke and Tyler's Southern Publicity Association to direct recruiting for the Klan. Simmons, a Methodist minister and former Methodist circuit rider, a high degree Mason, and a colonel in the Woodsmen of the World, agreed readily on recruiting methods with Clarke and Tyler, former publicity agents for the Salvation Army and the Anti-Saloon League. Organizers, called Kleagles, chosen primarily from the Protestant ministry or from recruiters for fraternal organizations, would work directly under Clarke and Tyler.

Klan membership held a strong attraction for large numbers of men who already belonged to secret white Protestant fraternal organizations, such as those to which Simmons belonged. The Klan offered a more blatant racism, anti-Catholicism, and anti-Semitism, as well as direct participation in politics to members of such societies as the Masons, Odd Fellows, and Knights of Pythias. Moreover, the basic objectives of these other orders resembled those of the Klan in respects more important than ritual and fraternity. The most recent and discerning historian of the Freemasons, Lynn Dumenil, summarized the fundamental Masonic aims: "Not only would America become homogenous again, but the perpetuation of the values of native, Protestant Americans would be assured.[11]

Kleagles received instructions to contact local ministers, fraternal lodge members, and potentially favorable newspaper editors upon entering a community. They were to ascertain the strongest needs of local white Protestants with the aid of these contacts and to begin enrolling members. They then would arrange an announcement of a chapter (Klavern) formation, preferably from a minister's pulpit and, if possible, by the minister himself. By early 1922, Clarke and Tyler had dispatched well over one thousand Kleagles.

Kleagles retained four dollars from each recruit's ten-dollar initiation fee. Clarke and Tyler received two dollars and fifty cents. The local leader (Exalted Cyclops) received a share also. In a good month, Clarke and Tyler made forty thousand dollars from initiation fees alone. Furthermore, members paid monthly dues and purchased for $6.50 white cotton paraphernalia manufactured in a large Klan-owned factory near Atlanta. These payments brought millions of dollars into the Klan's Atlanta headquarters. Too much was at stake to allow disruption of this business by impetuous violent members. The published "Ideals of the Ku Klux Klan," distributed to all members beginning in 1923 proclaimed: "This order does not take the law into its own hands and will not tolerate acts of lawlessness on the part of its members."[12]

The issues that Kleagles, Exalted Cyclopses, and early Klan members used to win additional members in a town or city varied from community to community. However, the basic Klan agenda remained fairly constant throughout the country. In the overwhelming majority of cases, achievement of this program required overcoming opposition from established business and political elites, which generally held stakes in the status quo. Members of these elites frequently owned or, through their banks, loaned money to purchase the land or buildings in which liquor was sold and the stores in which people who came to town to drink did their shopping. They wanted rapid growth of commercial and industrial districts and low taxes. Especially in cities of 50,000 or more, a significant proportion of the top echelons of these elites were employed by national corporations, whose needs often conflicted with the wishes of ordinary local citizens.

Elites were viewed by Klansmen as responsible for the bureaucracies which allegedly interfered with citizens' influence on political decisions. Bureaucracies, a national Klan pamphlet complained, created "government by political appointees rather than a government by elected representatives."[13]

These modernizing elites developed from the Victorian upper- and upper-middle-class urban groups represented by the materialistic Shaw family, whose behavior shocked old-fashioned Polly in Louisa May Alcott's novel, *An Old-Fashioned Girl*. Members of the enlarged elites placed great emphasis on the need for Victorian character traits in business. However, these individuals—large-scale farmers as well as financiers, industrialists, and merchants—gave their highest priority to those character traits which promoted business expansion, especially efficiency, order, and rationality. Robert H. Wiebe has explained how members of these elites operated comfortably despite inner conflicts:

> When that architect of a vast and impersonal business empire, J. P. Morgan, pronounced "character" the basis of all of his transactions, he signified not that he was a liar but that he could live at peace with his inconsistencies.[14]

❣|❣|❣

The most thorough statistical analyses of Klan membership during the 1920s have been written by Christopher Cocoltchos, Leonard Moore, and Robert Goldberg. A clear pattern emerges from Cocoltchos's information about Orange County, California, Moore's study of Indiana, and Goldberg's analysis of the Colorado Klan. Other recent books and articles support their conclusions.[15]

These studies of members' characteristics found that Klansmen represented a near cross section of the white Protestant male population in their communities. Everywhere, the Klan fought to overcome the power of business and professional elites, except in some small towns. Outside those towns, few members of these elites joined the Klan, and those who did tended to be the younger members who evidently believed that their ambitions could be best furthered by the Klan.

In these communities as a whole, Catholics, blacks, Jews, and recent immigrants formed a very small part of the population. The few exceptions were the black population of Indianapolis, which almost equaled the proportion of blacks in the country; the German Catholic population of Anaheim, California, which led the anti-Klan elite there; and the Mexican-American Catholic population of Orange County, which was thoroughly segregated when the Klan was organized and which the Klan consequently ignored altogether. The percentages of those minorities in these communities were insignificant compared with the proportions of these same minorities in major cities like New York, Chicago, Cleveland, and St. Louis, where native white Protestants constituted a minority of the residents (in some cases, less than one-quarter).

Klansmen were concentrated in middle white-collar positions and among small businessmen. Those who were blue-collar workers were overwhelmingly in skilled positions. Members belonged to all major Protestant denominations, but the Klan included very few members of fundamentalist sects. They attended services in Northern Methodist and Disciples of Christ churches especially. Klansmen generally had lived in their communities longer than nonmembers, usually at least ten years before they joined the order, yet they tended to be younger. Well over three-quarters of them were married. They belonged to more civic and fraternal organizations, particularly to the Masons. They possessed greater wealth, more property, and registered to vote in 1924 in much larger proportions than did nonmembers in their communities. Klansmen in the mid-1920s decidedly were not a fringe group of vigilantes; they were solid middle-class citizens and individuals of high Victorian character.

Indiana served as the focal point of Klan power in America. The Indiana Klan enrolled more members and a much larger proportion of the state population than did the Klaverns of any other state. The state capital, Indianapolis, was referred to by a leading historian of the Klan as the "Center of Klandom."[16]

Information about Klan members' characteristics in three Indiana communities, representative of the state's large and small cities and of its rural towns, illustrates the Klan's composition in Indiana. The three communities are Indianapolis, a major industrial and commercial city whose population in 1920 was 314,000; Richmond, an industrial city with a population of 27,000 in 1920; and Crown Point, a commercial township of 4,312, which served the surrounding farming area.[17]

Individuals in high white-collar occupations among Indianapolis's Klan members equalled almost exactly the proportion of men with that status in the city as a whole. However, the Indianapolis Klan contained none of the high executives of the city's largest corporations—such as Van Camp, one of the largest food canning companies in the nation; Eli Lilly, a major pharmaceutical manufacturer; and the Stutz and Dusenburg motor-car companies. Disciples of Christ, Lutheran, and United Brethren ranked highest among the church affiliations of Indianapolis's Klansmen.[18]

About 75 percent of Richmond's Klan members occupied white-collar or skilled-worker positions compared to 64 percent of non-Klansmen in such positions. However, non-Klansmen filled the city's highest white-collar jobs in considerably larger proportions than did Klansmen. The greatest differences between the Protestant church affiliations of Richmond's Klan members and those of Richmond's citizens as a whole lay in the much higher proportion of Klansmen who belonged to Presbyterian, United Brethren, Disciples of Christ, and Episcopal congregations.[19]

The occupational profile of Crown Point's Klan members resembled that of Indianapolis and Richmond Knights. Moore found that "Crown Point's wealthiest citizens did not appear to play any role in the Klan." Sixty-one percent of Crown Point's church-member Knights belonged to Methodist, Lutheran, Presbyterian, or Disciples of Christ congregations.[20]

In each of these three Indiana communities, Kleagles and local Klan organizers used vocal and written criticism of American Catholics, blacks, Jews, and recent immigrants as part of their recruiting rhetoric. However, Moore concluded that the Indiana Klan "did not employ violence as a strategy, and only a tiny fraction of the hooded order's membership ever engaged in violent or threatening acts."[21]

The characteristics of Orange County Klansmen differed little from those of the Indiana members. For fast growing Anaheim, the county seat, Cocoltchos derived statistical information for Klan, non-Klan, and active anti-Klan residents. The latter included those who had joined the club devoted to defeating the Klan politically and also those who had signed both of the petitions opposing the Anaheim Klan.[22]

A much higher proportion of Anaheim Klansmen held professional and administrative jobs than did non-Klansmen, but twice as high a percentage of active anti-Klansmen—who included the city's established business, professional and farming elite—occupied such positions as Klan members. Klansmen worked in trade, service, and skilled positions in greater proportions than did either of the other groups.

Over half the Anaheim Klansmen with a specific church affiliation belonged to Disciples of Christ and Northern Methodist congregations. Catholic was the largest single church affiliation among those actively opposed to the Klan—over 25 percent.[23]

Cocoltchos also collected statistics for Anaheim Klan leaders and the anti-Klan elite, which led activities in the city directed against the Klan. His data proved very informative for an understanding of the Klan's conflicts with the Anaheim business and professional elite.

The anti-Klan elite of three hundred individuals overlapped to a very large extent Anaheim's traditional elite. The median age of the elite in 1924 was fifty-four years compared to forty-two-and-a-half years for Klan leaders. The median years of prior residence in Anaheim was thirty-and-a-half years for the elite and fifteen years for Klan leaders in 1924. Ninety percent of elite members belonged to civic clubs, while 72 percent of Klan leaders did.

Forty-five percent of the elite occupied professional and administrative positions compared to 27 percent of the Klan leaders. Half of the latter worked in the retail and wholesale trades. The median wealth of Klan leaders amounted to $7,460 compared to $36,534 for members of the anti-

Klan elite. Seventy-two percent of Klansmen had already run for or held public office in 1924 compared to 55 percent of the elite. The Klan leaders, despite their role as prosperous community activists, faced a near united front of Anaheim's wealthy, well-entrenched business, professional, and large farmer elite.[24]

In the smaller city of Fullerton, California, Klansmen differed from the non-Klan population largely in their much larger proportion of members working in service and skilled jobs. Klan members owned more property and acknowledged much greater median wealth. A significantly higher proportion of them were married, belonged to civic clubs, and voted in 1924. Klansmen belonged predominantly to Disciples of Christ, Northern Methodist, Episcopalian, and Northern Baptist churches.[25]

Half of the Ku Klux Klan's members in Colorado lived in the capital and largest city, Denver. A much higher percentage of Denver's Klansmen worked in both high and middle white-collar occupations than did members of the male population as a whole. However, Goldberg found that "Denver's elite clubs listed only a handful of Klansmen among their members," and none belonged to the most prestigious social clubs, such as the Denver Club, the Denver Country Club, and the University Club. Only one Klan member was listed in Denver's Social Register. A much lower proportion of Klansmen than male citizens of Denver worked in skilled, semi-skilled, and unskilled labor jobs. Goldberg was unable to collect information about individual church membership, but over 70 percent of Denver's Disciples of Christ churches, 33 percent of its Methodist churches, and 25 percent of its Baptist churches actively supported the Klan.[26]

A Kleagle did not arrive in Canon City, Colorado (with a population of 4,551 in 1920) and surrounding rural Fremont County until 1923. Of the Klan's members between 1924 and 1928, 40 percent occupied high or middle white-collar positions. Only 1.5 percent worked at unskilled jobs. One-quarter of Canon City's Klansmen belonged to the Masons as well. Klan-member ministers guided the town's Methodist and Baptist churches and the fundamentalist Church of Christ congregation.[27]

These statistics bear out Leonard Moore's conclusions about the meaning of the latest books and articles about the Klan:

> Together, these recent works make it nearly impossible to interpret the 1920's Klan as an aberrant fringe group. . . . In-depth analysis of state and community Klans from different regions of the country make it clear . . .

that the Klan was composed primarily of average citizens representing nearly all parts of America's white Protestant society.[28]

❧|❧|❧

The rare seeming exceptions to the general patterns of Klan community organizing, upon close examination, tended to verify the rule. Grand Junction, Colorado—as described by Robert Alan Goldberg—provided an extreme example of these apparent exceptions.

Grand Junction, the largest city (1920 population of 8,865) on the western slope of Colorado's Rocky Mountains, served the retail shopping needs of the population in the vast area between the Rockies and the Wasatch Mountain Range in eastern Utah. That area's economy was based on cattle raising, general farming, and fruit raising. Few blacks or Jews lived in Grand Junction, and although the city's Catholic population increased 80 percent between 1916 and 1926 to 8 percent of the total, half of these Catholics were of Mexican descent, and they took no organized step to change their subservient position.[29]

Grand Junction, and Mesa County of which it was a part, seemed an ideal place for Klan organizing. Grand Junction Methodist minister Paul A. Shields wrote to Colorado governor William Sweet in 1924 that "Men, boys and girls are drinking in semi-public and often public places." Shields pleaded for state aid in enforcing prohibition. Despite assistance from state and federal Prohibition officers, Mesa County remained "soaked in moonshine and bootleg whiskey." The Grand Junction *Daily Sentinel* reported in May 1924: "Bootleggers are plying their trade in this city day in and day out with little attempt at concealing their work. If this city gets a black eye anywhere it gets it from the bootleggers.... Vagrants are picked up by the score—but not the bootleggers."

Grand Junction permitted prostitution in a regulated red-light district, despite efforts by moral reformers to close the district. Two motion-picture theaters remained open on Sunday, although eight local congregations, including the Catholic Church, tried to promote church attendance first by denouncing the theaters and then by litigation. All their efforts failed. Nor could they affect the nature of the films shown on Sunday, or any other day. Citizens watched movies entitled *The Truth about Husbands*, *Sinners in Silk*, *Pleasure Mad*, and *Sporting Youth*. Advertising in 1924 for the latter film promised "Young blood, young love, young ideas—bound recklessly pleasure-ward, jazz-stepping thrill chasing its way toward ever more vital sensations." A municipal dance hall opened in May 1924, raising further complaints from moral reformers.

In communities throughout the nation, the Klan at that point in time took a leading role in reducing or eliminating such sinful pleasures. In Grand Junction, however, the Klan protected sin. The city's leading citizens obtained the Klan franchise for Grand Junction, perhaps because they had read about the Klan's fight against moral offenses elsewhere. Walter Walker, editor and publisher of the *Daily Sentinel*, served as the Klavern's leader. Walker also owned the Avalon Theater, one of the city's two motion picture palaces. Mesa County's sheriff joined the Klan. Beer was served at Klavern meetings. The Klan disturbed nothing and nobody in the city, and pleasure seekers continued to flock to Grand Junction.

While the Klan deflected efforts to change the status quo, as part of its sound business practices, it attempted to enroll as many members as possible. Klan leaders followed the proven method of recruiting Protestant ministers and lodge members first. Klan membership grew rapidly, but the new members included many citizens attracted by the Klan's national agenda of overcoming elite resistance to punishing those who broke moral laws.

Late in October 1924, reformers led by Methodist minister W. C. Wasser took control of the Klan and retired Walter Walker. Walker's first anti-Klan editorial in the *Daily Sentinel* appeared on November 2, 1924. During a municipal election for members of the seven-man city council, Wasser urged all Christians in Grand Junction to join a crusade dedicated to eliminating bootlegging, prostitution, and gambling in the city and to changing the policies of the dance hall and movie theaters. With aid from the Woman's Christian Temperance Union, three candidates endorsed by Wasser won election to the city council. The county sheriff began enforcing Prohibition laws, averaging one raid on bootleggers every five days. These raids finally reduced the town's liquor traffic. The next Klavern election for Exalted Cyclops placed the Reverend George Rossman of Grand Junction's First Christian Church, an advocate of stern Prohibition enforcement, in that office. Thus, even Grand Junction's Klan evidently proved to be an aberration from the general Klan pattern for only a brief period of time.

❧❧❧

An editorial in the Indiana Disciples of Christ journal *Christian Evangelist*, published almost a year before the Klan took political control of the state of Indiana in 1924, captured the essence of the Klan's political message. The editor protested that Protestant churches alone could accomplish the Klan's mission but also acknowledged the Klan's national appeal: "Does the Klan stand for one hundred percent Americanism? So do I, not a Klansman," the editor declared. "Is it against the encroachment of the Roman hierarchy? So am I. . . . There is nothing it champions that I do not champion, though I wear no mask." The editorial continued:

> There are those who affirm that in its protests against lawlessness, against Roman Catholic domination, against Jewish monopolies here and there, against a divided allegiance to our country, it is doing a great and needed work; that it is the savior of Protestantism; that it is the defender of the Constitution; that it is a help to morals and religion; that its masks are but legitimate appeals to the dramatic within all of us . . . that it has "cleaned up" villages, towns and cities. . . . There can be no doubt that . . . tens of thousands of good people feel just this way about it and are fervent in its advocacy.[30]

Leonard Moore summarized what he called the Klan's "basic message":

> The average white Protestant was under attack: his values and traditions were being undermined; his vision of America's national purpose and social order appeared threatened; and his ability to shape the course of public affairs seemed to have been diminished.[31]

Basing its political activity upon this message and the failure of state and local elites to address it satisfactorily, the Klan won a high degree of political power and influence in the states of Alabama, California, Colorado, Georgia, Indiana, Kansas, Louisiana, Oklahoma, Oregon, and Texas. It took political control of hundreds of American cities and towns, including Akron, Atlanta, Birmingham, Dallas, Denver, El Paso, Evansville, Gary, Indianapolis, Little Rock, Oklahoma City, Portland, Oregon, Terre Haute, and Youngstown.

However, the powerful business elite of Richmond, Indiana, thwarted the Klan's political efforts. Richmond's major employers were International Harvester and the Pennsylvania Railroad. The successful anti-Klan forces were led by members of the Rotary Club, limited to representatives of the city's industrial corporations, top executives of its other businesses, and its most successful retail merchants. The Rotary received aid from the Kiwanis Club, dominated by small businessmen and city officials.[32]

Explaining the Klan's near-total triumph in Indiana, Moore concluded that the state and local elites "stood nearly alone as a white Protestant social group unwilling to support the Klan." That group, he declared, surpassed Indiana's Catholics, blacks, and Jews as the order's chief opponents. When Indiana's Klan chapters sought political power, Moore found "their most powerful rivals were . . . the Rotary Club and the Chamber of Commerce, not the powerless or nonexistent ethnic minorities." When the Klan swept the state election of 1924, "the real victims were not the state's Catholics but the Republican . . . political establishment, which, almost overnight, found itself removed from power."[33]

In Indianapolis, businessmen organized in the Chamber of Commerce and the Indiana Taxpayers' Association formed an important component of the Old Guard Republican establishment. School issues symbolized the conflict between the Old Guard and the Klan. Voters, led by the Klan, approved a series of school bond issues, meant to renovate dilapidated schools and to alleviate overcrowding in the city's elementary and high schools. The Chamber of Commerce and the Taxpayers' Association organized a Citizens' League to hide their own opposition to all spending for schools, except for a segregated high school to educate the city's black children. The school board refused to appropriate funds for any other construction. In the school-board election of 1925, the Klan elected all five of its candidates to replace the five Citizens' League incumbents. A school construction program started soon afterward. Aided by voter mobilization for the school-board election, the Klan won virtually every city political office in 1925.[34]

In Lake County, where Crown Point served as county seat, Moore concluded: "Prohibition enforcement and public corruption had a . . . preponderant influence on Klan political victories." Exports of liquor by Chicago criminal organizations had left Lake County soaked in alcohol and full of corruption. In the November 1924 elections, every Lake County candidate endorsed by the Klan—including those in Crown Point—won election.[35]

When the Klan in Orange County, California, turned to politics, its main task was overturning the power of local elites. Cocoltchos described the Klan as "totally unconcerned with the area's largest minority group, Mexican Catholics."[36] In Anaheim, the wealthiest businessmen had selected the city councilmen, the school-board members, and judges. Those officials chose the city manager, policemen, teachers, and court officials. Klansmen blamed these prominent businessmen for the city's flagrant Prohibition violations, poor enforcement of other laws, mediocre public-school education, poorly constructed school buildings, and business-oriented zoning regulations.

One of the Anaheim City Council's most egregious errors occurred when it voted in April 1923 to extend commercial North Zeyn Street through a residential area to the northern city limits. The residential population protested against the proposed intrusion that would endanger their quiet peaceful family lives and social relations. Anaheim's elite responded by declaring that "The march of progress has come upon them. . . . They must submit to the more modern idea of being put upon a highway. . . . " The residents would not submit. Rather, the voting precinct in which North Zeyn Street was located became a Klan stronghold.[37]

In 1924, the Klan led a city-wide political rebellion against Anaheim's business establishment. Directed largely by the Reverend Leon Meyers, a charismatic Disciples of Christ minister, assisted by Elmer Metcalf, a rancher and a trustee of Anaheim's grammar schools who had uncovered shoddy grammar-school construction, the Klan won control of Anaheim. On April 14, 1924, almost 75 percent of the city's registered voters went to the polls, the largest turnout in Anaheim's history. The five Klan-endorsed city-council candidates each obtained more votes in every election district than did any of their opponents. The new council quickly selected Metcalf as Anaheim's new mayor and replaced the city's chief of police, building inspector, and health inspector with Klansmen. It also added eleven Klansmen to the four-member police force.[38]

Fullerton's Klan based its political appeal on promises to stop the export of rum, Romanism, crime, and corruption both from Mexico and from the larger Orange County city of Anaheim. The Klan pledged itself especially to drive liquor out of the city's public schools. Fullerton's citizens, including many of its leading businessmen, supported the Klan in the hope that it could succeed where the police had failed. The Klan took control of the Fullerton City Council in 1924 and began enforcing Prohibition laws.[39]

The Denver city officials chosen by business groups also failed to reduce Prohibition violations. Evidence linked Republican Mayor Dewey Bailey to organized crime. Denver's Klan endorsed Democrat Benjamin F. Stapleton, Denver Klan member No. 1,128, to succeed Bailey. Stapleton, a political unknown, received support not only from the Klan but also from other groups opposed to the Denver business elite. The coalition included the Denver Labor County Central Committee, the Italian-American Social Club, the nonpartisan Denver *Post*, and liberal Democrats (including Governor William Sweet).

Stapleton easily defeated Bailey in an election held in May 1923. He soon appointed fellow Klansmen to every important city office. In addition, seven Klan members received appointments as police sergeants, and dozens more were selected as patrolmen. Less than a month after the election, the city's district attorney reported a dramatic drop in bootlegging, prostitution, and gambling.[40]

A former Klansmen in Canon City, Colorado, recalled:

The Klan came here for a definite positive purpose. There was an old
political group that had been here for years and years. . . . They had a . . .
death grip on politics. They owned all the real estate and the business houses
and controlled the two banks.

Well, our schools were no good, they didn't amount to anything. Our
streets were dirt, our sidewalks wooden. When I went to school . . . they
didn't even have electric lights. There were no lights in any of the public
schools.

We members of the Klan decided that we wanted to make a change in
that, which we did. We definitely did.[41]

The Klan announced its political objectives to the citizens of Canon City
and of rural Fremont County through an advertisement placed in the Canon
City *Daily Record* in October 1924. This declared that Klansmen "are on a
crusade for better government, one in which the old political ring shall be
done away with and the people shall rule as a real democracy."[42]

Before the Fremont County elections in November 1924, the established
business and political leaders formed the Independent Party to differen-
tiate its candidates from those endorsed by the Klan, who had captured
the Republican nominations. Independents described the Klan as aliens
and proclaimed in advertisements that a Klan victory would lead to "des-
potism equal to the darkest days of Soviet Russia." Klan ads responded:
"Do you know that you have been at the mercy of a political ring for
nearly a quarter of a century? Do you know that the leaders of the Independent Party and the candidates of that party have been that ring?"[43]

In the November elections, the Klan captured every contested office
but two. The Independent candidate for county treasurer won by four
votes, and its candidate for county judge won by twenty-one votes. On
April 7, 1925, the Klan captured every municipal office in Canon City.
The new Klan government built a new high school, a new sewer system,
paved streets and sidewalks, expanded the park system, and reorganized
the fire department.[44]

Although Klan speakers during the campaign had attacked the Pope
and the county's Catholic hierarchy, Klan public officials took no action
against Catholics, blacks, Jews, or immigrants. When the single Jewish
family in Canon City contributed one hundred dollars to the Klan to
insure its protection, the Klavern returned the money.[45]

❢|❢|❢

Starting in the mid-1920s, the Ku Klux Klan ebbed in numbers and in
influence. The three chief reasons for this decline were the inability of

the order to achieve its promises, the demoralization of members because of scandals involving Klan leaders and spokesmen (whom members expected to appear and act more honestly than their opponents), and counterattacks by the ethnic and religious groups and business elites which held political control of the nation's major cities.

After an initial burst of enthusiasm for the Klan, when it gained control of city, county, and state governments, inexperienced Klan elected officials found their programs rendered ineffective by professional politicians. Therefore voters—including Klan members—who had supported the Klan were disappointed by the order's accomplishments.

For example, in Indiana, where the Klan elected its candidate for governor and won large majorities in both houses of the legislature in 1925, Klansmen enacted only one of their proposals into law. That measure, obliging all public schools to teach their students about the United States Constitution, obtained bipartisan support.

Other bills introduced by Klan legislators—such as legislation mandating daily Bible reading in Indiana's schools, forcing parochial schools to use the same textbooks as public schools, and compelling public schools to hire only public-school graduates as teachers—failed to pass. Legislators, especially in the state senate, and the Klan governor killed such measures rather than face the controversy that such blatant attacks on religious liberty would cause. The near certainty of adverse judicial decisions increased the reluctance of these politicians (particularly those who hoped to seek national office) to risk their careers.[46]

Indiana Grand Dragon David C. Stephenson's crimes damaged the Klan most. Stephenson collected over a million dollars from Klansmen between 1922 and 1924. Most of this was used to support a most un-Klansmanlike life-style. He bought luxurious automobiles, an imposing suburban home, and a yacht on which he entertained numerous women. He also purchased a large liquor supply. Several times, his drinking binges brought him close to arrest by police.

In April 1925, Stephenson took one of his female companions, twenty-eight-year-old Madge Oberholtzer of Indianapolis, on an overnight train ride to Hammond, Indiana. During this trip, Stephenson repeatedly raped Oberholtzer. When they arrived in Hammond, she bought and swallowed a deadly poison. It took effect during the return trip to Indianapolis, but Stephenson refused to let the suffering woman see a physician until they reached Indianapolis. By then it was too late.

Before Oberholtzer died, she gave police a full statement. The State of Indiana charged Stephenson with causing her suicide because he had forced her to lose "that which she held dearer than life—her chastity."

Stephenson was indicted and convicted of kidnapping, rape, and second-degree murder. He received a sentence of life imprisonment.

Stephenson confidently expected a pardon from Indiana's Governor Ed Jackson, a Klansman. When Jackson refused his request, Stephenson offered to testify about the corruption of Jackson and other state and local Klan officials. As a result, Mayor John Duvall of Indianapolis went to prison for violating the Corrupt Practices Act—so did the county sheriff, its congressman, the city purchasing agent, and a large number of less important Klan officeholders. Based on Stephenson's testimony, a grand jury indicted Governor Jackson for bribery, but he escaped prison because the statute of limitations on his offenses had expired. Soon after these revelations Klan membership in Indiana began shrinking. Fewer than seven thousand members remained by 1928.[47]

Stephenson's trial, well publicized by newspapers and magazines, distressed Klansmen throughout America. Their outrage increased when they learned about the crimes of Dr. John Galen Locke, Colorado's Grand Dragon and Denver's Exalted Cyclops. In January 1925, Locke arranged the kidnapping of Klan member Keith Boehm, a high-school student. Taken to Locke's office and threatened with castration unless he married his pregnant girlfriend, Boehm agreed to the marriage. Locke explained to the Denver *Post* that "When I learned of what happened . . . I meant to see to it that young Boehm, as a Klansman, should do the manly thing." The district attorney brought kidnapping and conspiracy charges against Locke. Luckily for Locke, Klan opponent Judge Ben B. Lindsay of the juvenile court disqualified himself from the case. Locke's attorney engineered changes of venue until the case landed before a Klansman judge who found technical reasons to dismiss it.[48]

Then federal Treasury officials charged Locke with failing to report any income or to pay income taxes despite the fees he earned as a physician and from Klan initiation fees and commissions on the sale of Klan robes. Locke went to prison until Colorado's governor, who had been chosen by the Grand Dragon, established a fund to pay Locke's back taxes. Other Klansmen paid Locke's fine. Mass defections from Colorado's Klan began. Imperial Wizard Hiram Evans requested Locke's resignation, and Locke immediately complied.[49]

In Anaheim, the politically defeated Chamber of Commerce and Rotary Club collected sufficient signatures on petitions late in 1924 to force recently elected Klan city-council members into a recall election. Minor scandals and a failure to appreciably diminish Prohibition violations already had cost the Klan some support. Anaheim's Klan leader, Reverend

Mr. Meyers, sought to renew Klan members' enthusiasm by bringing Protestant evangelist E. E. Bulgin to the city in January 1925 to conduct revival meetings. Bulgin arrived on January 11, set up his tent, and began the services.

A group of Anaheim's ministers sent Bulgin and local newspapers a letter inquiring whether he had been brought to Anaheim "for the express purpose of assisting in the re-election of the members of the city council whose removal is being sought because of their Klan affiliations." Bulgin proclaimed his neutrality concerning the election. At the following evening's revival meeting, however, Bulgin told his assembled flock that "the way to vote right and never make a mistake is to find out what side the ex-saloonkeepers, the bootleggers and the harlots are on and get on the other side." Bulgin's nightly meetings attracted large and enthusiastic audiences.

Representatives of the Chamber of Commerce and of the Rotary and the Lion's clubs of Anaheim contacted the Knights of Columbus and the Catholic Truth Society in many parts of the West, asking for information about Bulgin. An Okmulgee, Oklahoma, attorney replied that Bulgin's real specialty was selling stock in fictitious or worthless mining companies. In return, he had taken deeds to some citizens' homes. Telegrams from Eastland, Texas, and Lewiston, Idaho, stated that Bulgin had been chased out of those cities after being charged with fraud in numerous lawsuits. Two of Anaheim's newspapers printed these replies.[50]

On February 3, 1925, almost 77 percent of Anaheim's voters—a larger proportion than the record turnout less than six months before that had elected the Klan councilmen—went to the polls. Every Klan-endorsed council member was recalled by a substantial margin.[51]

The Ku Klux Klan paid dearly for its obvious role in reinvigorating Victorian racism and religious bigotry. Kenneth Jackson pointed out that "Relatively few reports of Klan-related violence between 1915 and 1924 are contained in the files of United States Department of Justice." However, in September 1923, the *Literary Digest*, a Klan opponent, published an article entitled "The Klan as a Victim of Mob Violence." The Indiana state *Fiery Cross* complained in 1924 that "The list of the outrages against Klansmen is so long that it would take weeks to compile even an incomplete list."[52]

In dozens of cities—such as Fort Worth; San Antonio; Terre Haute; and Portland, Maine—Klan headquarters and meeting places were bombed and burned. After numerous warnings, the shop believed to be the publication headquarters of the Chicago Klan's journal, *Dawn*, was gutted by a bomb. An editorial in the *Fiery Cross* asked plaintively: Why does not anyone "ever read about halls of the Knights of Columbus being destroyed mysteriously?"[53]

Catholics and blacks had threatened the Klan with violence. The editor of the *Catholic World*, published by the Paulist Fathers, warned early in 1923 that because of the Klan, Catholics "may be driven to self-defense, even to the extent of bloodshed." The equally staid *Bulletin* of the National Catholic Welfare Council declared:

> In this struggle for the supremacy of law and order over lawlessness and despotism, no quarter should be given those self-appointed patriots who distort and disgrace our Americanism and whose weapons are darkness, the mask, violence, intimidation and mob rule.[54]

The Harlem-based radical black nationalist African Black Brotherhood proclaimed in its journal that "The nation-wide mobilization under the Christian cross and the Stars and Stripes of cracker America is plainly an act of war . . . , war of the cracker element of the white race against the whole Negro race." The Chicago *Defender*, the most widely read black newspaper in the United States, urged its readers in a front-page editorial to prepare to fight "against sons who now try to win by signs and robes what their fathers lost by fire and sword."[55]

When the Klan began organizing in and around the nation's largest cities, members of the order soon discovered that white Protestant authority no longer prevailed throughout the land. In these cities Catholics, blacks, Jews, and recent immigrants formed a majority of the population—sometimes a very large majority.

Soon after Kleagles ventured into New York City, Irish Catholic Mayor John F. Hylan told his police commissioner in 1922: "I desire you to treat this group of racial and religious haters as you would the Reds and bomb throwers. Drive them out of our city." Two New York City grand juries commenced investigations of the Klan, and the New York City Council quickly passed legislation forcing associations not incorporated in New York to file membership lists. Klan members in New York and suburban Westchester County during the 1920s totalled about 16,000, less than Klan membership in Akron or Youngstown, Ohio.[56]

Chicago's large Klan chapter did nothing to help enforce Prohibition laws. However, the West Suburban Ministers and Citizens Association organized to help enforce those laws in and around Chicago. Soon afterward, the association's leader, a minister, was found shot to death a block from Al Capone's headquarters in suburban Cicero. This warning ended private attempts to fight Prohibition offenses in Chicago.[57]

The Chicago City Council appointed a five-man committee in December 1922 to investigate the Klan and then report back to the council. The five members were identified as Ald. Robert J. Mulcahy, Irish; Ald. Louis B. Henderson, black; Ald. U. S. Schwartz, Jewish; Ald. S. S. Walkowiak, Polish; and Ald. Oscar H. Olsen, Norwegian. Largely as a result of the committee's unanimous report, the city council resolved by a vote of fifty-six to two to rid Chicago's municipal payroll of Klansmen. The Illinois legislature also received the report and consequently passed a bill prohibiting the wearing of masks in public. The measure cleared the Illinois House of Representatives by a vote of 100 to 2, and the Illinois State Senate by 26 to 1. Illinois's Klansmen were thus forced to hold most of their parades, picnics, and other gatherings in Indiana and Ohio.[58]

Boston's Mayor James Michael Curley barred Klan meetings in Boston, and the city council approved his order. He gave speeches before burning crosses and in an emotion-choked voice always proclaimed: "There it burns, the cross of hatred upon which Our Lord, Jesus Christ, was crucified—the cross of human avarice, and not the cross of love and charity...." Homes and stores of suspected Klansmen in Boston were bombarded with bricks and stones.[59]

On the outskirts of major cities, where the Klan sometimes dared to march or meet, the Knights received even worse treatment. Ten thousand Klansmen gathered near Carnegie, just outside Pittsburgh, on August 25, 1923, to witness an initiation featuring an address by Imperial Wizard Hiram Evans. When they tried to march back to the heavily Catholic, immigrant, and black town, however, a mob stood in their path. The Klansmen continued marching through a hail of rocks and bottles. Then a volley of shots rang out. One Klansman lay dead, a dozen others fell seriously wounded, and about a hundred more suffered minor injuries. The other Klan members turned and ran.[60]

Commenting on the Carnegie massacre, the Washington *Star* declared that "Parades of the Klan, with its masked and hooded members, tend to create disorder and rioting." An editorial in the Washington *Post* stated that the paper agreed with the *New York Times* that "The Klan is merely reaping as it has sown."[61]

Other Klan meetings were broken up by lethal shotgun blasts. In New York's suburban county of Queens, police ended a Memorial Day parade of 4,000 Klansmen by waving waiting cars through the whole parade line.[62]

Hiram Evans summarized the Klan's plight when he stated in March

1926 that "The Nordic American today is a stranger in large parts of the land his fathers gave him. Moreover, he is a most unwelcome stranger, and one most spat upon."[63]

Evans described accurately the result of the Klan's defense of Victorianism's essence. The most important social trends and the great social reform movements of the nineteenth and twentieth centuries had indeed left Klansmen strangers in most of the land their ancestors had settled.

CONCLUSION

Imperial Wizard Hiram Wesley Evans charged that "de-Americanized" intellectuals were undermining what the Klan sought to defend. Intellectuals, he declared, were sowing "confusion in thought and opinion" even among native white Protestants, whom he referred to as the "plain people." "The great mass of Americans of old pioneer stock," Evans acknowledged, was "very weak in the matter of culture, intellectual support and trained leadership. . . . It makes it very hard for us to state our case and advocate our crusade. If the Klan should ever fail, it would be from this cause."[1]

Other Klansmen traced the order's difficulties to women's increasing activities outside the home and to a general unwillingness by Americans to obey laws that sought to enforce a Victorian moral order, especially Prohibition legislation. Many Klan leaders charged that their most damaging opposition, especially in larger communities, came from corporate and professional elites and from business and government bureaucracies.

By the late twentieth century, those who supported the ascendancy of Victorian character faced additional conditions which undermined that concept. For example, civil-rights legislation and judicial decisions have changed the positions of females, African-Americans, Latinos, Asians, and other disadvantaged groups. Drastic shifts in life-styles since the early twentieth century have encouraged social lives vastly different from Victorian ideals and a highly un-Victorian hedonism.

Nevertheless, most Americans show a reluctance to surrender vital components of Victorian character as an ideal. They refuse also to give up many aspects of the Victorian conceptions of home and family. This reluctance seems due less to nostalgia than to the satisfactions still provided by these cornerstones of Victorianism. The assaults on Victorianism have eroded its conceptual foundations, but have left much of its structure largely intact. However, within this structure, the contradictions which led Elizabeth Cady Stanton to rebellion persist.

NOTES

‖‖‖

Introduction

1. Elizabeth Cady Stanton, *Eighty Years and More: Reminiscences 1815–1897* (New York: T. Fisher Unwin, 1898; reprint, New York: Schocken Books, 1971), 20–23; Alma Lutz, *Created Equal: A Biography of Elizabeth Cady Stanton, 1815–1902* (New York: John Day, 1940), 6–9. Stanton was the only female in the Greek, Latin, and advanced mathematics classes.

2. Theodore Stanton and Harriet Stanton Blatch, eds., *Elizabeth Cady Stanton As Revealed in Her Letters, Diary and Reminiscences* (New York: Harper, 1922), I: xiii; Lutz, *Created Equal*, 40, 45–50.

3. Stanton, *Eighty Years and More*, 54–55, 78–85; Lucretia Mott to Stanton, Mar. 16, 1855, Stanton and Blatch, eds., *Stanton, Letters, Diary and Reminiscences*, II: 18. In this letter, Mott, Stanton's collaborator in arranging the Seneca Falls meeting, wrote: "Remember the first convention originated with thee."

4. Ellen Carol Du Bois, *Feminism and Suffrage: The Emergence of an Independent Women's Movement in America, 1848–1869* (Ithaca: Cornell Univ. Press, 1978), 25–27, 31–34, 53, 110–25; Elizabeth Cady Stanton, "National Labor Congress," *Revolution*, I (Oct. 1868): 200.

5. Stanton and Blatch, eds., *Stanton, Letters, Diary and Reminiscences*, II: 232, 235, 333, 368–69; Lutz, *Created Equal*, 39, 47–49, 318.

1. Victorian Character

1. David P. Handlin presents a large volume of evidence about the relation between American Victorian culture and Victorian domestic architecture in *The American Home: Architecture and Society 1815–1915* (Boston: Little, Brown, 1979). An intelligent analysis of the typical Victorian home design, demonstrating its relationships to other aspects of Victorian culture can be found in Kathryn Kish Sklar, *Catharine Beecher: A Study in American Domesticity* (New Haven: Yale Univ., 1973), XI–XII, 277. Also, see Norma Prendergest, "The Sense of Home: Nineteenth-Century Domestic Architectural Reform," unpublished Ph.D. dissertation, Cornell Univ., 1981; Jan Cohn, *The Palace or the Poorhouse: The American House as a Cultural Symbol* (East Lansing: Michigan State Univ. Press, 1979); Chapter 5, "The Home," in Henry Seidel Canby, *The Age of Confidence* (New York: Farrar and Rinehart, 1934). William Dean Howells noted the relationship between the Victorian home and the value system of its occupants. See, for example, his discussion of the Hallecks' home in *A Modern Instance*, H. S. Commager, ed., *Selected Writings of William Dean Howells* (New York: Random House, 1950), 496–500. This topic is discussed also in Clifford E. Clark, "Domestic Architecture as an Index to Social History: The Romantic Revival and the Cult of Domesticity in America, 1840–1870," *Journal of Interdisciplinary History*, VII (Summer 1976): 33–56; and Jenni Calder, *The Victorian Home* (London: B. T. Batsford, 1977), which summarizes in popular fashion the place of the English home. In general, Calder finds that the English Victorian home filled most of the functions ascribed in this chapter to the American home.

2. My discussion of the Victorian family is indebted especially to Sklar, *Beecher*; Nancy F. Cott, *The Bonds of Womanhood, "Women's Sphere" in New England, 1780–1835* (New Haven: Yale Univ. Press, 1977); Carl N. Degler, *At Odds: Women and the Family in America from the Revolution to the Present* (New York: Oxford Univ. Press, 1980); Tamara K. Hareven, *Family Time and Industrial Time* (Cambridge: Cambridge Univ. Press, 1982); Daniel Walker Howe, "Victorian Culture in America," in Howe, ed., *Victorian America* (Philadelphia: Univ. of Pennsylvania Press, 1976), 3–28; Viola Klein, *The Feminine Character: History of an Ideology*, 2d edition (London: Routledge and Kegan Paul, 1971); Barbara A. Welter, *Dimity Convictions, The American Woman in the Nineteenth Century* (Athens, Ohio: Ohio Univ. Press, 1976); Joseph F. Kett, "Adolescence and Youth in Nineteenth-Century America," *Journal of Interdisciplinary History*, II (Summer 1971); Rosalind Rosenberg, *Beyond Separate Spheres, Intellectual Roots of Modern Feminism* (New Haven: Yale Univ. Press, 1982); Mary Patricia Ryan, "American Society and the Cult of Domesticity, 1830–1860," unpublished Ph.D. dissertation, Univ. of California, Santa Barbara, 1971; Ryan, *Cradle of the Middle Class: The Family in Oneida County, New York, 1790–1865* (New York: Cambridge Univ. Press, 1981); David E. Stannard, *The Puritan Way of Death: A Study in Religion, Culture, and Social Change* (New York: Oxford Univ. Press, 1977); Stannard, "Death and Dying in Puritan New England," *American Historical Review*, LXXVIII (Dec. 1973); Stephen Mintz, *A Prison of Expectations: The Family in Victorian Culture* (New York: New York Univ. Press, 1985), especially Chapter 3, "Literary Culture and the Need to Shape Character," 21–39; Bernard

Wishy, *The Child and the Republic* (Philadelphia: Univ. of Pennsylvania Press, 1968); and Michael Zuckerman, *Peaceable Kingdoms: New England Towns in the Eighteenth Century* (New York: Random House, 1970).

3. Howells, *Modern Instance*, 629.

4. An especially cogent discussion of this point can be found in Cott, *Bonds of Womanhood*, 2. For an early twentieth-century version of this literature, see E. E. Kellogg, *Studies in Character Building, A Book for Parents* (Battle Creek, Mich.: Good Health Publishing, 1905).

5. The term "romantic," which refers here to the dominant Western artistic style of the nineteenth century, served also as a general cultural style among the Victorian middle class. Use of the term "romanticized," therefore, for this period does not imply inaccuracy.

6. Whenever possible I have referred to published documents rather than to Louisa May Alcott's diary and letters in the Alcott Family Archive, Houghton Library, Harvard Univ.; her diary in the Fruitlands Museum, Harvard Univ.; and to letters, diaries, and journals written by members of Louisa May Alcott's immediate family, also housed mainly in the Alcott Family Archive. Ednah D. Cheney, ed., *Louisa May Alcott: Her Life, Letters and Journals* (Boston: Little, Brown, 1928), 132–36; Katherine Anthony, *Louisa May Alcott* (New York: Alfred A. Knopf, 1938), 158. One of the more perceptive reviews, written by Henry James, Jr., appeared in the *North American Review* and is reprinted in Henry James, *Notes and Reviews* (Cambridge, Mass.: Dunster House, 1921). Alcott's diary comments about James's criticism are printed in Cheney, *Alcott: Letters and Journals*, 135. James's critique was softened by his statement that with the possible exception of a few illustrious authors, he doubted that any American could write a better novel than Alcott's first effort. Alcott's extreme difficulties in writing *Moods* can be followed in her journal entries throughout Aug. 1860 and in January and Feb. 1861, Louisa May Alcott Journal, Alcott Family Archive, (hereafter referred to as LMA Journal). Also, see the scattered references in Martha Saxon, *Louisa May: A Modern Biography of Louisa May Alcott* (Boston: Houghton Mifflin, 1977).

7. Cheney, ed., *Alcott: Letters and Journals*, 36–38; Anthony, *Alcott*, 136–46.

8. Saxon points out that although nineteenth-century sales records for *Little Women* have been lost by the publisher, that publisher sold three million copies in 1929 alone. Saxon, *Louisa May*, 5. British author G. K. Chesterton wrote in 1922: "I know few women in England, from the most revolutionary Suffragette to the most carefully preserved Early Victorian, who will not confess to having passed a happy childhood with the Little Women of Miss Alcott." Gilbert Keith Chesterton, *What I Saw in America* (London: Dodd Mead, 1922), 84.

9. Cheney, ed., *Alcott: Letters and Journals*, 36–39, 54, 334; Anthony, *Alcott*, 136–46, 160–73. At Emerson's suggestion, Louisa May Alcott, while a young girl, made frequent use of his library. She became so friendly with Thoreau, beginning at age 12 when he served as her teacher, that Saxon identifies Alcott's *Moods* as "based on her long-term secret infatuation with Henry Thoreau." Saxon, *Louisa May*, 8; also, see Saxon, *Louisa May*, 278, and Saxon's footnotes and bibliography concerning *Moods*.

10. Cheney, ed., *Alcott: Letters and Journals*, 76, 115–21, 141–49, 158–59, 162,

165; Anthony, *Alcott*, 136. Louisa May Alcott, *Hospital Sketches* (New York: Sagamore Press, 1957). *Hospital Sketches* was published in book form in 1863. Alcott's ambiguous relationship to Ladislas Wisniewski can be followed most satisfactorily in Saxon, *Louisa May*, 286–89.

11. Cheney, ed., *Alcott: Letters and Journals*, 175, 228; Anthony, *Alcott*, 205–6. Madeline B. Stern, *Louisa May Alcott* (Norman: Univ. of Oklahoma Press, 1950) contains an excellent bibliography of contemporary accounts of these receptions given Alcott, especially see pp. 393–94. Newspaper clippings dealing with these events are deposited in the Alcott Family Archive. For Saxon's views of Alcott's reactions to her admirers, see Saxon, *Louisa May*, especially 16–17, 220, 306.

12. Anthony, *Alcott*, 205–6; Cheney, ed., *Alcott: Letters and Journals*, 252. Alcott slipped her defense of adolescent slang in her books into her novel *An Old-Fashioned Girl* (New York: Grosset and Dunlap, 1971), 203. Faced with multiple editions of almost all Alcott's books, I have referred to the most recent and most easily accessible editions, when those were available to me. These novels and collections of stories were published originally between 1865 and 1886.

13. Anthony, *Alcott*, 205–6.

14. Alcott, *Old-Fashioned Girl*, Preface. The idea that Victorian virtues remained dominant in small towns and villages, in contrast to wealthy areas of cities, is a theme developed convincingly in semi-autobiographical novels by Harriet Beecher Stowe, *Oldtown Folks* (Boston: Fields, Osgood & Co., 1869); and Lucy Larcum, *A New England Childhood* (Boston Houghton Mifflin, 1889).

15. Three years after publication of *An Old-Fashioned Girl*, Alcott wrote in her journal: "Work is and always has been my salvation," LMA Journal, July 1873. Also, see Alcott's novel *Work* (New York: Schocken Books, 1977). The quotation in the text is from Alcott, *Old-Fashioned Girl*, 142.

16. Alcott, *Old-Fashioned Girl*, 31, 34, 106.

17. *Ibid.*, 17–21, 32–33, 40–45, 119. The new urban middle class in this period is described in Sam Bass Warner, *The Private City: Philadelphia in Three Periods of its Growth* (Philadelphia: Univ. of Pennsylvania Press, 1968), 64–65. Alcott's version of the upper-middle-class urban girl's overconcern with clothes, parties, the theater, and romantic attachments is supported by Dio Lewis, *Our Girls* (New York: Harper and Bros., 1871).

18. Alcott, *Old-Fashioned Girl*, 13, 14, 40, 63–65.

19. *Ibid.*, 236–37, 244; Alcott, *Little Men* (Boston: Little, Brown, 1946), 236, 239–40. John Pratt, who married Louisa's older sister Anna in 1858 and died ten years later, served as a prototype for Brooke. Louisa May Alcott's feelings about Pratt, who, she claimed, "did more to make me trust and respect men than anyone I know," can be derived from the LMA Journal, Jan. and Feb. 1871, and L. M. Alcott to Anna Alcott Pratt, Dec. 1870, Henry W. Berg and Albert A. Berg Collection, New York Public Library. This collection contains many Alcott family papers not duplicated in the Alcott Archive, Harvard.

20. Alcott, *Little Women* (Boston: Little, Brown, 1946), 82.

21. Cheney, ed., *Alcott: Letters and Journals*, 26.

22. Alcott, *Little Women*, 260; Alcott, *Jo's Boys* (Boston: Little, Brown, 1946),

412; Clyde C. Griffen, "The Progressive Ethos," in Stanley Coben and Lorman Ratner, eds., *The Development of an American Culture*, 2d edition (New York: St. Martin's, 1983), 144–80. In evaluating the meaning of Jo's sermon, the high incidence of and slight protection against venereal disease and the absence of modern birth-control methods should be kept in mind. For an informative discussion of the alleged combined negative moral and economic effects of such vices as drinking and theater-going in Victorian America, see Irvin G. Wyllie, *The Self-Made Man in America: The Myth of Rags to Riches* (New York: Free Press 1954); and Richard Weiss, *The American Myth of Success: From Horatio Alger to Norman Vincent Peale* (New York: Basic Books, 1969; Champaign: Univ. of Illinois Press, 1990).

23. Bronson Alcott, "Researches on Childhood," 156–64, Bronson Alcott Journals, Alcott Family Archive. Part of this tale, plus sequels, can be found in Saxon, *Louisa May*, 90–93. Despite his qualms about the effectiveness of training through corporal punishment, Bronson Alcott sometimes found it necessary to spank Louisa when she refused to cease aggressive behavior. He succumbed also to the temptation of obtaining obedience through bribery, especially by offering apples. His more emotional wife resorted to spanking, bribery, and appeals based on her own sacrifices for the children; but she participated in the efforts to train the children's consciences through manipulation by granting and withholding affection, also. Saxon, *Louisa May*, 250, 273, 280. Certainly the tendency in training children during the mid- and late nineteenth century was in the direction of Bronson Alcott's emphasis on manipulation by affection. On this point, the works cited in note 2 essentially agree.

Carl Degler persuasively puts Bronson Alcott's experiments in indoctrinating his children with Victorian values and behavior patterns in fine perspective. Degler places these experiments within the context of other such mid-nineteenth-century personal journals, and the period's child-rearing manuals in *At Odds*, 89–101.

24. For an extreme example, see the incident in *Little Men*, when Jo's husband and beloved co-director of their school, Dr. Bhaer, forced a boy unable to stop lying to strike him until the boy collapsed because of mental anguish. Alcott, *Little Men*, 45–46. Bronson Alcott had used this technique to activate the consciences of his daughters. See also the similar account in Jo's "conscience book," *Little Men*, 26, 92.

25. Cheney, ed., *Alcott: Letters and Journals*, 47, 249.

26. Alcott, *Little Men*, 241; Alcott, *Old-Fashioned Girl*, 232.

27. Alcott, *Little Women*, 397–400. The statement about the "sacred words, husband and father" appears in *Little Women*, 244. On the subject of mutual responsibilities and activities by parents within the Victorian family, see Catharine Sedgwick, *Home* (New York: J. Munroe, 1850; first published in 1835).

28. Alcott, *Jo's Boys*, 416. A high-spirited tomboy who resembled Jo—Nan in *Jo's Boys*—became a physician and a spinster.

29. Thomas E. Hill, *Hill's Manual of Social and Business Forms* (Chicago: Quadrangle, 1971), 156–57. The manual was published first in 1873 by Moses Warren and Company. Page numbers are from the reprinted 1885 edition.

30. Catharine E. Beecher and Harriet Beecher Stowe, *The American Woman's*

Home, or Principles of Domestic Science (New York: J. B. Ford and Company, 1869), 299. A fine discussion of the development of Catharine Beecher's views on the Victorian family's role can be found in Sklar, *Beecher*, 160–63, 263–65. For a sample of statements by Victorian authors about the powerful influence upon American society exerted by women in the home, see Cott, *Bonds of Womanhood*, 85–100.

31. Beecher and Stowe, *American Woman's Home*, 192–93.

32. Howells, *Modern Instance*, 474. Howells's novels contain many related examples of the disabilities of Victorian wives when physical or business danger threatened or quick decisions had to be made. See, for example, *The Rise of Silas Lapham* in *Selected Writings*, 32, and *A Hazard of New Fortunes*, in *Selected Writings*, 161, 239. Kathryn Kish Sklar has described how female disability served as one strategy for exercising control within the Victorian home. Sklar, "Female Strategies in Victorian Families," paper delivered to the Conference on Lincoln's Thought and the Present, Springfield, Illinois, June 1976.

33. Howells, *Modern Instance*, 675–76. Especially perceptive comments about Howells's treatment of business morality can be found in Alan Trachtenberg, *The Incorporation of America, Culture and Society in the Gilded Age* (New York: Hill and Wang, 1982), 192–93.

34. Alcott, *Little Women*, 89.

35. *Ibid.*, 157. Some historians who have studied Victorian girls prefer to stress the success that Victorian females enjoyed in developing feelings of personal autonomy, especially when their attitudes and actions were reinforced by approval from other females. A case for this theme as a major one in Alcott's novels— especially in *Little Women*—has been made by Sarah Elbert, *A Hunger for Home: Louisa May Alcott and Little Women* (Philadelphia: Temple Univ. Press, 1984).

36. Beecher and Stowe, *American Woman's Home*, 314. For further discussion of Victorian females' unpreparedness for domestic duties, see Sklar, *Beecher*, 152–53; Carroll Smith-Rosenberg, "The Hysterical Woman: Sex Roles and Role Conflict in 19th-Century America," *Social Research*, XXXIX (Winter 1972): 657–58, 672, 673, 677, reprinted with revisions in Smith-Rosenberg, *Disorderly Conduct, Visions of Gender in Victorian America* (New York: Knopf, 1985), 197–216. Alcott's male character who showed the greatest understanding of the results of Victorian constraints on females—Dr. Alex Campbell, guardian of Rose in *Rose in Bloom*— also advised regular strenuous exercise for girls. Even Dr. Campbell, however, "considered house-work the best sort of gymnastics for girls." Alcott, *Rose in Bloom* (Boston: Roberts Brothers, 1876), 74–75; Alcott, *Eight Cousins* (Boston: Little, Brown, 1911), 25, 93. Judith Walzer Leavitt provides a fine analysis of the relationship between birth complications and the general health of all classes of nineteenth-century women in *Brought to Bed: Childbearing in America, 1750 to 1950* (New York: Oxford Univ. Press, 1986), 64–82.

37. The literature on prostitution in Europe and to a lesser extent in the United States during this period is enormous. Material about English prostitution has been used to comment on Victorian values by Steven Marcus, *The Other Victorians* (New York: Basic Books, 1966); Kellow Chesney, *The Victorian Underworld* (New York: Schocken, 1970), 307–65; and Judith K. Walkewitz, *Prostitution and Victorian*

Society: Women, Class, and the State (Cambridge: Cambridge Univ. Press, 1980). Indications of the extent of prostitution in the United States during the nineteenth century can be found in Ruth Rosen, *The Lost Sisterhood, Prostitution in America, 1900–1918* (Baltimore: Johns Hopkins Univ. Press, 1982); and Ronald G. Walters, *Primers for Prudery, Sexual Advice to Victorian America* (Englewood Cliffs, N.J.: Prentice Hall, 1974). A warning against factors that have caused historians to overestimate the extent of nineteenth-century prostitution in Europe and in the United States can be found in Mary Lynn McDougall, "Working-Class Women During the Industrial Revolution," in Renate Bridenthal and Claudie Koonz, eds., *Becoming Visible: Women in European History* (Boston: Houghton Mifflin, 1977), 271–72. Accounts of prostitution and of moral reform in American can be found in David J. Pivar, *Purity Crusade: Sexual Morality and Social Control, 1868–1900* (Westport, Conn.: Greenwood Press, 1973). The early twentieth-century Progressive attack against prostitution is described in John D'Emilio and Estelle B. Freedman, *Intimate Matters: A History of Sexuality in America* (New York: Harper and Row, 1988), 208–15. As the authors state, this organized drive "dwarfed all of its predecessors," p. 208.

38. Canby, *Age of Confidence*, 156–61.

39. Alcott, *Little Women*, 394.

40. Canby, *Age of Confidence*, 173–77. For elaboration see D'Emilio and Freedman, *Intimate Matters*, 179–83.

41. Howells, *Hazard of New Fortunes*, 27.

42. Cott's analysis of successive ideas advanced by historians of women concerning female roles can be found in *Bonds of Womanhood*, 197–201. Though brief, this cogent analysis conveys the most important and often the most subtle distinctions within this literature.

43. Canby, *Age of Confidence*, 51, 54.

44. *Ibid.*, 31, 79, 257–58.

45. These consequences of placing women in the role of "moral guardian" have been explored with fine insight by Glenda Gates Riley, "The Subtle Subversion: Changes in the Traditionalist Image of the American Woman," *The Historian*, XXII (Feb. 1970): 210–27. The same theme appears prominently in Barbara Welter's pioneering essay, "The Cult of True Womanhood," *American Quarterly*, XVIII (Summer 1966): 151–74, reprinted in Welter, *Dimity Convictions*, 21–41. Also, see Carroll Smith-Rosenberg, "The Female World of Love and Ritual: Relations Between Women in Nineteenth-Century America," *Signs*, I (Autumn 1975): 1–30, reprinted with revisions in Smith-Rosenberg, *Disorderly Conduct*, 53–76.

46. Beecher and Stowe, *American Woman's Home*, Dedication; Paul Monroe, *Founding of the American Public School System* (New York: Macmillan, 1940), I: 97, 478–92; Thomas Woody, *A History of Women's Education in the United States* (New York: Science Press, 1929), II: 321–28; Joseph A. Hill, *Women in Gainful Occupations, 1870–1920*, U.S. Census Monography IX (Washington, 1929): 41, 42, 65. See also Dee Garrison, "The Tender Technicians: The Feminization of Public Librarianship, 1876–1905," *Journal of Social History*, VI (Winter 1972–1973): 131–59.

47. Alcott, "My Girls," *Aunt Jo's Scrap Bag* (Boston: Little, Brown, 1900), 8–10.

48. Alcott, *Hospital Sketches*. A sizable literature exists dealing with obstacles placed before women seeking to enter the medical profession. For example, see Mary Roth Walsh, *Doctors Wanted: No Women Need Apply. Sexual Barriers in the Medical Profession, 1835–1875* (New Haven: Yale Univ. Press, 1977).

49. Alcott, *Old-Fashioned Girl*, 227–28.

50. For an example of Catharine Beecher's anger at the restrictions placed on women who chose careers, see Sklar, *Beecher*, 188–95.

51. Alcott, *Eight Cousins*, 126; *Little Women*, 404.

52. Howells, *Rise of Silas Lapham*, 58–59; *Modern Instance*, 368; *Hazard of New Fortunes*, 79.

53. Howells, *Hazard of New Fortunes*, 193–94. Also, see Howells, *Modern Instance*, 593–99; *Rise of Silas Lapham*, 46–48, 50.
Canby maintains that as a young man he sensed "the feeling among the women that the harsh necessities of business justified ethics quite different from the friendly code of ordinary life." *Age of Confidence*, 234.

54. Walter E. Houghton explores this theme comprehensively in terms largely applicable to the United States in his fine description of English Victorianism: *The Victorian Frame of Mind, 1830–1870* (New Haven: Yale Univ. Press, 1957), for example, 228–39. Houghton discusses the Puritan heritage in Victorian culture on pp. 51–52, 61–64, 125–26, and *passim*.

55. Alcott, *Little Women*, 426.

56. Alcott, *Little Men*, 238–41.

57. Alcott, *Little Women*, 84. A good introduction to the subject of Victorian women's religious attitudes and roles in American Protestantism is provided by Barbara Welter, "The Feminization of Religion in Nineteenth-Century America," in Mary Harman and Lois Banner, eds., *Clio's Consciousness Raised* (New York: Harper, 1973), 137–157.

58. Stannard, *Puritan Way of Death*, 171–74.

59. For many further examples of the religious activities of leading businessmen during this period, see Wylie, *Self-Made Man in America*, 55–74, 116–132.

60. Conflicts among early twentieth-century intellectuals between Victorian values and professional scientific values are described in Chapter 2.

61. Kenneth S. Lynn, *William Dean Howells, An American Life* (New York: Harcourt Brace Jovanovich, 1970), 242. David D. Hall pointed out that "John Stuart Mill approved Carlyle's description of the times as 'destitute of faith, but terrified of skepticism,'" Hall, "The Victorian Connection," Howe, ed., *Victorian America*, 81–94. Struggles like Howells's constitute an important theme in Hall's essay and in D. H. Meyer, "American Intellectuals and the Victorian Crisis of Faith," in Howe, ed., *Victorian America*, 59–80.

62. Howells, *Modern Instance*, 705.

63. For an account of Victorian religious life, see Collean McDannell, *The Christian Home in Victorian America, 1840–1900* (Bloomington: Univ. of Indiana Press, 1986). McDannell describes the development among Catholics after 1880

of what she calls "a Victorian domesticity similar to Protestant sensibilities." *Ibid.*, 52–76.

64. Gregory H. Singleton, "Protestant Organizations and the Shaping of Victorian America," *American Quarterly*, XXVII (Dec. 1975): 549–60; Singleton, "'Mere Middle-Class Institutions': Urban Protestantism in Nineteenth-Century America," *Journal of Social History*, VI (Summer 1973): 489–504; Singleton, "The Dynamics of WASP Culture: From Ethnic Cohesion to the Organization Man," unpublished paper presented at the annual meeting of the American Historical Association, New Orleans, Dec. 1972; also, Lawrence B. Davis, *Immigrants, Baptists, and the Protestant Mind in America* (Urbana: Univ. of Illinois Press, 1973).

65. The role of subcultures in relation to American Victorian culture is discussed in Howe, "Victorian Culture in America," 518–19. Also, see Stanley Coben and Lorman Ratner, "Culture, Society, Ethnicity, Class, Nation, and History" in Coben and Ratner, eds., *Development of an American Culture*, 1–15.

66. Nineteenth-century scientific theories about race are discussed in Chapter 2.

For a comprehensive analysis of early Western and colonial American attitudes toward blacks, see Winthrop D. Jordan, *White Over Black: American Attitudes Toward the Negro, 1550–1812* (Chapel Hill: Univ. of North Carolina Press, 1968). An excellent extension of the subject into the nineteenth and early twentieth centuries is available in George M. Fredrickson, *The Black Image in the White Mind. The Debate on Afro-American Character and Destiny, 1817–1914* (New York: Harper, 1971). Carl N. Degler presents a valuable comparison of the origins and development of racial ideas and behavior patterns in Brazil and the United States in *Neither Black Nor White: Slavery and Race Relations in Brazil and the United States* (New York: Macmillan, 1971). Degler carries his analysis of race relations into the second half of the twentieth century and assesses astutely the probable future of these relations. Bernard Farber found that inhabitants of Salem, Massachusetts, viewed Negroes as "nonpersons" in 1790. Farber, *Guardians of Virtue, Salem Families in 1800* (New York: Basic Books, 1972), 57.

On the development of attitudes in the U.S. toward Asians and Indians, see John Higham, *Strangers in the Land, Patterns of American Nativism, 1860–1925* (New Brunswick: Rutgers Univ. Press, 1955), especially 24–25; Gary B. Nash, *Red, White and Black: The Peoples of Early America* (Englewood Cliffs, N.J.: Prentice Hall, 1974); Stuart Creighton Miller, *The Unwelcome Immigrant: The American Image of the Chinese, 1785–1882* (Berkeley and Los Angeles: Univ. of California Press, 1969); and Alexander P. Saxton, *The Indispensible Enemy: Labor and the Anti-Chinese Movement in California* (Berkeley: Univ. of California Press, 1971).

67. E. R. Norman, *Anti-Catholicism in Victorian England* (London: George Allen and Unwin, 1968) contains an introductory essay entitled "The Anti-Catholic Tradition," pp. 13–22; Ronald Robinson and John Gallegher with Alice Denny, *Africa and the Victorians: The Climax of Imperialism* (New York: St. Martins, 1961); L. Perry Curtis, Jr., *Apes and Angels: the Irishman in Victorian Caricature* (Washington, D.C.: Smithsonian Institution, 1971); Nicholas Mansergh, *The Irish Question 1840–1921* (Toronto: Univ. of Toronto Press, 1966); Richard Ned Lebow,

White Britain and Black Ireland: The Influence of Stereotypes on Colonial Policy (Philadelphia: Institute for the Study of Human Issues, 1976); Douglas A. Lorimer, *Colour, Class and the Victorians: English Attitudes to the Negro in the Mid-Nineteenth Century* (Leicester: Holmes and Meier, 1978); Ray Allen Billington, *The Protestant Crusade, 1800–1860* (New York: Macmillan, 1938); Higham, *Strangers in the Land*.

68. Lyman Beecher, *A Plea for the West* (Cincinnati: Truman, 1835), 11–12.

69. Alcott, *Little Women*, 496.

70. Alcott, *Under the Lilacs* (Boston: Roberts Brothers, 1894), 43–44, 59–61. Amy, the youngest daughter in *Little Women*, was forced by a heartless teacher to dispose of a desk full of pickled limes—intended for distribution to her classmates—by throwing them out the schoolroom window. As the limes disappeared, a shout from the street "completed the anguish of the girls," for it told them that their delicacies now belonged to the "Irish children, who were their sworn foes. This—this was too much!" *Little Women*, 68.

71. Canby, *Age of Confidence*, 29.

72. *Ibid.*, 41–46.

73. *Ibid.*, 24–26, 28–29.

74. Good studies of this mobility include Bruce Laurie, Theodore Hershberg, and George Alter, "Immigrants and Industry: The Philadelphia Experience, 1850–1880," *Journal of Social History*, IX (Dec. 1975): 219–48. This article was reprinted with slight revisions in Theodore Hershberg, ed., *Philadelphia Work, Space, Family, and Group Experience in the Nineteenth Century* (New York: Oxford Univ. Press, 1981), a volume which includes several other outstanding essays. Also, Stephan A. Thernstrom, *Poverty and Progress* (Cambridge: Harvard Univ. Press, 1963); and Thernstrom, *The Other Bostonians* (Cambridge: Harvard Univ. Press, 1973). So far, most other studies of nineteenth-century American rural and urban communities have produced statistics essentially in agreement with Thernstrom's. For an example of a counterargument stressing economic as well as geographical mobility within a nineteenth-century southern European immigrant group, see Humbert S. Nelli, *The Italians in Chicago, 1880–1930: A Study in Ethnic Mobility* (New York: Oxford Univ. Press, 1970). More ambiguous evidence about the mobility of nineteenth-century Italian immigrants appears in John W. Briggs, *Immigrants to Three American Cities, 1890–1930* (New Haven: Yale Univ. Press, 1978).

75. W. E. B. Du Bois, *Darkwater: Voices from Within the Veil* (New York: Schocken, 1969; first published in 1920), 10–11; *The Autobiography of W. E. B. Du Bois* (New York: International Publishers, 1968), 75, 82–83; Du Bois, *Dusk of Dawn* (New York: Schocken, 1968), 25–27. See Francis L. Broderick, *W. E. B. Du Bois: Negro Leader in a Time of Crisis* (Stanford Univ. Press, 1959), 1–7, for further discussion of Du Bois's early almost uncritical acceptance of Victorian values.

76. Du Bois, *Darkwater*, 11, 54.

77. The classic examples of this literature include Max Weber, *The Protestant Ethic and the Spirit of Capitalism* (London: George Allen and Unwin, 1930; first published in German as articles in 1904 and 1905); Weber, *Ancient Judaism* (Glencoe: Free Press, 1952); Weber, *The City* (Glencoe: Free Press, 1958), both published first in German over thirty years earlier; Richard H. Tawney, *Religion and the Rise of Capitalism* (New York: Harcourt Brace 1947; first published in England in 1926);

Ernst Troeltsch, *The Social Teachings of the Christian Churches and Sects* (New York: Macmillan, 1931; first published in German in 1912); and Werner Sombart, *The Quintessence of Capitalism* (New York: Dutton, 1915; first published in German).

78. Theodore Roosevelt, "Character and Success," *Outlook*, LXIV (1900): 745.

79. Quoted in Carleton Putnam, *Theodore Roosevelt, the Formative Years, 1858–1886* (New York: Charles Scribner's Sons, 1958), 46, 56, 189.

80. My theme in this paragraph seems the chief implication of Richard L. McCormick's critique of scholarship dealing with the Progressive era, "The Discovery that Business Corrupts Politics: A Reappraisal of the Origins of Progressivism," *American Historical Review*, LXXXVI (Apr. 1981): 247–74.

81. Roosevelt, *Realizeable Ideals*, quoted in Griffen, "Progressive Ethos," 163–64. Roosevelt's entire lecture, a model of Progressive righteousness, illustrating the link between Victorianism and the origins of Progressivism is reprinted in Hermann Hagedorn, *The Works of Theodore Roosevelt* (New York: Scribner's, 1926), XIII. The quotation is from page 16. This lecture was one of a series delivered in Berkeley, California, in 1911; Leuchtenberg, *The Perils of Prosperity, 1914–32* (Chicago: Univ. of Chicago Press, 1958), 34.

82. Thomas G. Dyer, *Theodore Roosevelt and the Idea of Race* (Baton Rouge: Louisiana State Univ. Press, 1980), 19. Dyer found Roosevelt's ideas about race both complex and consistent. His book includes informative criticism of other historians' treatment of Roosevelt's racial concepts. For example, *ibid.*, XII-XIII, 28.

83. *Ibid.*, 2.

84. *Ibid.*, 6–9; John Higham, *Strangers in the Land*, 139–41.

85. Theodore Roosevelt, *The Winning of the West* (New York: G. P. Putnam's Sons, 1889); Dyer, *Roosevelt and the Idea of Race*, 45–81, 112–13; George Sinkler, *The Racial Attitudes of American Presidents from Abraham Lincoln to Theodore Roosevelt* (Garden City, N.Y.: Doubleday, 1972), 378–88, 403–5; William H. Harbaugh, *The Life and Times of Theodore Roosevelt*, rev. ed. (New York: Oxford Univ. Press, 1975), 61–64.

86. Dyer, *Roosevelt and the Idea of Race*, 9, 26–27, 67–68.

87. *Ibid.*, 13, 16–17.

88. *Ibid.*, 125–29. Harbaugh, *Theodore Roosevelt*, 28–29, 212–13.

89. Sinkler, *Racial Attitudes of American Presidents*, 435–46; Dyer, *Roosevelt and the Idea of Race*, 105.

90. Dyer, *Roosevelt and the Idea of Race*, 111–14; Sinkler, *Racial Attitudes of American Presidents*, 430–34.

91. For a broad summary of the rebellion against Victorian restraints in the 1890s and the failure of that rebellion to challenge the bases of conventional morality, see John Higham, "The Reorientation of American Culture in the 1890s" in John Weiss, ed., *The Origins of Modern Consciousness* (Detroit: Wayne State Univ. Press, 1965), 25–48.

2. The Development of an American Intelligentsia

1. The term "intelligentsia" possesses the connotations that I wish to impart. In his enlightening chapter "Prophecy: The Emergence of an Intelligentsia," es-

pecially, James Billington traced the development of this transnational concept. Billington, *Fire in the Minds of Men: Origins of the Revolutionary Faith* (New York: Basic Books, 1980), 208–42. Billington's account of the concept's early meanings, particularly, coincides closely with the ideas I intend to convey. For example, Billington states, "The activist [Russian] intellectuals of the 1870's called themselves the 'true,' the 'new,' and the 'young' intelligentsia, and brought with them in their westward diaspora the image of pure truth opposing unbridled power." *Ibid.*, 415. Also, "Mikhailovsky insisted that there was deep meaning in the fact that the Russian word for truth, *pravda*, meant both objective, scientific truth (*pravda-istina*) and justice (*pravda-spravedlivost*). The intelligent had to be committed to both." *Ibid.*, 401. The implications of "intelligentsia" in this book largely coincide also with Karl Mannheim's definition of a "free intelligentsia" elaborated in his section "The Sociological Problem of the 'Intelligentsia,'" in Mannheim, *Ideology and Utopia: An Introduction to the Sociology of Knowledge* (New York: Harcourt Brace, 1949; first printed in large part in Bonn by F. Cohen in 1929), 136–46. On the broad modern origins of the concept, see Martin Malia, *Alexander Herzen and the Birth of Russian Socialism 1812–1855* (Cambridge: Harvard Univ. Press, 1961), 4–6, 115–19, 184–86, 412–20.

Richard Hofstadter commented accurately about the United States: "After 1890 it became possible to speak of intellectuals as a class." And "Alienation became a kind of fixed principle among young intellectuals during the years preceding the war [World War I]." Hofstadter, *Anti-Intellectualism in American Life* (New York: Knopf, 1962), 408–10.

2. The most comprehensive treatment of U.S. universities during the second half of the nineteenth century is by Laurence R. Veysey, *The Emergence of the American University* (Chicago: Univ. of Chicago Press, 1965). The quoted statement by Johns Hopkins president Daniel Coit Gilman appears in *ibid.*, 163. The quoted statement by Columbia president Butler and the comment by Chicago's Harper can be found in *ibid.*, 364, 368.

3. After Harvard philosopher George Santayana addressed an audience at the Sorbonne in 1905, he wrote to his Harvard colleague William James that the experience had been "exhilarating. You can say what is *really* true. You needn't remember that you are in Cambridge, or are addressing the youth entrusted to your personal charge. . . . After our atmosphere, this is liberty." Santayana returned permanently to Europe in 1912. Douglas L. Wilson, ed., *The Genteel Tradition, Nine Essays by George Santayana* (Cambridge: Harvard Univ. Press, 1967), 2–3.

4. Veysey, *Emergence of the American University*, 161.

5. John R. Commons, *Myself* (Madison: Univ. of Wisconsin Press, 1963), 52–53.

6. Richard Hofstadter and Walter P. Metzger, *The Development of Academic Freedom in the United States* (New York: Columbia Univ. Press, 1955), 335. The most valuable source of published information about the teaching of evolution in American colleges is Hamilton Cravens, *The Triumph of Evolution: American Scientists and the Heredity-Environment Controversy, 1900–1941* (Philadel-

phia: Univ. of Pennsylvania Press, 1978). Also, Edward J. Larson, *Trial and Error: The American Controversy over Creation and Evolution* (New York: Oxford Univ. Press, 1985).

7. I. A. Newby, *Jim Crow's Defense: Anti-Negro Thought in America, 1900–1930* (Baton Rouge: Louisiana State Univ. Press, 1965), 12–13. Especially valuable analyses among the enormous literature concerning "scientific" racism are Stephen Jay Gould, *The Mismeasure of Man* (New York: W.W. Norton, 1981); Richard Hofstadter, *Social Darwinism in American Thought, 1860–1915* (Philadelphia: Univ. of Pennsylvania Press, 1945); Higham, *Strangers in the Land;* and Barbara Miller Solomon, *Ancestors and Immigrants* (Cambridge: Harvard Univ. Press, 1956).

8. Thomas F. Gossett, *Race, The History of an Idea in America* (New York: Schocken, 1965), 155–59; Newby, *Jim Crow's Defense,* 12–13; Gould, *Mismeasure of Man,* 75–77. For an attempt at a fair yet critical account of Galton's thought and influence, see D. W. Forrest, *Francis Galton, The Life and Work of a Victorian Genius* (London: Elek, 1974). Franz Boas served as the leading spokesman early in the twentieth century for American social scientists who opposed the idea of a genetically determined racial hierarchy (see Chapter 3). American biologists converted to the concept that man was the product of both biological and cultural evolution. See Cravens, *Triumph of Evolution,* 157–90.

9. Gossett, *Race,* 60; Gould, *Mismeasure of Man,* 42–50. The quotation is from Gould, *Mismeasure of Man,* 44–45. Gould translated the entire letter "verbatim, for the first time so far as I know."

10. *Ibid.,* 284; Newby, *Jim Crow's Defense,* 66–67. Students either working under the direction of William A. Dunning at Columbia University or inspired by the books and essays of Dunning and his students wrote the most thorough and persuasive history of Reconstruction from what had been the southern point of view. Their well-documented interpretations persuaded almost all scholars, except a few isolated recalcitrants such as W. E. B. Du Bois.

11. Gossett, *Race,* 109.

12. George W. Stocking, *Race, Culture, and Evolution. Essays in the History of Anthropology* (New York: Free Press, 1968), 122–23, 127–28. Bean theorized also that what he called the "Jewish nose" developed because of the "habitual indignation" of that race. Stocking, *Race, Culture, and Evolution,* 188.

13. Gossett, *Race,* 160–72; Murray Kranz, "The Emergence of a Sociological View Toward the Negro," unpublished Ph.D. dissertation, Univ. of California, Los Angeles, 1973, pp. 28–34; Stanford M. Lyman, *The Black American in Sociological Thought, A Failure of Perspective* (New York: Capricorn, 1973), 15–22. For Commons's conventional views on racial and ethnic groups, see his *Races and Immigrants in America* (New York: Macmillan, 1907); Solomon, *Ancestors and Immigrants,* 131–32; Gossett, *Race,* 172–74. Naturalists Frank Norris and Jack London contributed as much as any novelists to the spread of Social Darwinist racist attitudes.

14. In his history of these genteel authors and editors, John Tomsich wrote: "They were the ones . . . who sat in day-by-day control of what passed into the

hands of America's better-informed readers. It is this attitude and values . . . that shaped cultural life in Victorian America." Tomsich, *A Genteel Endeavor: American Culture and Politics in The Gilded Age* (Stanford: Stanford Univ. Press, 1971), 6–9. The quotation above appears on p. 9.

15. *Ibid.*, 5–6, 81–83; also, Arthur John, *The Best Years of the Century: Richard Watson Gilder, Scribner's Monthly, and the Century Magazine, 1870–1909* (Urbana-Champaign: Univ. of Illinois Press, 1981); Gossett, *Race*, 198–227, 305, 335–36, 434–36.

16. Theodore Dreiser, *Sister Carrie* (New York: Doubleday and Page, 1900). The most thorough account of Dreiser's writing of *Sister Carrie*, his conflict with Doubleday, and the book's reception can be found in W. A. Swanberg, *Dreiser* (New York: Scribner's, 1965), 85–93. For supplementary information, see Robert H. Elias, *Theodore Dreiser: Apostle of Nature* (New York: Knopf, 1949); Malcolm Cowley, "Sister Carrie's Brother," originally published in the *New Republic*, May 26, 1947, but reprinted as the first part of "Sister Carrie: Her Fall and Rise" in Alfred Kazin and Charles Shapiro, eds., *The Stature of Theodore Dreiser: A Critical Survey of the Man and His work* (Bloomington: Indiana Univ. Press, 1955), 171–81; George Steinbrecher, Jr., "Inaccurate Accounts of Sister Carrie," *American Literature*, XXIII (Jan. 1952): 490–93; Stephen Stepanchev, *Dreiser Among the Critics* (New York: New York Univ. Press, 1950). The interview with Dreiser by a *New York Times* reporter was reprinted in Kazin and Shapiro, eds., *The Stature of Theodore Dreiser*, 59–60; it appeared in the *Times* on Jan. 15, 1901.

17. Twain left three versions of *The Mysterious Stranger*, but separated from these the chapter he entitled "Conclusion of the Book." John S. Tuckey, in *Mark Twain and Little Satan: The Writing of the Mysterious Stranger* (West Lafayette: Purdue Univ. Press, 1963), estimates that Twain wrote this concluding chapter in 1905 and believes that the author then considered the novel completed.

18. Dwight Macdonald, "Mark Twain: An Unsentimental Journey," in Justin Kaplan, ed., *Mark Twain: A Profile* (New York: Hill and Wang, 1967), 120–22. The conclusion of *The Mysterious Stranger* expressed beliefs that Twain had held long before the personal tragedies which marred his later years. See Sholom Kahn, *Mark Twain's Mysterious Stranger: A Study of the Manuscrpt Texts* (Columbia: Univ. of Missouri Press, 1978), viii; and Henry Nash Smith, *Mark Twain: The Development of a Writer* (Cambridge: Harvard Univ. Press, 1962); as well as Tuckey, *Mark Twain and Little Satan*.

19. Henry F. May, *The End of American Innocence: A Study of the First Years of Our Own Time: 1912–1917* (New York: Knopf, 1959); Tomsich, *Genteel Endeavor*, 4; Stanley Coben, "The Assault on Victorianism in the Twentieth Century," *American Quarterly*, XXVII (Dec. 1975): 604–25; Peter Novick, *That Noble Dream: The "Objectivity Question" and the American Historical Profession* (New York: Cambridge Univ. Press, 1988).

20. Pound's words were published first in the *New Freewoman* and are reprinted in Frederick J. Hoffman, *The Twenties: American Writing in the Postwar Decade* (New York: Viking, 1955), 165–66.

21. Stanley Coben, "The Scientific Establishment and the Transmission of

Quantum Mechanics to the United States, 1919–1932," *American Historical Review*, LXXVI (Apr. 1971): 442–66; Max Jammer, *The Conceptual Development of Quantum Mechanics* (New York: McGraw-Hill, 1966), 323–45. Two examples of the acceptance during the 1920s of the uncertainty principle and of probability in quantum mechanics by American theoretical physicists can be found in Percy W. Bridgman, *The Logic of Modern Physics* (New York: Macmillan, 1927), 92; and Edward U. Condon and Philip M. Morse, *Quantum Mechanics* (New York: Macmillan, 1929), Preface. For an abundance of further evidence, see Jammer, *Conceptual Development of Quantum Mechanics*, 326–45.

J. W. Grove observed that T. H. Huxley was obliged to defend science in what for most of his lifetime (1825–95) was a hostile social environment. Grove, *In Defense of Science: Science, Technology, and Politics in Modern Society* (Toronto: Univ. of Toronto Press, 1989), 13. Huxley argued that science was only rigorously applied commonsense. Grove, *In Defense of Science*, 13–14.

22. See the large volume of correspondence between DeKruif and Mencken concerning this collaboration and the circumstances leading up to it in the file marked DeKruif, Paul, the Papers of H. L. Mencken, New York Public Library (hereafter referred to as Mencken Papers). Several letters from DeKruif to Loeb also refer to DeKruif's relations with Lewis and Mencken, file marked DeKruif, Paul, Loeb Papers, New York Public Library. Also, see Mark Schorer, *Sinclair Lewis: An American Life* (New York: McGraw-Hill, 1961), 305, 361–69, 372–73, 381, 385, 389, 406–7, 414–20. Schorer seems inclined toward the view that Lewis's contact with DeKruif was Dr. Morris Fishbein.

Lewis may well have been inspired to write a novel about medical research by DeKruif's articles about Loeb and about medical research. For an especially good example of these articles, see DeKruif, "Jacques Loeb, the Mechanist," *Harper's Magazine*, CXLVI (Jan. 1923): 182–90, an account which describes Loeb as possessing characteristics Lewis later attributed to Gottlieb.

On Dreiser and Croly's interest in Loeb's work and its influence on their writing, see Dreiser to Loeb, May 29, 1919; Loeb to Dreiser, Sept. 11, 1920; Loeb to Croly, Mar. 5, 1920; Croly to Loeb, Mar. 11, 1920. All in Loeb Papers, New York Public Library.

23. Sinclair Lewis, *Arrowsmith* (New York: Harcourt Brace, 1925), 267–68. On the probable combination in Gottlieb of Loeb's characteristics with those of Professor Frederick G. Novy, Univ. of Michigan bacteriologist, see Schorer, *Lewis*, 364–65. DeKruif also had served on the Univ. of Michigan faculty.

24. Lewis's "Self Portrait" quoted in Hoffman, *Twenties*, 368; Hemingway to Fitzgerald, May 28, 1934, Papers of F. Scott Fitzgerald, Firestone Library, Princeton Univ.

25. Schorer, *Lewis*, 268–74, 301–4, 364–69, 440–41, 446–51; D. J. Dooley, *The Art of Sinclair Lewis* (Lincoln: Univ. of Nebraska Press, 1967), 59–60, 99–103.

26. A. Scott Berg, *Max Perkins, Editor of Genius* (New York: E. P. Dutton, 1978), 123–25, 177–79, 198.

27. Ernest Hemingway, *Death in the Afternoon* (New York: Charles Scribner's Sons, 1932), 2–3.

3. A Structure to Support Intellectual Dissent

1. A case history of the concurrence during the 1920s of these conditions in one important field—theoretical atomic physics—can be found in Coben, "The Scientific Establishment and the Transmission of Quantum Mechanics to the United States."

2. U.S. Department of Commerce, Bureau of the Census, *Historical Statistics of the United States, Colonial Times to 1957* (Washington, D.C.: U.S. Government Printing Office, 1960), 210–11.

3. U.S. Department of the Interior, Office of Education, *Biennial Survey of Education, 1926–1928* (Washington, D.C.: U.S. Government Printing Office, 1928), 698; U.S. Department of Commerce, Bureau of Census, *Biennial Survey*, 207–11; Paul Forman, John L. Heilbron, and Spencer R. Weart, "Physics circa 1900: Personnel, Funding, and Productivity of the Academic Establishment," *Historical Studies in the Physical Sciences*, vol. 5 (Princeton: Princeton Univ. Press, 1975), esp. Tables II, A.2, and A.7, on pp. 8, 13, 34–35; George J. Stigler, *Employment and Compensation in Higher Education*, Occasional Paper no. 33 (New York: National Bureau of Economic Research, 1950), 210.

4. Joseph Ben-David, *Fundamental Research and the Universities* (Paris: Organization for Economic Cooperation and Development, 1968), esp. 29–34; Ronald C. Tobey, *The American Ideology of National Science, 1919–1930* (Pittsburgh: Univ. of Pittsburgh Press, 1971), 6–7; Spencer R. Weart, "The Physics Business in America, 1919–1940: A Statistical Reconnaissance" in Nathan Reingold, ed., *The Sciences in the American Context: New Perspectives* (Washington, D.C.: Smithsonian Institution Press, 1979), 295–358; Kendall Birr, "Industrial Research Laboratories," in Reingold, ed., *The Sciences in the American Context: New Perspectives*, 193–208; W. H. G. Armytage, *The Rise of the Technocrats: A Social History* (London: Routledge and Kegan Paul, 1965), 246.

5. For representative evidence of this change in attitudes, see Robert and Helen Lynd, *Middletown: A Study in Modern American Culture* (New York: Harcourt Brace, 1929), 182–87. The Lynds summarized the replies of informants among ambitious elements of the working class. "Over and over again one sees both parents working to keep their children in college. 'I don't know how we're going to get the children through college, but we're *going* to. A boy without an education today just ain't *anywhere!*' was the emphatic assertion of one father," p. 187.

6. Henry May reached similar conclusions in *End of American Innocence*, especially 298–303. I am grateful to my former research assistant, Gregory M. Singleton, for his carefully prepared data concerning the educational attainments of those generally considered members of the Harlem Renaissance. Material collected by another former research assistant, Emory Tolbert, confirmed Professor Singleton's and my own conclusions.

7. J. Robert Oppenheimer, *Science and the Common Understanding* (New York: Simon and Schuster, 1953), 36.

8. "Plans for the Promotion of Research in Physics and Chemistry Prepared

by the Research Fellowship Board of the National Research Council, May 1920";
Papers of Robert A. Millikan, California Institute of Technology, box 5; Arthur
A. Noyes to Robert A. Millikan, May 7, 1920, Millikan Papers; Abraham Flexner
to George Ellery Hale, Sept. 18, 1919, Papers of George Ellery Hale, California
Institute of Technology, microfilm roll 14; Raymond B. Fosdick, *The Story of the
Rockefeller Foundation* (New York: Harper, 1952), 145–46.

9. The best single source for following these changes in the history of American
philanthropy are the correspondence and reports in the Rockefeller Foundation
Archives, Rockefeller Archive Center, Hillcrest, Pocantico Hills, North Tarrytown, New York (hereafter referred to as Rockefeller Archive). The shifts are
traced and their meaning discussed in Stanley Coben, "American Foundations as
Patrons of Science: The Commitment to Individual Research," in Nathan Reingold, ed., *The Sciences in the American Context: New Perspectives* (Washington, D.C.:
Smithsonian Institution, 1979), 229–47; Barry D. Karl, *Charles E. Merriam and the
Study of Politics* (Chicago: Univ. of Chicago Press, 1974), 118–39, 153, 182–84,
201–13; Barry D. Karl and Stanley N. Katz, in their account of foundations'
development, "The American Private Philanthropic Foundations and the Public
Sphere, 1890–1930," *Minerva*, XIX (1981): 236–70, discuss some of the foundations
only mentioned in this book, such as the Russell Sage Foundation; Raymond B.
Fosdick, *Story of the Rockefeller Foundation;* Milton Lomask, *Seed Money: The Gug-
genheim Story* (New York: Farrar, Straus, 1964); Roger L. Geiger, *To Advance
Knowledge: The Growth of American Research Universities, 1900–1940* (New York:
Oxford Univ. Press, 1986), 140–73; and John Higham, "The Schism in American
Scholarship," *American Historical Review*, LXXII (Oct. 1966): 1–21.

10. Lewis B. Cooper, *Sabbatical Leaves for College Teachers*, Univ. of Florida
Education Series, I, 1932. The Papers of H. L. Mencken, on microfilm, Firestone
Library, Princeton Univ., contain a number of letters from writers holding positions as visiting teachers at universities and letters from writers on lecture tours,
including a complaint from Sherwood Anderson in 1926 that he had received
more money from one talk before a Univ. of California audience than Mencken's
American Mercury had paid him for one of his best short stories. Anderson to
Mencken, marked "1926," Mencken Papers. Even Pound, hardly known in America outside intellectual circles, was tempted. He wrote from Rapallo in 1926: "As
to a lecture tour: the question is simply: What wd. it pay? I can not afford to do
it on the cheap. If I blow all that energy, I have got to have a few years from
worry *after it*." D. D. Paige, ed., *The Selected Letters of Ezra Pound, 1907–1941*
(New York: New Directions Publishing Co., 1971), 204. In 1921, Pound had
replied to William Carlos Williams in a similar fashion: if guaranteed expenses
and "leisure for a year after the whirlwind campaign—I will listen to the stern
voice of duty and save as much of the country as is ready to be snatched from
the yawning maw of gum shoes, YMCA. . . ." *Selected Letters of Pound*, 165. Major
literary journals associated with colleges and universities either started or expanded
during the period after 1912 included the *Texas Review*, the *Yale Review*, the *Sewanee
Review*, and the *Virginia Quarterly Review*. Frederick J. Hoffman, *The Little Magazine: A History and Bibliography* (Princeton: Princeton Univ. Press, 1946), 2; and

supplementary descriptions of literary journals in the bibliography. Almost every major scholarly discipline added new journals.

11. Hoffman, et al., *The Little Magazine;* Charles Allen, "The Advance Guard," *Sewanee Review,* LI (July/Sept. 1943): 410–20; Austin Warren, "Some Periodicals of the American Intelligentsia," *The New English Weekly,* I (Oct. 6, 1932): 595–97; Arthur J. Wertheim, *New York Little Renaissance* (New York: New York Univ. Press, 1976), 227–46.

12. Walker Gilmer, *Horace Liveright, Publisher of the Twenties* (New York: David Walker, 1970); Charles A. Madison, *Book Publishing in America* (New York: McGraw-Hill, 1966).

13. Cowley reported also that after Perkins brought Fitzgerald to Scribner's, even before publication of the author's first novel, *This Side of Paradise,* some of Scribner's executives and editorial staff recognized the book as "the terrifying voice of a new age...." Berg, *Perkins,* 22, 108.

For sensitive accounts of Perkins as an editor, see the cogent essay by John Kuehland and Jackson R. Bryer in John Kuehl and Jackson R. Bryers, eds., *Dear Scott/Dear Max: The Fitzgerald-Perkins Correspondence* (New York: Scribner, 1971), especially 13–14; also Berg, *Perkins.* Alfred Harcourt's successful effort to win Faulkner from Liveright is described in Gilmer, *Liveright,* 125–27. Harcourt's long ordeal as Lewis's publisher can be followed in Schorer, *Lewis,* and in a volume of letters between Harcourt and Lewis in Lewis, *From Main Street to Stockholm* (New York: Harcourt Brace, 1952). Also, Alfred Harcourt, *Some Experiences* (Riverside, Conn., 1951).

14. Henry Dan Piper, *F. Scott Fitzgerald: A Critical Portrait* (New York: Holt, Rinehart and Winston, 1965), 72–74, 79; Robert Sklar, *F. Scott Fitzgerald: The Last Laocoön* (New York: Oxford Univ. Press, 1967). Although authors' incomes notoriously are difficult to uncover, Swanberg observed that in his federal income-tax return for 1926, Dreiser *declared* income of over $91,000 in royalties, and in 1927, over $97,000. Swanberg, *Dreiser,* 318, 340.

15. Piper, *Fitzgerald,* 71–79; Frank Luther Mott, *History of American Magazines* (Cambridge: Harvard Univ. Press, 1957), 671–711; John Tebbe, *George Horace Lorimer and the Saturday Evening Post* (New York: Doubleday, 1948); Sklar, *Fitzgerald,* 108–34, 184, 216–17; Swanberg, *Dreiser,* 318, 340.

Dreiser had written for the mass-circulation magazines since the early twentieth century; he served as editor of the *Delineator,* June 1907–Sept. 1910. Both as writer and magazine editor, however, he had kept his ideas about society and politics severely in check. During the 1920s, on the contrary, he was encouraged to give nearly free rein to his views. The *Saturday Evening Post* paid Dreiser handsomely in 1928 for a series of sympathetic articles about Bolshevik rule in the Soviet Union. Swanberg, *Dreiser,* 340.

16. Malcolm Cowley, *Exile's Return: A Literary Odyssey of the 1920's* (New York: Viking, 1934), 65, 225.

17. Margaret Mead, *Coming of Age in Samoa* (New York: William Morrow, 1928), 158–60, 205–9, 212–14.

18. Mead, *Growing Up in New Guinea* (New York: William Morrow, 1930), 158–73.

19. Benedict, "Psychological Types in the Cultures of the Southwest," *Proceedings, Twenty-Third Annual Congress of Americanists* (1928), 572–81; "The Science of Custom," *Century Magazine*, 117 (1929): 641–49; *Patterns of Culture* (Boston: Houghton Mifflin, 1934), 128, 133, 140, 152, 158; Margaret Mead, ed., *An Anthropologist at Work: Writings of Ruth Benedict* (Boston: Houghton Mifflin, 1959), 211–12; Eric R. Wolf, *Anthropology* (Englewood Cliffs: Prentice Hall, 1964), 42.

20. Edward Sapir, "Culture, Genuine and Spurious," *American Journal of Sociology*, XXIX (1924): 401–29. Sapir widened his audience for this message further by publishing condensed versions of this essay in the literary journals the *Dial*, LXVII (1919): 233–36; and the *Dalhousie Review*, II (1922): 165–78. The quotations can be found on pp. 408–9, 411, and 413–14 of the essay in the *American Journal of Sociology*.

21. On the Chicago school of sociology, the most relevant works are James T. Carey, *Sociology and Public Affairs: The Chicago School* (Beverly Hills: Sage, 1975); the essays by James F. Short, Jr., Harvey W. Zorbaugh, Ellsworth Faris, and W. I. Thomas in Short, ed., *The Social Fabric of the Metropolis: Contributions of the Chicago School of Urban Sociology* (Chicago: Univ. of Chicago Press, 1971); Thomas V. Smith and Leonard D. White, eds., *Chicago, An Experiment in Social Science Research* (New York: Greenwood, 1929); and Robert Farris, *Chicago Sociology, 1920–1930* (San Francisco: Chandler, 1967).

22. See Rupert Vance's perceptive essay on Odum in the *International Encyclopedia of the Social Sciences* (New York: Crowell, 1968), 11, 270–71.

23. Robert S. Lynd and Helen M. Lynd, *Middletown*, vi.

24. *Ibid.*, 32–34, 59–60, 84–87, 118–19, 120–30, 148–49.

25. *Ibid.*, 330, 493–95.

26. The most thorough studies of the Boas school's role in shifts in attitudes toward race among social scientists have been carried out by George W. Stocking, Jr., especially in his *Race, Culture and Evolution: Essays in the History of Anthropology* (New York: Free Press, 1968); his "American Social Scientists and Race Theory: 1890–1915," unpublished Ph.D. dissertation, Univ. of Pennsylvania, 1960; and Stocking, ed., *Malinowski, Rivers, Benedict and Others, Essays on Culture and Personality* (Madison: Univ. of Wisconsin Press, 1986), 95–183.

27. Stocking, *Race, Culture and Evolution*, 163–80; Mead, "The Methodology of Racial Testing," *American Journal of Sociology*, 31 (Feb. 1926): 657–67; Herskovits, "The Racial Hysteria," *Opportunity*, II (June 1924): 166–68; "Some Effects of Social Selection on the American Negro," *Publications of the American Sociological Society*, XX (1926): 77–80; "Some Physical Characteristics of the American Negro Population," *Journal of the Social Forces*, VI (Sept. 1927): 93–98; "Race Relations," *American Journal of Sociology*, XXXIV (May 1929): 1129–39; *The American Negro* (New York: Knopf, 1928); Klineberg, "An Experimental Study of Speed and Other Factors in Racial Differences," *Archives of Psychology*, No. 93 (1928). (Klineberg's earlier research is summarized in Klineberg, ed., *Characteristics of the American Negro* (New York: Harper, 1944); and in his *Race Differences* (New York: Harper, 1935). Also, see Boas to Klineberg, Feb. 6, 1928, Oct. 25, 1929, Papers of Franz Boas, American Philosophical Society, Philadelphia.

28. These processes are described in Coben, "Assault on Victorianism," 611–

14. This article also contains an account of the rewriting of textbooks renouncing the authors' previous statements about racial differences in favor of the conclusions of Boas and his students and an account of the major article renouncing previous views.

29. Charles H. Thompson, "The Conclusion of Scientists Relative to Racial Differences," *Journal of Negro Education*, III (July 1934): 494–512.

30. Eliot, who during the 1930s wrote the play *Murder in the Cathedral* and poetry which also showed an Anglo-Catholic perspective, might seem, therefore, out of place in this list. However, Eliot characterized his earliest work as "atheistical." He specifically denied any "Christian" content in *The Waste Land*, and few literary critics disagree. Malcolm Cowley, ed., *Writers at Work: The Paris Review Interviews* (New York: Viking, 1965), 91–97.

31. Condon and Morse, *Quantum Mechanics*; C. Cajori, *A History of Physics* (New York: Macmillan, 1929); Max Jammer, *The Conceptual Development of Quantum Mechanics*, 281–92, 323–61; Katherine Sopka, *Quantum Physics in America, 1920–1935* (New York: Arno Press, 1980); Hans Reichenbach, *Philosophic Foundations of Quantum Mechanics* (Berkeley and Los Angeles: Univ. of California Press, 1944), v–vii, 1–44.

32. Harlow Shapley, *Galaxies* (Cambridge: Harvard Univ. Press, 1961); Helen Wright, *Explorer of the Universe, A Biography of George Ellery Hale* (New York: Dutton, 1966).

33. For a more lengthy discussion of Rose, Ruml, and Moe as foundation officials than the one below, see Coben, "American Foundations as Patrons of Science: The Commitment to Individual Research," in Reingold, ed., *The Sciences in the American Context: New Perspectives*, 229–48.

34. Buttrick to Rose, May 8, 1909, Rose Papers, Rockefeller Archive; Frederick T. Gates to Rose, Dec. 17, 1909, Rockefeller Sanitary Commission Collection, Rockefeller Archive; John Ettling, *The Germ of Laziness: Rockefeller Philanthropy and Public Health in the New South* (Cambridge: Harvard Univ. Press, 1981), 113–17.

35. Rockefeller Sanitary Commission, "Organization, Activities and Results, 1910," copy in papers of Simon Flexner, BF 365, American Philosophical Society Library, Philadelphia. See the maps in this report of Central and South America, Europe, Africa, and Asia. Rose conducted the survey at Gates's request. See Ettling, *Germ of Laziness*, 187–89. Gerald Jonas, *The Circuit Riders: Rockefeller Money and the Rise of Modern Science* (New York: Norton, 1989), 73–74. On the recruitment of Rose, see Ettling, *Germ of Laziness*, 114.

36. Simon Flexner, "On the Etiology of Tropical Dysentery," *Philadelphia Medical Journal*, VI (July–Dec. 1900): 414–24; Flexner with L. F. Barker, "Report upon an Expedition sent by the Johns Hopkins University to Investigate the Prevalent Diseases in the Philippines," *Johns Hopkins Hospital Bulletin*, XI (1900): 37; Flexner, "The Pathology of Bubonic Plague," *University of Pennsylvania Medical Bulletin*, XIV (1901): 205; Flexner with L. F. Barker and F. G. Novy, "Report of the Commission Appointed by the Secretary of the Treasury for the Investigation of Plague in San Francisco, under Instructions from the Surgeon-General, Marine-Hospital Service, Treasury Department, U.S. Marine Hospital Service"

(Washington: Government Printing Office, 1901); James Thomas Flexner, *An American Saga: The Story of Helen Thomas and Simon Flexner* (Boston: Little, Brown, 1984), 244–53, 334–40. Flexner to Rose, July 5, 1913, BF 365, box 1, file 1, Simon Flexner Papers, American Philosophical Society, Philadelphia. The quotation is from Burton J. Hendrick, *The Life and Letters of Walter H. Page* (Garden City, N.Y.: Doubleday, Page and Co., 1923), I: 126–27.

37. Simon Flexner, address prepared for delivery at the memorial ceremony for Wickliffe Rose, Feb. 15, 1932, BF 365, box 1, file 24, Simon Flexner Papers.

38. Stiles is quoted in Ettling, *Germ of Laziness*, 147.

39. Rose to Simon Flexner, Dec. 30, 1913, BF 365, box 1, file 1, Simon Flexner Papers; Jonas, *The Circuit Riders*, 134–35.

40. References to material in the Rockefeller Foundation Archives which provided much of the information for the summary above of Rose's role in the development of the sciences—especially physics—during the 1920s can be found in Coben, "Transmission of Quantum Mechanics," and Coben, "American Foundations as Patrons of Science," 233–36. Also, see Raymond B. Fosdick, *Adventure in Giving* (New York: Harper and Row, 1962); Fosdick, *Story of the Rockefeller Foundation;* and George W. Gray, *Education on an International Scale: A History of the International Education Board, 1923–1938* (New York: Harcourt Brace, 1941).

41. References for this summary of Ruml's career in the Rockefeller Foundation can be found in Coben, "American Foundations as Patrons of Science," 236–37. Also see Joan Bulmer and Martin Bulmer, "Philanthropy and Social Science in the 1920's: Beardsley Ruml and the Laura Spelman Rockefeller Memorial, 1922–29," *Minerva*, XIX (1981): 347–407; and Fosdick, *Story of the Rockefeller Foundation*, 194–202.

42. Further information about Moe's career during the 1920s can be found in Coben, "American Foundations as Patrons of Science," 237–39, 242–43; Lomask, *Seed Money;* and in the Moe Papers. Most of Moe's administrative papers, however, remain closed to scholars by the Guggenheim Foundation, which retains them.

The list of later eminent Guggenheim Fellows was taken from "John Simon Guggenheim Memorial Foundation, Some Fellows of Past Years in Various Fields," undated document in the Moe Papers, Box M722, folder #13, American Philosophical Society, Philadelphia. The foundation selected very few female Fellows until its second decade when Martha Graham, Gwendolyn Brooks, Marjoire Hope Nicholson, Violet Barbour, and Eudora Welty were among those chosen, "John Simon Guggenheim Memorial Foundation."

4. The Problem of the Twentieth Century

1. See Chapter 1, pp. 27–31, concerning the Victorian color caste system.

2. E. Franklin Frazier, *Black Bourgeoisie* (New York: Collier, 1962); Oliver C. Cox, *Caste, Class and Race: A Study in Social Dynamics* (Garden City, N.Y.: Doubleday, 1948); W. E. B. Du Bois, *Philadelphia Negro: A Social Study* (Philadelphia,

Univ. of Pennsylvania Press, 1899); W. E. B. Du Bois, *Souls of Black Folk* (Chicago: A. C. McClurg, 1903); Julie Winch, *Philadelphia's Black Elite: Activism, Accommodation, and the Struggle for Autonomy: 1787–1848* (Philadelphia: Temple Univ. Press, 1988).

3. Chicago Commission on Race Relations, *The Negro in Chicago: A Study of Race Relations and a Race Riot* (Chicago: Univ. of Chicago Press, 1922); William M. Tuttle, Jr., *Race Riot: Chicago in the Red Summer of 1919* (New York: Atheneum, 1972); Herbert J. Seligman, *The Negro Faces America* (New York: Harper and Bros., 1920); Arthur I. Waskow, *From Race Riot to Sit In* (Garden City, N.Y.: Doubleday, 1966); August Meier, *Negro Thought in America, 1880–1915* (Ann Arbor: Univ. of Michigan Press, 1963).

4. U.S. Department of Commerce, Bureau of the Census, *Historical Statistics of the United States, Colonial Times to 1970* (Washington, D.C.: Government Printing Office, 1975), I: 22–23; Charles S. Johnson, *The Shadow of the Plantation* (Chicago: Univ. of Chicago Press, 1966); Emmett J. Scott, *Negro Migration During the War* (New York: Oxford Univ. Press, 1920); Scott, "Letters of Negro Migrants of 1916–18," *Journal of Negro History*, IV (July 1919): 290–340; Scott, "Additional Letters of Negro Migrants of 1916–18," *Journal of Negro History*, IV (Oct. 1919), 412–65; Louise Venable Kennedy, *The Negro Peasant Turns Cityward: Effects of Recent Migrations to Northern Centers* (New York: Columbia Univ. Press, 1934); Kennedy and Frank A. Ross, *A Bibliography of Negro Migration* (New York: Columbia Univ. Press, 1922); Thomas J. Woofter, *Negro Migration* (New York: W. D. Gray, 1922); Woofter, *Negro Problems in Cities* (Garden City, N.Y.: Doubleday, 1928); Mary White Ovington, *Half a Man: The Status of the Negro in New York* (New York: Longmans, Green, 1911); Chicago Commission on Race Relations, *Negro in Chicago;* U.S. Bureau of the Census, *Negro Population: 1790–1915* (Washington, D.C.: Government Printing Office, 1918), Introduction.

5. Du Bois, *Souls of Black Folk*, reprinted in *Three Negro Classics* (New York: Avon, 1965). The quotations are from pp. 282, and 312–15 of this edition respectively.

6. See note 4 above.

7. Stanley Coben, "The Failure of the Melting Pot," in Gary Nash and Richard Weiss, eds., *The Great Fear* (New York: Holt, Rinehart and Winston, 1970), 144–64.

8. U.S. Department of Labor, Division of Negro Economics, *Negro Migration in 1916–17* (Washington, D.C.: Government Printing Office, 1919), 33.

9. U.S. Department of Commerce, Bureau of the Census, *Historical Statistics*, I: 22–23.

10. See notes 4 and 8 above. Walter Laidlaw, ed., *Population of the City of New York 1890–1930* (New York: City Census Committee, 1932); Laidlaw, ed., *Statistical Sources for Demographic Studies of Greater New York* (New York: The New York City 1920 Census Committee, Inc., 1923); New York City Tenement House Department, *Tenth Report 1918–29* (New York: Martin Brown Press, 1929); Gilbert Osofsky, *Harlem: The Making of a Ghetto* (New York: Scribner's, 1963); Seth M. Scheiner, *Negro Mecca: A History of the Negro in New York City, 1865–1920* (New

York: New York Univ. Press, 1965); U.S. Department of Commerce, Bureau of the Census, *Negroes in the United States, 1920–32* (Washington, D.C.: Government Printing Office, 1935); Allan H. Spear, *Black Chicago: The Making of a Negro Ghetto 1890–1920* (Chicago: Univ. of Chicago Press, 1967); Reynolds Farley, "The Urbanization of Negroes in the United States," *Journal of Social History*, I (Spring 1968): 50.

11. Osofsky, *Harlem*, 83–123; James Weldon Johnson, *Black Manhattan* (New York: Knopf, 1930), 145–59; Roy Ottley and William J. Weatherby, eds., *The Negro in New York: An Informal Social History, 1626–1940* (New York: Praeger, 1967), 183–88. This informative volume was edited from manuscripts originally prepared by the WPA Federal Writers Project under the working title, "Harlem—The Negroes of New York! An Informal Social History." A related process in Chicago can be followed in Spear, *Black Chicago*, 11–27, 129–66. Some of the difficulties blacks encountered during these efforts are described in Coben, "The Failure of the Melting Pot"; Osofsky, *Harlem*, 105–10; Spear, *Black Chicago*, 201–22; Scheiner, *Negro Mecca*, 113–36; and Kenneth L. Kusmer, *A Ghetto Takes Shape* (Urbana: Univ. of Illinois Press, 1976) on the Cleveland black ghetto.

12. James Weldon Johnson, "Harlem: The Culture Capital," in Alain Locke, ed., *The New Negro* (New York: Albert and Charles Boni, 1925), 301–2. Johnson elaborated on this theme in his *Black Manhattan*, 145–48; and in an article (clipping in his scrapbook), "New York *Age*: Views and Reviews, 1920–23," dated Jan. 10, 1920, headed "The Future Harlem," James Weldon Johnson Scrapbooks, p. 4, James Weldon Johnson Papers, Yale Univ. Library.

13. Osofsky, *Harlem*, 136–43; New York Urban League, "Twenty-Four Hundred Negro Families in Harlem: An Interpretation of the Living Conditions of Small Wage Earners," unpublished manuscript, Schomberg Library, New York City, dated 1923.

14. E. K. Jones, "The Negro's Struggle for Health," *Proceedings of the National Council on Social Work, 1923* (Chicago: Univ. of Chicago Press, 1923), 68–72; New York State, Commission of Housing and Regional Planning, *Report . . . to Governor Alfred E. Smith and to the Legislature . . . on the Present Housing Emergency, December 12, 1923* (Albany, N.Y.: J. B. Lyon, 1924); New York City Tenement House Department, *Tenth Report, 1918–29;* Spear, *Black Chicago;* Benjamin Brawley, *A Social History of the American Negro* (New York: Macmillan, 1921), especially 299.

15. Daniel Mason Gregory, "Stravinsky as a Symptom," *American Mercury*, 4 (Apr. 1925): 465–68.

16. "Stokowski Defends Jazz," *New York Times*, May 16, 1924. My explanation of why whites entered black areas of cities in order to hear "real" jazz owes much to conversations and correspondence with Professor Harold R. Battiste, Jr., Jazz Studies Program, Department of Music, Univ. of New Orleans, especially Battiste to the author, Nov. 10, 1989.

17. Gunther Schuller, *Early Jazz: Its Roots and Musical Developments* (New York: Oxford Univ. Press, 1968), 203–4.

18. Schuller, *Early Jazz*, 54.

19. "Why Jazz Sends Us Back to the Jungle," *Current Opinion*, LXV (Sept.

1918): 165; "Jazz," *Living Age*, CCCVI (July 21, 1920): 280–81. These themes and the related ideas mentioned below are ubiquitous among the objections to jazz cited in Neil Leonard, *Jazz and the White Americans* (Chicago: Univ. of Chicago Press, 1962), Chapter II, "Traditionalist Opposition," 29–46.

20. Clive Bell, "Plus De Jazz," *New Republic*, XXVIII (Sept. 21, 1921): 92–96; "Jazz Played Out," *Literary Digest*, LXX (Jan. 14, 1922): 27.

21. "Where the *Étude* Stands on Jazz," *Étude*, 42 (Aug. 1924): 514–20; "Where is Jazz Leading America," *Ibid.* (Sept. 1924), 595.

22. "Accursed Jazz—An English View," *Literary Digest*, 91 (Oct. 2, 1926): 28.

23. Schuller, *Early Jazz*, 10.

24. A. M. Jones, *Studies in African Music* (London: Oxford Univ. Press, 1959). The quotation is from Jones, *Studies in African Music*, I: 38. Schuller points out that Jones lived in Africa for a large portion of his life and obtained opinions from African master musicians about his transcriptions of their music and his analyses of these. Thus, his volumes incorporate African perspectives, which saved him from many of the most common errors in earlier studies of African music, Schuller, *Early Jazz*, 10. Also see Francis Bebey, *African Music: A People's Art* (Westport: Lawrence Hill and Co., 1975; English translation).

25. A large literature on this topic exists now. Good starting points are Henry Louis Gates, Jr., *The Signifying Monkey* (New York: Oxford Univ. Press, 1988), especially 63–64, 100–105, and particularly 123–24; Robert Farris Thompson, *Flash of the Spirit: African and Afro-American Art and Philosophy* (New York: Random House, 1983); Paul Oliver, *Savannah Syncopators: African Retentions in the Blues* (New York: Stein and Day, 1970); Samuel Charters, *The Roots of the Blues: An African Search* (New York: Perigee Books, 1981); Richard A. Waterman, "African Influences on the Music of the Americas," in Charlotte M. Otten, ed., *Anthropology and Art: Readings in Cross-cultural Aesthetics* (Garden City, N.Y.: Natural History Press, 1971), 227–44.

26. For this discussion of the development of jazz and blues artists, I have depended largely on transcripts, tapes, and summaries of interviews at Tulane University's Archive of New Orleans Jazz, which is not limited to musicians born or raised in New Orleans. I am grateful for the friendly assistance provided by the staff, particularly by Connie Griffith, director of Special Collections, and by Richard Binion Allen, curator of the Archive of New Orleans Jazz. Most published autobiographies and biographies of jazz musicians verify the patterns discussed here. Especially see the taped and transcribed autobiography of Jelly Roll Morton, conducted and edited by Alan Lomax, *Mister Jelly Roll*, 2d ed. (Berkeley: Univ. of California Press, 1973).

27. Mezz Mezzrow, *Really the Blues* (New York: Random House, 1946), 2–3, 15; for a story similar in many respects to Mezzrow's, see Max Kaminsky, *My Life in Jazz* (New York: Harper, 1963). The discussion of Teagarten's early career is taken from his taped interview in the Tulane Archive of New Orleans Jazz. Also see the taped interview with trumpeter Harry James, who, like Teagarten, learned to play jazz while growing up in Texas.

28. These conclusions were drawn largely from my own discussions with jazz

musicians, including their recollections of earlier musicians. Again, I am indebted especially to conversations with Harold R. Battiste, Jr., during 1988–89. The same conclusions could be abstracted from published autobiographies. For a particularly good example, see Sidney Bechet, *Treat it Gentle, An Autobiography*, (New York: Da Capo, 1978; original edition, New York: Twayne, 1960).

29. Martin Williams, "King Oliver in New York," RCA Vintage LPV-529, reprinted in Williams, *Jazz in Its Time* (New York: Oxford Univ. Press, 1989), 173–77.

30. This computer study was carried out with the skillful assistance of my research assistant William Barth, using information in directories of jazz and blues artists such as John Chilton, *Who's Who of Jazz: Storyville to Swing Street* (Philadelphia: Chilton Book Company, 1972; first published in London by Bloomsbury Book Shop in 1970).

31. Nathan Irvin Huggins, *Harlem Renaissance* (New York: Oxford Univ. Press, 1971), 9–11.

32. Langston Hughes, "Negro Artist and the Racial Mountain," *Nation*, 122 (June 16, 1926): 662–63. Hughes's most recent biographer, Arnold Rampersad considers "Negro Artist and the Racial Mountain" "the finest essay of Hughes' life," *The Life of Langston Hughes*, I, *1902–41. I Too Sing America* (New York: Oxford Univ. Press, 1986), 130–31.

33. Langston Hughes, *Fine Clothes to the Jew* (New York: Knopf, 1927), 21, 41, 82, 84. The influence of the oral-blues tradition on Hughes's poetry is discussed comprehensively in Steven C. Tracy, *Langston Hughes and the Blues* (Urbana: Univ. of Illinois Press, 1988).

34. The development of my opinions about Garvey and Du Bois was assisted by the Center for Afro-American Studies at UCLA which generously provided funds for my research concerning these men. My opinions have been informed also by reading Tolbert, *The UNIA and Black Los Angeles* (Los Angeles: Center for Afro-American Studies, Univ. of California, Los Angeles, 1980). This book still is the only lengthy study of UNIA division.

35. Du Bois's theories about a distinct black culture and, to some extent, black education have been evaluated from a recent perspective in Darwin T. Turner, "W. E. B. Du Bois and the Theory of a Black Aesthetic"; and Wilson J. Moses, "The Poetics of Ethiopianism: W. E. B. Du Bois's Struggle to Reconcile Folk and High Art," both reprinted in William L. Andrews, *Critical Essays on W. E. B. Du Bois* (Boston: G. K. Hall, 1985), 73–122. See also, Du Bois, "The Negro in Literature and Art," *Annals of the American Academy of Political and Social Science;* XLIX (Sept. 1913): 233–37; Du Bois, "Criteria of Negro Art," *Crisis*, XXXII (Oct. 1926): 290–97; and Du Bois, "Negro Art," *Crisis*, XXIII (June 1921): 55–56.

A good example of Du Bois's ideas about the education of black youth can be found in Herbert Aptheker, ed., *W. E. B. Du Bois, The Education of Black People: Ten Critiques 1906–60* (Amherst: The Univ. of Massachusetts Press, 1973).

36. The destruction of most of Garvey's personal records and those of the UNIA and BSL are described in Judith Stein, *The World of Marcus Garvey: Race and Class in Modern Society* (Baton Rouge: Louisiana State Univ. Press, 1986), 2. Stein states

accurately that "The incomplete record, the accidental survival of papers that might not be representative, and the heavy weight of [dubious] sources from government investigatory bodies makes writing about Garvey a hazardous undertaking."

37. Robert A. Hill, ed., *The Marcus Garvey and Universal Negro Improvement Association Papers, I, 1826–August 1919* (Berkeley: Univ. of California Press, 1983), 94, 95–99, 112, 532–36. The quotation is from the Kingston *Daily Gleaner*, Feb. 17, 1930, p. 12, which was given to me by Boyd James. It is reprinted in Hill, ed., *Garvey and UNIA Papers*, I: 94; Amy Jacques Garvey, "The Early Years of Marcus Garvey," in John Henrik Clarke, *Marcus Garvey and the Vision of Africa* (New York: Random House, 1974), 32–33.

38. Stein, *World of Marcus Garvey*, 64–72, 78–85; Amy Jacques Garvey, *Garvey and Garveyism* (London: Collier-Macmillan, 1963), 34.

39. Stein, *World of Marcus Garvey*, 78–84; *Negro World*, Aug. 1, 1920. The stock circular and advertisement are quoted in E. David Cronon, *Black Moses: The Story of Marcus Garvey* (Madison: Univ. of Wisconsin Press, 1955), 51–52, 77–78.

40. Hill, ed. *Garvey and the UNIA Papers*, I: 452–53.

41. Stein, *World of Marcus Garvey*, 89–104; Cronon, *Black Moses*, 57–60.

42. Stein, *World of Marcus Garvey*, 94–98; Cronon, *Black Moses*, 84–92; Tony Martin, *Race First: The Ideological and Organizational Struggles of Marcus Garvey and the Universal Negro Improvement Association* (Westport: Greenwood Press, 1976), 156–60. The BSL circular is reprinted in Hill, ed., *Garvey and the UNIA Papers*, III: 441.

43. Stein, *World of Marcus Garvey*, 93–98, 137, 153.

44. Cronon, *Black Moses*, 78–79; Stein, *World of Marcus Garvey*, 77–78, 93–98; Martin, *Race First*, 153–59.

45. My account of this convention is derived from the *Negro World*, July–Sept. 1920; *New York Times*, Aug. 2–Sept. 1, 1920; New York *Age*, Sept. 2, 1920; New York *World*, Aug. 2–5, 1920; First International Convention of the Negro Peoples of the World, "Convention Program," UNIA Central Division Papers, UNIA Papers, New York Public Library, Schomburg Center for Research in Black Culture, New York City. The quotation from Garvey's convention speech on Aug. 2 is from the *New York Times*, Aug. 3, 1920. The "Declaration of Rights . . ." is reprinted in Amy Jacques Garvey, *Philosophy and Opinions of Marcus Garvey* (New York: Universal Publishing House, 1923), 2, 135–43.

46. Tolbert, *UNIA and Black Los Angeles*, 58–66; *New York Times*, Jan. 13, 1922; *Negro World*, June 13 and July 8, 1923; *New York Times*, June 19, 21, 22, 1923; Stein, *World of Marcus Garvey*, 135, 192–204, 206–7. Stein found the efforts of the Department of Justice to bring about Garvey's arrest and deportation ineffective. Stein, *World of Marcus Garvey*, 137. The associates indicted with Garvey were found not guilty.

47. Du Bois, *Souls of Black Folk*, 221; Vincent Harding, "A Black Messianic Visionary," in Rayford W. Logan, ed., *W. E. B. Du Bois, a Profile* (New York: Hill and Wang, 1971), 274–93; Du Bois, *Dusk of Dawn*, 199, 220, 268; Du Bois, *The Autobiography of W. E. B. Du Bois*, 216–19; B. Joyce Ross, *J. E. Spingarn and the Rise of the N.A.A.C.P., 1911–1929* (New York: Atheneum, 1972), 65.

48. Herbert Aptheker, ed., *The Correspondence of W. E. B. Du Bois*, I, *Selections, 1877–1934* (Amherst: Univ. of Massachusetts Press, 1973), 214–15.

49. Aptheker, ed., *Correspondence of Du Bois*, I: 245–46.

50. W. E. B. Du Bois, "Marcus Garvey," *Crisis*, XXI (Dec. 1920): 58–60 and XXI (Jan. 1921), 112–15. For Garvey's apparently vindictive response to these articles, see Manning Marable, *W. E. B. Du Bois: Black Radical Democrat* (Boston: Twains Publishers, 1986), 117. Du Bois continued to view Garvey's "plan to unite Negrodom by a line of steamships" as a "brilliant suggestion" even after the demise of the BSL. Du Bois looked into the possibility of starting such a line himself in Jan. 1921. Stein, *World of Marcus Garvey*, 84. After Garvey's deportation, Du Bois wrote: "When Garvey was sent to Atlanta, no word or action of ours accomplished the result. . . . We have, today, no enmity against Marcus Garvey. He has a great and worthy dream." Du Bois, *Autobiography*, 273–74.

51. Du Bois to J. Spingarn, Oct. 28, 1914; preceded by an earlier exchange of letters related to the same subjects, Du Bois to Spingarn, Oct. 23, 1914; J. Spingarn to Du Bois, Oct. 24, 1914—all in Joel Spingarn file, Papers of W. E. B. Du Bois, Fisk Univ. Ross, *Spingarn*, 61–65, discusses the relationship between Du Bois and Spingarn. Spingarn had been persuaded to accept the board chairmanship—then the most powerful position in the NAACP—not long before this correspondence with Du Bois.

52. Editorial, "Close Ranks," *Crisis*, XVI (July 1918): 111. Du Bois repented this article before the war ended and later attributed much of his temporary patriotism to Joel Spingarn's enthusiasm. *Dusk of Dawn*, 253–56. Du Bois describes the War Department's request for his own enlistment in *Dusk of Dawn*, 256–58. Du Bois's wartime activities are sketched in Broderick, *Du Bois*, 106–12. Spingarn's efforts to gain a commission for Du Bois are described in Ross, *Spingarn*, 98–101. Du Bois describes his wartime and postwar alienation in his *Autobiography*, 274; and in *Dusk of Dawn*, 262.

53. Du Bois, *Darkwater*, "The Riddle of the Sphinx," 53–54.

54. Du Bois, *Darkwater*, "The Hands of Ethiopia," 56–74. The quotations are from pp. 60–61.

5. The Dilemma of American Feminists

1. Stanton and Blatch, eds. *Stanton, Letters, Diary and Reminiscences*, II: 59–60. Alma Lutz, *Crusade for Freedom: Women of the Antislavery Movement* (Boston: Beacon Press, 1968), 162, 242. On Sept. 20, 1855, Stanton wrote to a feminist friend about a recent conversation with her father: "He asked me: 'Elizabeth, are you getting ready to lecture before lyceums?' 'Yes, Sir,' I answered. 'I hope,' he continued, 'you will never do it during my lifetime, for if you do, be assured of one thing. Your first lecture will be a very expensive one.'" Stanton and Blatch, eds., *Stanton, Letters, Diary and Reminiscences*, II: 61.

2. Du Bois, *Feminism and Suffrage*, 28.

3. *Ibid.*, 27–28.

4. Stanton, *Eighty Years and More*, 78–83; Kraditor, *The Ideas of the Woman Suffrage Movement, 1890–1920* (New York: Columbia Univ. Press, 1965), 1–3.

5. Stanton, *Eighty Years and More*, 148–49; *Proceedings of the Women's Rights Conventions, held at Seneca Falls and Rochester, New York, July and August, 1848* (New York: R. J. Johnston, 1870); Du Bois, *Feminism and Suffrage*, 23–24; Eleanor Flexner, *Century of Struggle: The Woman's Rights Movement in the United States* (Cambridge: Harvard Univ. Press, 1959), 74–77.

6. Flexner, *Century of Struggle*, 76–77.

7. *Proceedings of the Women's Rights Conventions . . . 1848*; Flexner, *Century of Struggle*, 75.

8. Du Bois, *Feminism and Suffrage*, 27–28. For Anthony's letter to Stanton, see Stanton and Blatch, eds., *Stanton, Letters, Diary and Reminiscences*, II: 64–66.

9. "The Ballot—Bread, Virtue, Power," *Revolution*, I (Jan. 8, 1868); *Revolution*, I (Jan. 22, 1868). *Revolution* was edited and published by Anthony and Stanton from Jan. 1868 to May 1970. On the breadth of the topics it covered, see Flexner, *Century of Struggle*, 150–51. Stanton's letter to Anthony is quoted in Stanton's diary entry of Dec. 3, 1899, reprinted in Stanton and Blatch, eds., *Stanton, Letters, Diary and Reminiscences*, II: 346. For Stanton's views in 1876 of women's progress toward achieving the demands in the 1848 "Declaration of Sentiments," see Lutz, *Created Equal*, 238–39. Stanton declared in 1876 that "I feel the degradation of sex more bitterly than I did on July 19, 1848."

10. Du Bois, *Feminism and Suffrage*, 163–64; 201–2. Inclusion of the word "male" in section two of the Fourteenth Amendment prevented use of the amendment to enfranchise women.

11. U.S. Congress, Senate, *Arguments Before the Committee on Privileges and Elections of the United States Senate in Behalf of a Sixteenth Amendment to the Constitution of the United States Prohibiting the Several States from Disenfranchising United States Citizens on Account of Sex, January 11 and 12, 1878* (Washington: Government Printing Office, 1878), 44.

12. U.S. Department of the Interior, Census Office, *Ninth Census: The Statistics of the Wealth and Industry of the United States* (Washington: Government Printing Office, 1872), Part III: 831–42, especially Table 20; U.S. Department of the Interior, Census Office, *Compendium of the Tenth Census: June 1, 1880* (Washington: Government Printing Office, 1883), especially Part II: 1368–77, Table CIII; U.S. Department of the Interior, Census Office, *Report on the Population of the United States at the Eleventh Census, 1890* (Washington: Government Printing Office, 1895), Part II, especially Table 78 and pp. 304–5; Kraditor, *Ideas of the Woman Suffrage Movement*, 5–6; Carl Degler, *At Odds*, 178–209, 307–15, 377. Alice Kessler-Harris, *Out to Work: A History of Wage-Earning Women in the United States* (New York: Oxford Univ. Press, 1982), 118–19.

13. Kraditor, *Ideas of the Woman Suffrage Movement*, 3–4; Flexner, *Century of Struggle*, 151–52, 219–20; Du Bois, *Feminism and Suffrage*, 163–64, 188–200.

14. Kraditor, *Ideas of the Woman Suffrage Movement*, 6–7.

15. Carrie Chapman Catt and Nettie Rogers Shuler, *Woman Suffrage and Politics*

(New York: Charles Scribner & Sons, 1923) 107–31, 227–34; Flexner, *Century of Struggle*, 175, 262–63; Kraditor, *Ideas of the Woman Suffrage Movement*, 4–5.

16. David Mitchell, *The Fighting Pankhursts: A Study in Tenacity* (London: Jonathan Cape, 1967), 32–33; Christine A. Lunardini, *From Equal Suffrage to Equal Rights: Alice Paul and the National Woman's Party, 1910–1928* (New York: New York Univ. Press, 1986), 5–9, 13–17.

17. Lunardini, *Equal Suffrage to Equal Rights*, 4–5, 20–21.

18. *Ibid.*, 1–17.

19. Kraditor, *Ideas of the Woman Suffrage Movement*, 239–40.

20. Christine A. Lunardini and Thomas A. Knock, "Woodrow Wilson and Woman Suffrage: A New Look," *Political Science Quarterly*, XCV (Winter 1980–81): 655–71.

21. Interviews by the author with Alice Paul, July 1–3, 1971, Washington, D.C. (hereafter referred to as Coben, Interviews with Paul); Lunardini, *Equal Suffrage to Equal Rights*, 25–31; 63rd Cong., 1st Sess., *Report of the Committee on the District of Columbia, United States Senate, Pursuant to Senate Resolution 499 of March 4, 1913, Directing Said Committee to Investigate the Conduct of the District Police and the Police Department of the District of Columbia in Connection with the Woman Suffrage Parade on March 3, 1913*, Senate Report No. 53, May 29, 1913 (Washington: Government Printing Office, 1913); Harriot Stanton Blatch and Alma Lutz, *Challenging Years: The Memoirs of Harriot Stanton Blatch* (New York: G. P. Putnam's Sons, 1940), 194–97.

22. Catt and Shuler, *Woman Suffrage and Politics*, 244–46; Lunardini, *Equal Suffrage to Equal Rights*, 41–49; Flexner, *Century of Struggle*, 265–70; Blatz and Lutz, *Challenging Years*, 244–51.

23. Jacqueline Van Voris, *Carrie Chapman Catt: A Public Life* (New York: Feminist Press, 1987), 120–21.

24. Coben, Interviews with Paul; Lunardini, *Equal Suffrage to Equal Rights*, 123; Catt and Shuler, *Woman Suffrage and Politics*, 242–43. On Jan. 10, 1916, Catt wrote to presidents of NAWSA state suffrage organizations: "There is no doubt but that the Congressional Union has pushed the Federal Government to the front, no matter what anybody says about it." The quotation is from Flexner, *Century of Struggle*, 366 n. 10.

25. Doris Stevens, *Jailed for Freedom* (New York: Boni and Liveright, 1920), 91–157; Lunardini, *Equal Suffrage to Equal Rights*, 121–37, 141, 145–46; Sherna Gluck, ed., *From Parlor to Prison: Five American Suffragists Talk about Their Lives* (New York: Random House, 1976), 244–45; Blatch and Lutz, *Challenging Years*, 274–82.

26. Arthur S. Link, *Wilson: The Road to the White House* (Princeton: Princeton Univ. Press, 1947), 2, 322–23, 519; Link, *Wilson: The New Freedom* (Princeton: Princeton Univ. Press, 1956), 257–58; Lunardini, *Equal Suffrage to Equal Rights*, 99–101, 123–24.

27. Wilson's intercession may also have been decisive in the House of Representatives' vote on the suffrage amendment. Lunardini, *Equal Suffrage to Equal Rights*, 139–49.

28. *Suffragist*, X (Jan.–Feb. 1921), special convention issue.

29. Jill Conway, "Women Reformers and American Culture, 1870–1930," *Journal of Social History*, V (Winter 1971–72): 164.

30. U.S. Department of Commerce, Bureau of the Census, *Fifteenth Census of the United States: 1930*, V, *General Report on Occupations* (Washington: Government Printing Office, 1933), "Sex and Occupations of Gainful Workers . . . for the United States: 1930, 1920, and 1910," 38–61; Janet M. Hooks, *Women's Occupations Through Seven Decades*, U.S. Department of Labor, Women's Bureau Bulletin No. 218 (Washington: Government Printing Office, 1947), 214–22.

31. Washington *Evening Star*, Nov. 9, 1922. The story headed "Stunning Blow Dealt Women Politicians" was copyrighted by the Consolidated Press.

32. U.S. Office of Education, *Biennial Survey of Education* (Washington: Government Printing Office, 1929), 698–99; Mabel Newcomber, *A Century of Higher Education for American Women* (New York: Harper, 1959), 46; Jessie Bernard, *Academic Women* (University Park, Pa.: Pennsylvania State Univ. Press, 1964), 69–71, 73, 126.

33. Virginia C. Gildersleeve, "The College Girl of the Crisis," unpublished manuscript of address delivered Feb. 4, 1934, Virginia C. Gildersleeve Papers, Columbia Univ. Library; Bernard, *Academic Women*, 36; Jessie Bernard to the author, Nov. 6, 1975. For Dean Gildersleeve's efforts to win admission for Barnard College students to Columbia's graduate departments, see Gildersleeve, *Many a Good Crusade: Memoirs of Virginia Croceron Gildersleeve* (New York: Macmillan, 1954), 97–109.

34. Ella Lonn, "Academic Status of Women on University Faculties," *Journal of the American Association of University Women*, XVII (Jan.–Mar. 1924): 5–11.

35. For these advertisements, see *Good Housekeeping*, 88 (Jan. 1929): 183, 189, 128, 121, 147; *McCall's*, LVI (Aug. 1926): 53, 66.

36. *Women Lawyer's Journal*, XV (Apr. 1924): 4.

37. Hill, *Women in Gainful Occupations, 1870–1920*, 36–44; Bureau of the Census, "Sex and Occupations . . . 1930, 1920, and 1910," 38–61; Janet M. Hooks, *Women's Occupations Through Seven Decades*, 214–22.

38. *Proceedings of the Women's Rights Conventions . . . 1848*, "Declaration of Sentiments," reprinted in *Equal Rights*, I (Feb. 24, 1923): 6. The resolutions adopted by the 1848 convention are reprinted on the same page. "The Ballot—Bread, Virtue, Power," *Revolution*, I (Jan. 8, 1868).

39. Christine A. Lunardini, *Equal Suffrage to Equal Rights*, 152–53, 202; Coben, Interviews with Paul; "Conversations with Alice Paul: Woman Suffrage and the Equal Rights Amendment," interviewed by Amelia Fry, 1972–73, Suffragists Oral History Project, Bancroft Library, Univ. of California, Berkeley (1976), 256 (hereafter, Fry, Paul Interview).

40. *Suffragist*, VIII (Sept. 1920): 191. Before the convention met, the NWP Executive Committee already had committed itself to working for an ERA. *National Executive Committee Minutes*, Jan. 21, 1921, NWP Papers, Library of Congress.

41. "Report of the National Convention of the National Woman's Party, February 15–18, 1921," NWP Papers, Library of Congress.

42. "What Next," *Suffragist*, VIII (Oct. 1920): 235; Kelley and Josephine Gold-

mark had persuaded Louis D. Brandeis in 1907 to defend an Oregon eight-hour-day law for women before the U.S. Supreme Court. Aided by Kelley and Goldmark—Brandeis's sister-in-law—especially, Brandeis had presented evidence of women's physical and emotional weaknesses, their deficiencies in powers of "persistent attention and application," and the consequences of these for female workers. This unique brief, filed in *Muller v. Oregon*, 208 U.S. 412 (1908), became known as the first "Brandeis Brief." Brandeis's victory in court, in a decision handed down Feb. 24, 1908, established the constitutionality of protective legislation for women and children. Josephine Goldmark, *Impatient Crusader: Florence Kelley's Life Story* (Urbana: Univ. of Illinois Press, 1953), 51–65; Eleanor Flexner, *Century of Struggle*, 214–15; Judith A. Baer, *The Chains of Protection: The Judicial Response to Women's Labor Legislation* (Westport: Greenwood Press, 1978), 57–61, 75–76. Baer's is the most thorough examination of Brandeis's arguments and their consequences.

43. "Report of the National Convention of the NWP . . . 1921," NWP Papers, Library of Congress; Blanche Wiesan Cook, ed., *Crystal Eastman on Women and Revolution* (New York: Oxford Univ. Press, 1978), 60–63.

44. "Report of the National Convention of the NWP . . . 1921," NWP Papers, Library of Congress.

45. Lunardini, *Equal Suffrage to Equal Rights*, 162.

46. Fry, Paul Interview, 265–66. In 1943, Paul revised the proposed amendment for submission to the Senate Judiciary Committee. This final draft stated: "Equality of rights under the law shall not be denied or abridged by the United States or by any State on account of sex."

47. *Equal Rights*, XI (Feb. 16, 1924): 2; XI (Feb. 23, 1924): 11.

48. *Journal of the American Association of University Women*, XVIII (Mar. 1924): 21–28.

49. Editorial, "Which Will be the Next?" *Equal Rights*, XI (May 10, 1924): 99–100.

50. J. Stanley Lemons, *The Woman Citizen: Social Feminism in the 1920's* (Urbana: Univ. of Illinois Press, 1973), 200–204.

51. Lemons, *Woman Citizen*, 203–4.

52. Coben, Interviews with Paul; 68th Cong., 2d Sess., U.S. House of Representatives, Committee on the Judiciary, *Hearing on H. J. Res., Equal Rights Amendment to the Constitution*, testimony by NWP witnesses, 1–42. Powerful arguments against protective legislation can be found also in Harriot Stanton Blatch, "Do Women Want Protection? Wrapping Women in Cotton-Wool," the *Nation*, CXXVI (Jan. 31, 1923), 115–16; and in Blatch and Lutz, *Challenging Years*, 320–35, which includes a portion of Blatch's article in the *Nation*.

53. House Judiciary Committee, *Hearing on . . . Equal Rights Amendment*, 42–43. Catt's role in organizing the League of Women Voters is described in Van Voris, *Catt*, 153–58. Nancy F. Cott relates the arguments during the 1920s between advocates of "equal rights" and "special protections" for females to recent divisions within the women's liberation movement in Nancy F. Cott, "Feminist Theory and Feminist Movements: The Past Before Us," in Juliet Mitchell and Ann Oakley,

eds., *What is Feminism: A Reexamination* (New York: Pantheon Books, 1986), 49–62, especially 55–60.

54. House Judiciary Committee, *Hearing on . . . Equal Rights Amendment*, 44. Alice Paul declared: "We were [laughing] really *thunderstruck* when we heard . . . that they wanted to preserve their alimony. Of course they could [already] have alimony given to the husband, and it has been given to the husbands over and over again since." Fry, Paul Interview, 450. Also, see Baer, *Chains of Protection*, 4–5, 108–9, 216.

55. Susan M. Hartmann, *From Margin to Mainstream: American Women and Politics Since 1960* (New York: Knopf, 1989), 113–14; Carol C. Parr, "Women in the Military," in Irene Tinker, ed., *Women in Washington: Advocates for Public Policy* (Beverly Hills: Sage Publications, 1983), 240–41. On child-support payments, see Hartman, *From Margin to Mainstram*, 159, 164.

56. House Judiciary Committee, *Hearing on . . . Equal Rights Amendment*, 56, 58.

57. *Ibid.*, 64–80.

58. *Ibid.*, 89–91.

59. 70th Cong., 2d Sess., U.S. Senate Subcommittee of the Committee on the Judiciary, *S. J. 64, A Joint Resolution Proposing an Amendment to the Constitution of the United States Relative to Equal Rights for Men and Women, February 1, 1929*, p. 23. The subcommittee was composed of Senator Charles W. Waterman of Colorado, acting as chairman; Senator Frederick Steiwer of Oregon; and Senator M. M. Neely of West Virginia.

60. *Ibid.*, 66–67.

61. *Ibid.*, 56.

62. For a discussion of the sculpture of the ideal woman in *An Old-Fashioned Girl*, see Ch. 1, p. 21. Just after she published the first magazine supplement of *Little Women*, Louisa May Alcott attended the founding convention of the New England Woman Suffrage Association in 1868. Du Bois, *Feminism and Suffrage*, 168. In a letter to Lucy Stone in 1885, Alcott declared: "It is a great cross to me that ill health and home duties prevent my devoting heart, pen and time to this most vital question [woman suffrage] of the age." Alcott to Lucy Stone, Aug. 31, 1885, the Papers of Alma Lutz, the Arthur and Elizabeth Schlesinger Library on the History of Women in America, Radcliffe College, Cambridge, Massachusetts.

63. Lunardini, *Equal Suffrage to Equal Rights*, 169–70. Paul sent an emissary to Eleanor Roosevelt in 1936 because, she believed, "As one observes her work in the White House one cannot but feel that she belongs with us and not against us." Cott, *The Grounding of Modern Feminism* (New Haven: Yale Univ. Press, 1977), 364.

64. Cynthia Harrison, *On Account of Sex: The Politics of Women's Issues, 1945–1968* (Berkeley and Los Angeles: Univ. of California Press, 1988); Gallup poll, "Equality: the Enemy is Within," *Los Angeles Times*, Apr. 22, 1976, Part IV, 5. This poll found that men favored the ERA in a proportion greater than did women. It found also that 60 percent of women in the nationwide sample and 63 percent of men preferred to work for a man. Also, see Hartmann, *From Margin to Mainstream*, 160, 184–85, 189–90, about attitudes of women in the 1980s; and Jane J. Mansbridge, *Why We Lost the ERA* (Chicago: Univ. of Chicago Press, 1986), Ap-

pendix: "Support for the ERA, 1970–1982," 201–18. Mansbridge's tables show that such characteristics as gender, race, family income, occupational prestige, education, and Catholicism/Protestantism made little difference in determining support for the ERA in 1982. Categories such as Jewish or no religion, rare or no church attendance, few or no children, youth, urban habitation, and residence on the East or West coasts *did* make a difference.

6. Toward a New Economic and Political Order

1. The separation of economic policy from Victorian virtues was carried forward by the New Deal. The New Deal also brought together the major segments of La Follette's coalition, See pp. 134–35; n. 70, 197.

For an excellent symposium on the question of why the United States lacks a strong labor, farmer-labor, or socialist political party, see John H. Laslett and Seymour Martin Lipset, eds., *Failure of a Dream? Essays in the History of American Socialism* (Garden City, N.Y.: Doubleday, 1974). The movements most comparable to La Follette's—the Populist Party's 1892 presidential campaign and the Socialists at their peak behind Eugene Debs in 1912—earned significantly lower percentages of the total vote than did La Follette.

La Follette's distinguished career as a farmer-labor oriented Progressive is traced in Patrick J. Maney, *"Young Bob" La Follette* (Columbia: Univ. of Missouri Press, 1987); David P. Thelen, *Robert La Follette and the Insurgent Spirit* (Boston: Little, Brown, 1976); and Kenneth Campbell MacKay, *The Progressive Movement of 1924* (New York: Columbia Univ. Press, 1947), 123–33.

2. The history of the British Labour Party, to the point at which it became a significant political factor, can be followed in Henry Pelling, *The Origins of the Labour Party, 1880–1900* (London: Oxford Univ. Press, 1965); Beatrice Webb, *Our Partnership* (New York: Longmans, Green, 1948); Philip P. Poirier, *The Advent of the British Labour Party* (New York: Columbia Univ. Press, 1958); Norman and Jeanne MacKenzie, *The First Fabians* (London: Weidenfeld and Nicolson, 1977); and Eric Thomas Chester, *Socialists and the Ballot Box: A Historical Analysis* (New York: Praeger, 1985), 20–29.

The AFL kept abreast of developments in Great Britain through exchanges of fraternal delegates with the British labor movement. Both the British and American delegates presented reports to the AFL annual conventions, reprinted in *Report of the Proceedings of the Thirty-ninth Annual Convention of the American Federation of Labor, 1919* (Washington, D.C.: Law Reporter Printing Co., 1919), 324, 333–39, and in subsequent annual reports (hereafter referred to as *AFL Proceedings*).

3. Henry Pelling, *A Short History of the Labour Party* (London: Macmillan, 1961); C. F. Brand, *The British Labour Party* (Stanford: Stanford Univ. Press, 1964); Poirier, *Advent of the British Labour Party.*

4. *Proceedings, Third Conference for Progressive Political Action . . . February 11–12, 1924* (hereafter referred to as *Proceedings, CPPA, 1924*).

5. *Proceedings, CPPA, 1924;* Nathan Fine, *Labor and Farmer Parties in the United States, 1828–1928* (New York: Rand School, 1928), 407–8.

6. Stone to La Follette, June 25, 1923, La Follette Family Papers, Library of Congress, Series B-97 (hereafter referred to as La Follette Papers); Edward Keating, *The Story of "LABOR"* (Washington, D.C.: Edward Keating, 1923), 25.

7. Steffens to La Follette, Aug. 15, 1923, La Follette Papers, Series B-97.

8. *Labor,* Nov. 10, 1923, p. 3. The article stressed La Follette's enthusiasm for what he had observed in Europe.

9. This and the following summary of Gompers's views are taken largely from his many expressions of them in the *American Federationist,* for which he regularly wrote editorials, and from his speeches at AFL annual conventions.

10. For example, see Gompers's editorial, "Industry's Self-Determination," *American Federationist,* XXXI (May 1924): 399–402.

11. This event is described in Philip Taft, *The A.F. of L. in the Time of Gompers* (New York: Harper, 1957), 484.

12. For a more detailed account of the coal strike, its relation to other disturbances during the immediate postwar era, and to Palmer's political ambitions, see Stanley Coben, *A. Mitchell Palmer: Politician* (New York: Columbia Univ. Press, 1963; reprint, New York: DaCapo, 1972), especially pp. 177–84; and Coben, "A Study in Nativism: The American Red Scare of 1919–20," *Political Science Quarterly,* LXXIX (Mar. 1964), 52–75.

13. *AFL Proceedings, 1922,* 58, 291–96, 371–78.

14. Pelling, *Origins of the Labour Party,* 213–15.

15. *AFL Proceedings, 1922,* 292.

16. A thorough and perceptive account of this judicial assault on union activities can be found in Irving Bernstein, *The Lean Years, A History of the American Worker, 1920–33* (Boston: Houghton Mifflin, 1966; first edition, 1960), 190–242. Also, see Felix Frankfurter and Nathan Green, *The Labor Injunction* (New York: Macmillan, 1930; reprint, Gloucester: P. Smith, 1963), 253–63.

17. AFL Proceedings, 1923, 66–73, 273–74; Leonard Painter, *Through Fifty Years with the Brotherhood Railway Carmen of America* (Kansas City, Mo.: Railway Carmen, 1941), 152–72; Robert G. Zieger, "From Hostility to Moderation: Railroad Labor Policy," *Labor History,* IX (Winter 1968): 28–31; Bernstein, *Lean Years,* 211–12; John D. Hicks, *Republican Ascendancy 1921–1933* (New York: Harper, 1960), 71–73; Keating, *The Story of "LABOR",* 110–14.

18. Even before the shopmen struck, the railroad unions, angered by rejection of the Plumb Plan and enaction of the Esch-Cummins measure, participated in plans for a farmer-labor conference to discuss joint political activity and the possibility of a new political party in 1919. Warren S. Stone, chief executive officer of the Brotherhood of Locomotive Engineers, and James F. Forrester, head of the Brotherhood of Railroad Signalmen served as the chief promoters of this idea among union leaders. These two, the most politically active brotherhood leaders at that time, requested that the AFL Executive Council send Gompers to this conference, and the council agreed. When Gompers discovered that a political party might be formed, he declined to attend. In deference to him, the council

reversed its instructions. This and other conflicts between Gompers and railroad union leaders over working toward a third party are described in Taft, *A.F. of L. in the Time of Gompers*, 477–80.

19. *AFL Proceedings, 1923*, 273–74.

20. *AFL Proceedings, 1922*, 296.

21. Note the instructions given Gompers by the Executive Council and the override of his opposition to the Plumb Plan by the 1919 convention, described in Taft, *A.F. of L. in the Time of Gompers*, 477–80.

22. Lee Wolman, *The Growth of American Trade Unions, 1880–1923* (New York: National Bureau of Economic Research, 1924), 119; Bernstein, *Lean Years*, 84; *AFL Proceedings, 1924*, 23.

23. Taft, *A.F. of L. in the Time of Gompers*, 484.

24. The account that follows of the North Dakota Nonpartisan League and its offshoots is based largely on Robert L. Morlan, *Political Fire, The Nonpartisan League, 1915–1922* (Minneapolis: Univ. of Minnesota Press, 1955).

25. *Ibid.*, 36–43, 65–66, 84–85, 161–62, 177, 194, 200–201, 279–83, 297, 301, 345.

26. *Ibid.*, 343–46; James Weinstein, *The Decline of Socialism in America, 1912–1925* (New York: Random House, 1967), 29–95; Fine, *Labor and Farmer Parties*, 373–74. Keating discusses the aid directed into campaigns such as those in North Dakota and Minnesota for Nonpartisan League and Farmer-Labor candidates by the railroad brotherhoods, largely organized by Warren Stone, in *The Story of "LABOR"*, 114–23. On the large-scale work of the brotherhoods on behalf of Shipshead and Magnus Johnson, see Stone to La Follette, June 25, 1923, and Keating to La Follette, June 29, 1923, La Follette Papers.

27. Millard Gieske, *Minnesota Farmer Laborism: The Third-Party Alternative* (Minneapolis: Univ. of Minnesota Press, 1979); Richard M. Valelly, *Radicalism in the States: The Minnesota Farmer-Labor Party and the American Political Economy* (Chicago: Univ. of Chicago Press, 1989).

28. U.S. Department of Commerce, Bureau of the Census, *Historical Statistics of the United States, Colonial Times to 1970*, I: 11–30, 480–519; II: 1038.

29. Excellent brief accounts of the crimes and strongly suspected crimes of high Harding administration officials can be found in William E. Leuchtenburg, *The Perils of Prosperity, 1914–32* (Chicago: Univ. of Chicago Press, 1958), 90–94; and Richard M. Abrams, *The Burdens of Progress, 1900–1929* (Glenview, Ill.: Scott, Foresman, 1978), 144–46.

30. "Labor's Political Demands," document presented to the platform committees of the Republican and Democratic conventions, reprinted in *American Federationist*, XXXI (July 1924): 554–55. According to Gompers, well before the Democratic and Republican conventions AFL leaders had given up hope of much success. *Ibid.*, XXXI (Sept. 1924): 742. Gompers added: "It is no fantastic thing to look for the success of Senator La Follette in the coming election. America is seething with protest against the machinations of Big Business, the betrayal of public trust. . . ."

31. William H. Harbaugh, *Lawyer's Lawyer, The Life of John W. Davis* (New

York: Oxford Univ. Press, 1973), 197–98; David H. Stratton, "Splattered With Oil: William G. McAdoo and the 1924 Democratic Presidential Election," *Southwestern Social Sciences Quarterly*, XLIV (June 1963): 62–75.

32. Harbaugh, *John W. Davis*, 212; *Proceedings, Democratic National Convention, held at New York, N.Y., June 24–July 9, 1924* (New York: n.p., 1924), 310; *New York Times*, July 1, 1924. This issue is disclosed perceptively in David Burner, *The Politics of Provincialism: The Democratic Party in Transition, 1918–1932* (New York: Norton, 1967), 117–18.

33. *New York Times*, July 2, 1924.

34. *Proceedings, Democratic National Convention, 1924*, 338–969.

35. Otis L. Graham, Jr., *The Great Campaigns: Reform, and War in America, 1900–1928* (Englewood Cliffs, N.J.: Prentice Hall, 1971). 112. The full meaning of such statements, made before Wilson's illness removed him from political activity temporarily, probably will remain unclear until publication of Arthur S. Link's one-volume biography of Wilson.

36. The account that follows of the Farmer-Labor Party is based largely on Fine, *Labor and Farmer Parties*; Morlan, *Political Prairie Fire*; and Weinstein, *Decline of Socialism in America*.

37. La Follette-Wheeler Progressive Campaign Headquarters, Releases Numbers 137, 138, 145, dated Oct. 24, 26, 31, 1924, La Follette Papers, Series B-206; Shorer, *Lewis*, 408; Nick Salvatore, *Eugene V. Debs, Citizen and Socialist* (Urbana: Univ. of Illinois Press, 1982), 334–37. Lippmann was placed under great pressure to back La Follette. He explained to Frankfurter, who viewed La Follette as moving in directions necessary for America's future, that he preferred Davis's "strong Jeffersonian bias against the concentration and exaggeration of government. . . ." Harbaugh, *John W. Davis*, 243.

38. Belle C. and Fola La Follette, *Robert M. La Follette* (New York: Macmillan, 1953), 110, 113.

39. Roe to La Follette, June 17, 1924, La Follette Papers, Series B-119. Several weeks earlier, writing on behalf of himself and other friends of La Follette in Washington, D.C., Roe reported "very strong" feelings on the part of all of them that "a straight third-party ticket, and this means candidates for the House and Senate from all the states," must be nominated if the La Follette campaign were to be successful. Roe to Robert La Follette, Jr., May 23, 1924, La Follette Papers, Series B-101.

40. La Follette to Nelson, Aug. 7, 1924, La Follette Papers, Series B-119.

41. Keating, *The Story of "LABOR"*, 156. When the CPPA's third conference in Feb. 1924 decided on a July 1 convention, a story in *Labor* declared that delegates at that time would "determine whether the time is ripe for launching a new political party." *Labor*, Feb. 23, 1924.

42. *Proceedings, CPPA Convention held at Cleveland, Ohio, July 4–5, 1924* (1924), II: 163; *New York Times*, July 5, 6, 1924. The CPPA platform is reprinted in MacKay, *Progressive Movement of 1924*, Appendix 4. For a good analysis of the platform, see David Waterhouse, "The Failure of Working-Class Politics in America: The Case of the Progressive Movement of 1924," unpublished Ph.D. disser-

tation, Univ. of California, Los Angeles, 1982, 8–14, revised for publication, forthcoming from Garland Press; also Thelen, *La Follette*, 182.

43. Bernstein, *Lean Years*, 346–47; Vivian Vale, *Labour in American Politics* (London: Routledge and Kegan Paul, 1971), 30–31.

44. Taft, *A.F. of L. in the Time of Gompers*, 484; Gompers, "We Are in to Win," *American Federationist*, XXXI (Sept. 1924): 742; Gompers, "Why Labor Should Support La Follette and Wheeler," *Ibid.*, XXXI (Oct. 1924): 808–9.

45. MacKay describes much of this fiasco in *Progressive Movement of 1924*, 149, 156–57, 175–96. La Follette's headquarters in Washington, D.C., acknowledged that he could not start campaigning until Oct. 6 because he lacked funds, reported the *New York Herald Tribune*, Oct. 6, 1924. Senator Frank Walsh, during a post-election Senate investigation, placed Republican expenditures for the presidential campaign at $15,700,000, or seventy times what La Follette collected or spent. MacKay, *Progressive Movement of 1924*, 185.

46. Negley D. Cochran, *E. W. Scripps* (New York: Harcourt Brace, 1933), 186.

47. MacKay, *Progressive Movement of 1924*, 156–59.

48. *Ibid.*, 148.

49. *Ibid.*, 168–69.

50. Many of these red-baiting articles and ads, including a series of articles in the *Saturday Evening Post*—one of which stated inaccurately that William Z. Foster and the Communists were campaigning for La Follette—are quoted in MacKay, *Progressive Movement of 1924*, 162–74. When a list of 213 college and university professors who supported La Follette was released by La Follette's publicity bureau, which consisted largely of Director Ernest Gruening, the Cincinnati *Enquirer* in an editorial called for the discharge of all these advocates of "recognized heresies." MacKay, *Progressive Movement of 1924*, 166. This list of professors included Felix Frankfurter, Paul H. Douglas, Franz Boas, John Dewey, and Harvard astronomer Harlow Shapley. La Follette-Wheeler Campaign Headquarters, Release No. 138, Oct. 31, 1924, La Follette Papers, Series B-206.

51. Dawes's energetic attempt to bring every red-fearing voter to the polls in order to protect America—and to elect Coolidge—is described in Paul R. Leach, *That Man Dawes* (Chicago: The Reilly & Lee Co., 1930). The quotation is from pp. 232–34.

52. John W. Davis, appalled by the Republican attempt to stamp La Follette as a dangerous "Red," pointed out that the proposal that would enable Congress to legalize measures declared unconstitutional by the Supreme Court was not "Bolshevistic," but rather application of "the old British theory of supremacy of Parliament." Harbaugh, *John W. Davis*, 245.

53. Quoted in Leuchtenburg, *Perils of Prosperity*, 134.

54. Norman C. Meier, "Motives in Voting: A Study in Public Opinion," *American Journal of Sociology*, XXXI (Sept. 1925): 199–212.

55. The best statistical analyses can be found in Waterhouse, "The Estimation of Voting Behavior from Aggregate Data: A Test," *Journal of Social History*, XVI (Spring 1983): 35–53; Waterhouse, "The Failure of Working-Class Politics in America," 194–238, Tables 1–48, 51; Jerome N. Clubb and Howard W. Allen,

"The Cities and the Election of 1928," *American Historical Review*, LXXIV (Apr. 1969): 1205–20; Allan J. Lichtman, *Prejudice and the Old Politics, The Presidential Election of 1928* (Chapel Hill: Univ. of North Carolina Press, 1979); Lichtman, "Critical Election Theory and the Reality of American Presidential Politics, 1916–40," *American Historical Review*, LXXXI (Apr. 1976): 317–51; and David Burner, *The Politics of Provincialism*.

56. Burner, *The Politics of Provincialism;* MacKay quotes a communication to him from Norman Thomas describing the situation in New York State, *Progressive Movement of 1924*, 201–2. Cahan's name appeared frequently in the La Follette-Wheeler press releases prepared by Gruening and Wheeler. Cahan was listed as a speaker ready to travel where needed.

57. John M. Allswang, *A House for All Peoples; Ethnic Politics in Chicago, 1890–1936* (Lexington: Univ. of Kentucky Press, 1971), 191–93, 200–201.

58. Lichtman, "Critical Election Theory and American Presidential Politics," 333.

59. MacKay, *Progressive Movement of 1924*, Appendix 5, pp. 274–75, gives the vote for each state in percentiles. On California, *ibid.*, 181–82. Regarding the state of Washington, see Weinstein, *Decline of Socialism in America*, 227, 292, and 292 n. 8. On the 1924 election in the South, see Waterhouse, "The Failure of Working-Class Politics in America," 204–5.

60. MacKay broke the election returns down by region and analyzed these tabulations. See his statistics in *Progressive Movement of 1924*, 222. These are analyzed on pp. 221–29. MacKay concludes: "The Congressional results in the 1924 election did not sustain the appearance of an overwhelming Republican endorsement, so vividly suggested by the Electoral College totals." *Ibid.*, 228. Also see H. Keenleyside, "The American Political Revolution of 1924," *Current History*, XXI (Mar. 1925): 833–40.

61. La Follette-Wheeler Campaign Headquarters press release for Sept. 9, 1924; La Follette to Roe, Oct. 7, 1924, La Follette Papers, Series B-205; Mark Harrison to George Norris, May 28, 1924, Papers of George W. Norris, Library of Congress; *Labor*, Sept. 20, 1924. Stone presided over the labor leaders' meeting, which was called for campaign-planning purposes.

62. Keating's editorial appeared in *Labor*, Nov. 8, 1924.

63. Taft, *The A.F. of L. in the Time of Gompers*, 485; *Labor*, Nov. 15, 1924; *Labor*, Feb. 28, 1925.

64. The failure to vote on Sheppard's resolution, seconded by Manion of the Telegraphers' Union and Robertson of the Firemen's Union, which would have retained the coalition somewhat bruised but intact for the next election, is discussed in Fine, *Labor and Farmer Parties*, 415–16.

65. Ellis W. Hawley, "Herbert Hoover and Economic Stabilization, 1921–22," in Hawley, ed., *Herbert Hoover as Secretary of Commerce* (Iowa City: Univ. of Iowa Press, 1981), 47.

66. The decision by Norris to withdraw from his Senate contest in which he was the Republican nominee so that he could campaign in good conscience for La Follette, and La Follette's arguments persuading him not to do so, can be followed in Richard Lowitt, *George W. Norris: the Persistence of a Progressive, 1913–*

1933 (Urbana: Univ. of Illinois Press, 1971), 221–23, 237–39. Norris's decision to support Smith is explained in Lowitt, *Norris*, 410–14.

67. *AFL Proceedings, 1923*, 52–53.

68. Taft, *A.F. of L. in the Time of Gompers*, 487.

69. Waterhouse, "The Failure of Working-Class Politics in America," 251–77, especially 277.

70. Lichtman, "Critical Election Theory and American Presidential Politics," 345. Waterhouse, Burner, Richard Oestreicher, and V. O. Key agree with Lichtman. See Waterhouse, "The Failure of Working-Class Politics in America," 287–320; Burner, "The Election of 1924," in Arthur M. Schlesinger, Jr., ed., *The History of American Presidential Elections*, VI (New York: Chelsea House, 1971), 2459–80; and Burner, *Politics of Provincialism*, 69, 137, 227–31; and Oestreicher, "Urban Working-Class Political Behavior and Theories of American Electoral Politics, 1870–1940," *The Journal of American History*, LXXIV (Mar. 1988): 1281; V. O. Key, *Politics, Parties and Pressure Groups*, 5th ed. (New York: Thomas Y. Crowell, 1964), 261–62. Carl N. Degler expressed views similar to Lichtman's in "American Political Parties and the Rise of the City," *Journal of American History*, LI (June 1964): 56.

7. The Guardians

1. Estimates of Klan membership by scholars who have studied the order range from Kenneth T. Jackson's personal estimate of just over two million to Robert Alan Goldberg's assay of "perhaps as many as six million." Jackson, *The Ku Klux Klan in the City, 1915–1930* (New York: Oxford Univ. Press, 1967), 237; Goldberg, *Hooded Empire: The Ku Klux Klan in Colorado* (Urbana: Univ. of Illinois Press, 1981), vii.

2. Jackson, *Ku Klux Klan in the City*, 237, 239.

3. Charles C. Alexander concluded that in the Southwest, particularly in Oklahoma and Texas where most alleged vigilante activity took place, "Probably the preponderance of Klan vigilante acts featured a handful of Klansmen acting precipitately and without the sanction of local officers of the order." Alexander, *The Ku Klux Klan in the Southwest* (Lexington: Univ. of Kentucky Press, 1965), 59.

4. U.S. House of Representatives, 76th Cong., 1st Sess., *The Ku Klux Klan, Hearings Before the Committee on Rules* (Washington, D.C.: Government Printing Office, 1921). The committee did not find sufficient evidence of wrongdoing by Klan members to recommend further action by Congress or by the U.S. Department of Justice.

A series of articles in the New York *World* during Sept. 1921 brought the allegations of Klan vigilante actions, including violence, to the attention of the American public and of Congress. A reporter for the *World*, who had participated in the newspaper's three-month investigation of the Klan, appearing as a witness before the Rules Committee, stated about the sixty-five cases uncovered by the *World:* "They are all marked by those two sets of characteristics. There are punishments and there are punishments inflicted under the protection of masks, and local report and local belief in all these communities is that they were Ku Klux work. . . . The whole subject is so exceedingly difficult that light needs to be let in on the thing to the very fullest degree possible." *Ku Klux Klan, Hearings Before the Committee on Rules*, 8–9.

5. Savannah *Tribune*, July 13, 1922. Charles Alexander declared that "The actions of the Klan in those four states [Arkansas, Louisiana, Oklahoma and Texas] indicated a strikingly small amount of hostility toward Negroes." He reported the statement of a traveler through the Southwest in 1922 who summarized his findings for the *Survey* magazine: "Negroes with whom I have had an opportunity to talk are not greatly disturbed by it [the Klan] so far as the security of their own people is concerned. They say, as others do, that it is mainly an anti-bootlegging and anti-homebreaking organization." Alexander, *Klan in the Southwest*, 23.

6. *Searchlight*, Mar. 1, 15, 29, 1924. For further comment about Christ as a model of Victorian character see Mintz, *A Prison of Expectations*, 33.

7. "Kloran, Knights of the Ku Klux Klan" (Atlanta: Imperial Palace, 1916).

8. Christopher Nickolas Cocoltchos, "The Invisible Government and the Viable Community: The Ku Klux Klan in Orange County, California, During the 1920's," unpublished Ph.D. dissertation, Univ. of California, Los Angeles, 1979; Goldberg, *Hooded Empire;* Peter Akin, "The Ku Klux Klan in Georgia, 1915–1930," unpublished paper presented to the Workshop on Quantitative, Political History, California Institute of Technology, June 23, 1989; Leonard Joseph Moore, "White Protestant Nationalism in the 1920's: The Ku Klux Klan in Indiana," unpublished Ph.D. dissertation, Univ. of California, Los Angeles, 1985; William D. Jenkins, "The Ku Klux Klan in Youngstown, Ohio: Moral Reform in the Twenties," *Historian*, XLI (Nov. 1978):76–93; and Jenkins's forthcoming book on the Youngstown Klan; Eckard V. Toy, "The Ku Klux Klan in Oregon," in G. Thomas Edwards and Carlos A. Schwantes, eds., *Experiences in a Promised Land: Essays in Pacific Northwest History* (Seattle: Univ. of Washington Press, 1986), 269–86; Toy, "Robe and Gown: The Ku Klux Klan in Eugene, Oregon," in Shawn Lay, ed., *The Invisible Empire in the West: Toward a New Historical Appraisal of the Klan in the 1920s* (forthcoming from the Univ. of Illinois Press in 1991), 226–327; David A. Horowitz, "The Klansman as Outsider: Ethnocultural Solidarity and Antielitism in the Oregon Ku Klux Klan of the 1920s," *Pacific Northwest Quarterly*, LXXX (Jan. 1989): 12–20. Horowitz, "Order, Solidarity and Vigilance: The Ku Klux Klan in La Grande, Oregon," in Lay, ed. *The Invisible Empire in the West*, 328–80. William Toll, "Progress and Piety: The Ku Klux Klan and Social Change in Tillamook, Oregon," *Pacific Northwest Quarterly*, LXIX (Apr. 1978) 75–85; Kenneth D. Wald, "The Visible Empire: The Ku Klux Klan as an Electoral Movement [on Memphis, Tennessee]," *The Journal of Interdisciplinary History*, XI (Summer 1980): 217–37; Shawn Lay, *War, Revolution and the Ku Klux Klan: A Study of Intolerance in a Border City* (El Paso: Texas Western Press, 1985); Larry R. Gerlach, *Blazing Crosses in Zion: The Ku Klux Klan in Utah* (Logan: Utah State Univ. Press, 1982).

9. Goldberg, *Hooded Empire*, 127.

10. *Fiery Cross of Indiana*, December 29, 1922.

11. These and other psychic rewards of fraternal lodge membership are ana-

lyzed perceptively in Lynn Dumenil, *Freemasonry and American Culture, 1880–1939* (Princeton: Princeton Univ. Press, 1984); and Mark C. Carnes, *Secret Ritual and Manhood in Victorian America* (New Haven: Yale Univ. Press, 1989). The quotation is from Dumenil, *Freemasonry*, 147. Dumenil discusses the popularity of the Klan among Masons in *Freemasonry*, 122–23, 261 n. 35.

12. David M. Chalmers, *Hooded Americanism: The History of the Ku Klux Klan*, 2d ed. (New York: New Viewpoints, 1981, 31–35; Charles C. Alexander, "Kleagles and Cash: The Ku Klux Klan as a Business Organization, 1915–1930," *Business History Review*, XXXIX (Autumn 1965), 351–53; Jackson, *Klan in the Cities*, 9–10; Goldberg, *Hooded Empire*, 3–4; "Ideals of the Ku Klux Klan" (Atlanta: Imperial Palace, 1923), 6; Alexander, *Klan in the Southwest*, 107.

13. Leonard Joseph Moore, "Citizen Klansmen: Ku Klux Klan Populism in Indiana During the 1920's," Chapter 1, pp. 55–56, manuscript scheduled for publication by the Univ. of North Carolina Press in 1991. I am grateful to Professor Moore for allowing me to read the final version of this manuscript.

14. An account of the Shaw family and of Polly's reaction to it are discussed in Chapter 1 of this book, pages 7–8. Robert H. Wiebe, *The Search for Order: 1877–1920* (New York: Hill and Wang, 1967), 134. The development and characteristics of modern business elites are analyzed in Alfred D. Chandler, *The Visible Hand: The Managerial Revolution in American Business* (Cambridge: Harvard Univ. Press, 1977);

15. See note 8 above.

16. Jackson, *Klan in the City*, 144.

17. U.S. Department of Commerce, Bureau of the Census, *Fourteenth Census of the United States, Indiana Compendium* (Washington, D.C.: Government Printing Office, 1924), 43.

18. Moore, "Citizen Klansmen," Chapter 2, Tables 7, 12. Gregory Holmes Singleton discussed the vague border separating fundamentalist and many non-fundamentalist churches during the 1920s in Singleton, "Fundamentalism and Urbanization: A Quantitative Critique of Impressionistic Interpretations," in Leo F. Schnore and Eric E. Lambard, eds., *The New Urban History: Quantitative Explorations by American Historians* (Princeton: Princeton Univ. Press, 1975), 205–27. While serving as the author's research assistant, Singleton reported evidence that a sizable proportion of church members as well as ministers in almost every Protestant denomination accepted the fundamentals.

19. Moore, "Citizen Klansmen," 25–68; also, *Ibid.*, Chapter 2, Tables 8, 13, 18.

20. *Ibid.*, 25–68; also, *Ibid.*, Chapter 2, Tables 9, 14. The quotation about Crown Point's wealthiest citizens is from *Ibid.*, Chapter 3, p. 91. Information about the proportion of Catholics, blacks, Jews, and immigrants in Crown Point's population was given to the author during a conversation with Moore, Nov. 2, 1989.

21. *Ibid.*, Chapter 2, p. 37.

22. Cocoltchos, "Invisible Government and the Viable Community," Appendix A.

23. *Ibid.*, Tables 39–44.

24. *Ibid.*, Tables 20, 21.

25. *Ibid.*, Tables 30, 31.

26. Goldberg, *Hooded Empire*, 12–48. Information about the absence of Klansmen in Denver's elite clubs can be found on p. 36.

27. Goldberg, *Hooded Empire*, 118–48.

28. Leonard Joseph Moore, "Historical Interpretations of the 1920's Klan: The Traditional View and the Populist Revision," 22, manuscript scheduled for publication in the *Journal of Social History* in Dec. 1990. I am grateful to Professor Moore for allowing me to read the final version of this manuscript.

29. The following discussion of Grand Junction's Klan was condensed from the account in Goldberg, *Hooded Empire*, 149–62.

30. *Christian Evangelist*, Dec. 13, 1923, quoted in Moore, "Citizen Klansmen," Chapter 2, p. 42.

31. Moore, "Citizen Klansmen," Chapter 2, p. 36.

32. Moore, "Ku Klux Klan in Indiana," 179–85.

33. Moore, "Citizen Klansmen," Chapter 1, p. 18.

34. *Ibid.*, Chapter 5, pp. 216–20.

35. Moore, "Ku Klux Klan in Indiana," 266–69.

36. Cocoltchos, "Invisible Government and the Viable Community," xii.

37. *Ibid.*, 5–6.

38. *Ibid.*, 337–58. For a brief biography of Meyers and an account of his career until he accepted the leadership of Anaheim's Klan, see pp. 126–38.

39. *Ibid.*, 209–307, 333–37, 370–72.

40. Goldberg, *Hooded Empire*, 28–30, 32–35.

41. *Ibid.*, 28–30, 120–21.

42. *Ibid.*, 118.

43. *Ibid.*, 127.

44. *Ibid.*, 128, 144.

45. *Ibid.*, 119, 122.

46. Moore, "Ku Klux Klan in Indiana," 274–76.

47. Chalmers, *Hooded Americanism*, 171–72; Jackson, *Klan in the City*, 157; Moore, "Ku Klux Klan in Indiana," 278–80.

48. Goldberg, *Hooded Empire*, 98–99.

49. *Ibid.*, 104–6.

50. Cocoltchos, "Invisible Government and the Viable Community," 539–42, 547–48.

51. *Ibid.*, 552.

52. Jackson, *Klan in the City*, 290; "The Klan as a Victim of Mob Violence," *Literary Digest*, LXXVIII (Sept. 8, 1923): 12–13; Stanley Coben, "The First Years of Modern America, 1918–1933," in William E. Leuchtenburg, ed., *The Unfinished Century* (Boston: Little, Brown, 1973), 301.

53. Alexander, *Klan in the Southwest*, 222; *Dawn*, Oct. 20, 1923; Jackson, *Klan in the City*, 123; Coben, "First Years of Modern America," 301; Stanley Coben, "The Assault on Victorianism in the Twentieth Century," *American Quarterly*, XXVIII (Dec. 1975): 623.

54. Coben, "First Years of Modern America," 297.

55. *Ibid.*, 297–98; Jackson, *Klan in the City*, 102.

56. Jackson, *Klan in the City*, 176–77, 239.

57. *Ibid.*, 125; Coben, "Assault on Victorianism," 623.

58. Jackson, Klan in the City, 106–10, 117–19.

59. Ibid., 182.

60. "The Klan as the Victim of Mob Violence," 12–13; Jackson, *Klan in the City*, 171.

61. "The Klan as the Victim of Mob Violence," 12.

62. A lengthy account of this incident was published in the *New York Times*, May 31, 1927.

63. Hiram Wesley Evans, "The Klan's Fight for Americanism," *North American Review*, CCXXIII (Mar. 1926): 39.

Conclusion

1. Evans, "The Klan's Fight for Americanism," 43, 49. The connotation of the phrase "plain people" in Evans's article is, in most respects, similar to that of Canby's in *The Age of Confidence*. See Chap. 1 of this work, pp. 17–20, 30.

Selected Bibliography

Manuscript Collections

American Philosophical Society Library
    Franz Boas Papers
    Simon Flexner Papers
    Henry Allen Moe Papers
    Elsie Clews Parsons Papers

Archives of the National Woman's Party, Washington, D.C.
    National Woman's Party Papers, on microfilm

Bancroft Library, University of California, Berkeley
    Alfred L. Kroeber Papers
    Robert H. Lowie Papers
    Sources for History of Quantum Physics, Center for History of Science
        and Technology
    Suffragists Oral History Project
    Mabel Vernon Papers

California Institute of Technology Library
    George Ellery Hale Papers
    Robert A. Millikan Papers

Columbia University Library
    Virginia C. Gildersleeve Papers

Firestone Library, Princeton University
    F. Scott Fitzgerald Papers
    H. L. Mencken Papers
    H. L. Mencken Papers, on microfilm
    Woodrow Wilson Papers

Fruitlands Museum, Harvard University
    Louisa May Alcott Diary

History of Physics Collection, Neils Bohr Library, American Institute of Physics, New York, New York
    Transcripts of Interviews Conducted by Charles Weiner

Herbert Hoover Presidential Library, West Bend, Iowa
    Herbert Hoover, Commerce Department Papers
    Herbert Hoover, Presidential Papers

Houghton Library, Harvard University
    Alcott Family Archives

Library of Congress
    La Follette Family Papers
    National Association for the Protection of Colored People Papers
    National Woman's Party Papers, 1913–1920
    George Norris Papers

New York Public Library
    Henry W. Berg and Albert A. Berg Collection
    Jacques Loeb Papers
    H. L. Mencken Papers
    Joel E. Spingarn Papers

Rockefeller Archive Center, Hillcrest, Pocantico Hills, North Tarrytown, N.Y.
    General Education Board Papers
    International Education Board Papers
    Laura Spelman Rockefeller Memorial Papers
    Rockefeller Family Archives
    Rockefeller Foundation Papers
    Rockefeller Sanitary Commission Papers
    Wickliffe Rose Papers

The Arthur and Elizabeth Schlesinger Library on the History of Women in America, Radcliffe College
    Doris Stevens Papers

Schomburg Center for Research in Black Culture, New York Public Library
    Marcus Garvey and Universal Negro Improvement Association Papers
    Works Projects Administration Research Papers

University of Massachusetts Library, Amherst
    W.E.B. Du Bois Papers

Vassar College Library
    Ruth Benedict Papers

Yale University Library
James Weldon Johnson Papers

Public Documents

Boas, Franz. *Changes in the Bodily Form of Descendants of Immigrants.* 61st Cong., 2nd Sess. Senate Document No. 208. Washington, D.C.: GPO, 1910.

Chicago Commission on Race Relations. *The Negro in Chicago: A Study of Race Relations and a Race Riot.* Chicago: Univ. of Chicago Press, 1922.

Hooks, Janet M. *Women's Occupations Through Seven Decades.* U.S. Department of Labor. Women's Bureau. Bulletin No. 218. Washington, D.C.: GPO, 1947.

New York City Tenement House Department. *Tenth Report 1918–1929.* New York: Martin Brown Press, 1929.

New York State. Commission of Housing and Regional Planning. *Report to Governor Alfred E. Smith and to the Legislature on the Present Housing Emergency, December 12, 1923.* Albany: J.B. Lyon, 1924.

United States Census Bureau. *Negro Population in the United States, 1920–1932.* Washington, D.C.: GPO, 1935.

U.S. Congress. House. 68th Cong., 2nd Sess. Committee on the Judiciary. *Hearings on H. J. Res., Equal Rights Amendment to the Constitution.* Washington, D.C.: GPO, 1925.

U.S. Congress. House. 76th Cong., 1st Sess. *The Ku Klux Klan, Hearings Before the Committee on Rules.* Washington, D.C.: GPO, 1921.

U.S. Congress. Senate. *Arguments Before the Committee on Privileges and Elections of the United States in Behalf of a Sixteenth Amendment to the Constitution of the United States Prohibiting the Several States from Disenfranchising United States Citizens on Account of Sex, January 11 and 12, 1878.* Washington, D.C.: GPO, 1878.

U.S. Congress. Senate. 63rd Cong., 1st Sess. *Report of the Committee on the District of Columbia, United States Senate, Pursuant to Senate Resolution 499 of March 4, 1913, Directing Said Committee to Investigate the Conduct of the District Police and the Police Department of the District of Columbia in Connection with Woman Suffrage Parade on March 3, 1913.* Senate Report No. 53, May 29, 1913, Washington, D.C.: GPO, 1913.

U.S. Congress. Senate. 70th Cong., 2nd Sess. U.S. Senate Subcommittee of the Committee on the Judiciary. *S.J. 64, A Joint Resolution Proposing an Amendment to the Constitution of the United States Relative to Equal Rights for Men and Women, February 1, 1929.* Washington, D.C.: GPO, 1929.

U.S. Department of Commerce. Bureau of the Census. *Fourteenth Census of the United States, Indiana Compendium.* Washington, D.C.: GPO, 1924.

U.S. Department of Commerce. Bureau of the Census. *Fifteenth Census of the United*

States: 1930, V, General Report on Occupations. Washington, D.C.: GPO, 1933.

U.S. Department of Commerce. Bureau of the Census. *Historical Statistics of the United States, Colonial Times to 1957.* Washington, D.C.: GPO, 1960.

U.S. Department of Commerce. Bureau of the Census. *Historical Statistics of the United States, Colonial Times to 1970.* Washington, D.C.: GPO, 1975.

U.S. Department of Commerce. Bureau of the Census. *Negroes in the United States, 1920–1932.* Washington, D.C.: GPO, 1935.

U.S. Department of the Interior. Census Office. *Ninth Census: The Statistics of the Wealth and Industry of the United States.* Washington, D.C.: GPO, 1872.

U.S. Department of the Interior. Census Office. *Compendium of the Tenth Census: June 1, 1880.* Washington, D.C.: GPO, 1883.

U.S. Department of the Interior. Census Office. *Report on the Population of the United States at the Eleventh Census, 1890.* Washington, D.C.: GPO, 1895.

U.S. Department of the Interior. Office of Education. *Biennial Survey of Education, 1926–1928.* Washington, D.C.: GPO, 1928.

U.S. Department of Labor. Division of Negro Economics. *Negro Migration in 1916–17.* Washington, D.C.: GPO, 1919.

U.S. Office of Education. *Biennial Survey of Education.* Washington, D.C.: GPO, 1929.

Other Unpublished Sources

Akin, Peter. "The Ku Klux Klan in Georgia, 1915–1930." Paper presented to the Workshop on Quantitative, Political History, California Institute of Technology, June 23, 1989.

Cocoltchos, Christopher Nickolas. "The Invisible Government and the Viable Community: The Ku Klux Klan in Orange County, California, During the 1920's." Ph.D. diss., Univ. of California, Los Angeles, 1979.

Gildersleeve, Virginia C. "The College Girl of the Crisis." Unpublished manuscript of address delivered Feb. 4, 1934. Virginia C. Gildersleeve Papers, Columbia Univ. Library.

Kranz, Murray. "The Emergence of a Sociological View Toward the Negro." Ph.D. diss., Univ. of California, Los Angeles, 1973.

Moore, Leonard Joseph. "White Protestant Nationalism in the 1920's: The Ku Klux Klan in Indiana." Ph.D. diss., Univ. of California, Los Angeles, 1985.

———. "Citizen Klansmen: Ku Klux Klan Populism in Indiana During the 1920's." Unpublished manuscript scheduled for publication by the Univ. of North Carolina Press in 1991.

———. "Historical Interpretations of the 1920's Klan: The Traditional View and the Populist Revision." Manuscript scheduled for publication in the *Journal of Social History* in Dec. 1990.

New York Urban League. "Twenty-Four Hundred Negro Families in Harlem: An Interpretation of the Living Conditions of Small Wage Earners." Unpublished manuscript, Schomberg Library, New York City, dated 1923.

Prendergest, Norma. "The Sense of Home: Nineteenth-Century Domestic Architectural Reform." Ph.D. diss., Cornell Univ., 1981.

Ryan, Mary Patricia. "American Society and the Cult of Domesticity, 1830–1860." Ph.D. diss., Univ. of California, Santa Barbara, 1971.

Singleton, Gregory H. "The Dynamics of WASP Culture: From Ethnic Cohesion to the Organization Man." Paper presented at the annual meeting of the American Historical Association, New Orleans, Dec. 1972.

Sklar, Kathryn Kish. "Female Strategies in Victorian Families." Paper delivered to the Conference on Lincoln's Thought and the Present, Springfield, Ill., June 1976.

Stocking, George W., Jr. "American Social Scientists and Race Theory: 1890–1915." Ph.D. diss., Univ. of Pennsylvania, 1960.

Waterhouse, David. "The Failure of Working-Class Politics in America: The Case of the Progressive Movement of 1924." Ph.D. diss., Univ. of California, Los Angeles, 1982; revised for publication, forthcoming from Garland Press.

Books and Articles

Abrams, Richard M. *The Burdens of Progress, 1900–1929*. Glenview, Ill.: Scott, Foresman, 1978.

Alcott, Louisa May. *Rose in Bloom*. Boston: Roberts Brothers, 1876.

———. *Moods*. Boston: Roberts Brothers, 1882.

———. *Under the Lilacs*. Boston: Roberts Brothers, 1894.

———. *Aunt Jo's Scrap Bag*. Boston: Little, Brown, 1900.

———. *Eight Cousins*. Boston: Little, Brown, 1911.

———. *Jo's Boys*. Boston: Little, Brown, 1914.

———. *Little Men*. Boston: Little, Brown, 1946.

———. *Little Women*. Boston: Little, Brown, 1946.

———. *Hospital Sketches*. New York: Sagamore Press, 1957.

———. *An Old-Fashioned Girl*. New York: Grosset and Dunlap, 1971.

———. *Work*. New York: Schocken Books, 1977.

Alexander, Charles C. "Keagles and Cash: The Ku Klux Klan as a Business Organization, 1915–1930." *Business History Review* XXXIX (Autumn 1965): 348–67.

———. *The Ku Klux Klan in the Southwest*. Lexington: Univ. of Kentucky Press, 1965.

Allen, Charles. "The Advance Guard." *Sewanee Review* LI (July/Sept. 1943): 410–20.

Allswang, John M. *A House for All Peoples: Ethnic Politics in Chicago, 1890–1936.* Lexington: Univ. of Kentucky Press, 1971.

Anderson, Mary. *Women at Work.* Minneapolis: Univ. of Minnesota Press, 1951.

Andrews, William L. *Critical Essays on W.E.B. Du Bois.* Boston: G.K. Hall, 1985.

Anthony, Katherine. *Louisa May Alcott.* New York: Alfred A. Knopf, 1938.

Aptheker, Herbert, ed. *W.E.B. Du Bois, The Education of Black People: Ten Critiques 1906–1960.* Amherst: The Univ. of Massachusetts Press, 1973.

———, ed. *The Correspondence of W.E.B. Du Bois, Selections, 1877–1934.* Amherst: The Univ. of Massachusetts Press, 1973.

Armytage, W.H.G. *The Rise of the Technocrats: A Social History.* London: Routledge and Kegan Paul, 1965.

Baer, Judith A. *The Chains of Protection: The Judicial Response to Women's Labor Legislation.* Westport: Greenwood Press, 1978.

Bannister, Robert C. *Social Darwinism: Science and Myth in Anglo-American Social Thought.* Philadelphia: Temple Univ. Press, 1979.

Bebey, Francis. *African Music: A People's Art.* Westport: Lawrence Hill and Co., 1975. English translation.

Bechet, Sidney. *Treat It Gentle, An Autobiography.* New York: DaCapo, 1978.

Becker, Susan D. *The Origins of the Equal Rights Amendment: American Feminism Between the Wars.* Westport: Greenwood Press, 1981.

Beecher, Catharine E., and Harriet Beecher Stowe. *The American Woman's Home, or Principles of Domestic Science.* New York: J.B. Ford and Company, 1869.

Beecher, Lyman. *A Plea for the West.* Cincinnati: Truman, 1835.

Bell, Clive. "Plus De Jazz." *New Republic* XXVIII (Sept. 21, 1921): 92–96.

———. "Jazz Played Out." *Literary Digest* LXX (Jan. 14, 1922): 27–28.

Ben-David, Joseph. *Fundamental Research and the Universities.* Paris: Organization for Economic Cooperation and Development, 1968.

Benedict, Ruth. "The Concept of the Guardian Spirit in America." *Memoirs of the American Anthropological Association* XXIX (1923): 1–97.

———. "Psychological Types in the Cultures of the Southwest." *Proceedings, Twenty-Third Annual Congress of Americanists* (1928): 572–81.

———. "The Science of Custom." *Century Magazine* 117 (1929): 641–49.

———. *Patterns of Culture.* Boston: Houghton Mifflin, 1934.

Berg, A. Scott. *Max Perkins, Editor of Genius.* New York: E.P. Dutton, 1978.

Bernard, Jessie. *Academic Women.* University Park, Pa.: Pennsylvania State Univ. Press, 1964.

Bernstein, Irving. *The Lean Years, A History of the American Worker, 1920–33.* Boston: Houghton Mifflin, 1966.

Billington, James. *Fire in the Minds of Men: Origins of the Revolutionary Faith.* New York: Basic Books, 1980.

Billington, Ray Allen. *The Protestant Crusade, 1800–1860.* New York: Macmillan, 1938.

Birr, Kendall. "Industrial Research Laboratories." In Nathan Reingold, ed. *The*

Sciences in the American Context: New Perspectives. Washington, D.C.: Smithsonian Institution Press, 1979.

Blatch, Harriot Stanton. "Do Women Want Protection? Wrapping Women in Cotton Wool." *The Nation* CXVI (Jan. 31, 1923): 115–16.

———, and Alma Lutz. *Challenging Years: The Memoirs of Harriot Stanton Blatch.* New York: G.P. Putnam's Sons, 1940.

Brand, C. F. *The British Labour Party.* Stanford: Stanford Univ. Press, 1964.

Brawley, Benjamin. *A Social History of the American Negro.* New York: Macmillan, 1921.

Bridenthal, Renate, and Claudie Koonz, eds. *Becoming Visible: Women in European History.* Boston: Houghton Mifflin, 1977.

Bridgman, Percy W. *The Logic of Modern Physics.* New York: Macmillan, 1927.

Briggs, John W. *Immigrants to Three American Cities, 1890–1930.* New Haven: Yale Univ. Press, 1978.

Broderick, Francis L. *W.E.B. Du Bois: Negro Leader in a Time of Crisis.* Stanford: Stanford Univ. Press, 1959.

Brown, Sterling A. "The Blues as Folk Poetry." In Langston Hughes and Arna Bontemps, eds. *Book of Negro Folklore.* New York: Dodd, Mead, 1958.

Bulmer, Joan and Martin. "Philanthropy and Social Science in the 1920's: Beardsley Ruml and the Laura Spelman Rockefeller Memorial, 1922–1929." *Minerva* XIX (1981): 347–407.

Burner, David. *The Politics of Provincialism: The Democratic Party in Transition, 1918–1932.* New York: Norton, 1967.

———. "The Election of 1924." In Arthur M. Schlesinger, Jr., ed. Vol. VI. *The History of American Presidential Elections.* New York: Chelsea House, 1971.

Caffrey, Margaret. *Ruth Benedict: Stranger in this Land.* Austin: Univ. of Texas Press, 1989.

Cajori, C. *A History of Physics.* New York: Macmillan, 1929.

Calder, Jenni. *The Victorian Home.* London: B.T. Batsford, 1977.

Canby, Henry Seidel. *The Age of Confidence.* New York: Farrar and Rinehart, 1934.

Carey, James T. *Sociology and Public Affairs: The Chicago School.* Beverly Hills: Sage, 1975.

Carnes, Mark C. *Secret Ritual and Manhood in Victorian America.* New Haven: Yale Univ. Press, 1989.

Catt, Carrie Chapman, and Nettie Rogers Shuler. *Woman Suffrage and Politics.* New York: Charles Scribner & Sons, 1923.

Chafe, William Henry. *The American Woman: Her Changing Social, Economic, and Political Roles, 1920–1970.* New York: Oxford Univ. Press, 1972.

Chalmers, David M. *Hooded Americanism: The History of the Ku Klux Klan.* New York: New Viewpoints, 1981.

Chandler, Alfred D. *The Visible Hand: The Managerial Revolution in American Business.* Cambridge: Harvard Univ. Press, 1977.

Charters, Samuel. *The Roots of the Blues: An African Search.* New York: Perigree Books, 1981.

Cheney, Ednah D., ed. *Louisa May Alcott: Her Life, Letters and Journals.* Boston: Little, Brown, 1928.

Chesney, Kellow. *The Victorian Underworld.* New York: Schocken, 1970.

Chester, Eric Thomas. *Socialists and the Ballot Box: A Historical Analysis.* New York: Praeger, 1985.

Chesterton, Gilbert Keith. *What I Saw in America.* London: Dodd, Mead, 1922.

Chilton, John. *Who's Who of Jazz: Storyville to Swing Street.* Philadelphia: Chilton Book Co., 1972.

Clark, Clifford E. "Domestic Architecture as an Index to Social History: The Romantic Revival and the Cult of Domesticity in America, 1840–1879." *Journal of Interdisciplinary History* VII (Summer 1976): 33–56.

Clarke, John Hendrik. *Marcus Garvey and the Vision of Africa.* New York: Random House, 1974.

Clubb, Jerome N., and Howard W. Allen. "The Cities and the Election of 1928." *American Historical Review* LXXIV (Apr. 1969): 1205–20.

Coben, Stanley. *A. Mitchell Palmer: Politician.* New York: Columbia Univ. Press, 1963.

———. "A Study In Nativism: The American Red Scare of 1919–1920." *Political Science Quarterly* LXXIX (Mar. 1964): 52–75.

———. "The Failure of the Melting Pot." In Gary Nash and Richard Weiss, eds. *The Great Fear.* New York: Holt, Rinehart and Winston, 1970.

———. "The Scientific Establishment and the Transmission of Quantum Mechanics to the United States, 1919–1932." *American Historical Review* LXXVI (Apr. 1971): 442–66.

———. "The First Years of Modern America, 1918–1933." In William E. Leuchtenburg, ed. *The Unfinished Century.* Boston: Little, Brown, 1973.

———. "The Assault of Victorianism in the Twentieth Century." *American Quarterly* XXVII (Dec. 1975): 604–25.

———. "American Foundations as Patrons of Science: The Commitment to Individual Research." in Nathan Reingold, ed. *The Sciences in the American Context: New Perspectives.* Washington, D.C.: Smithsonian Institution Press, 1979.

———, and Lorman Ratner. "Culture, Society, Ethnicity, Class, Nation, and History." In Coben and Ratner, eds. *Development of an American Culture.* New York: St. Martin's, 1983.

Cochran. Negley D. *E.W. Scripps.* New York: Harcourt Brace, 1933.

Cohn, Jan. *The Palace or the Poorhouse: The American House as a Cultural Symbol.* East Lansing: Michigan State Univ. Press, 1979.

Commager, H.S., ed. *Selected Writings of William Dean Howells.* New York: Random House, 1950.

Commons, John R. *Races and Immigrants in America.* New York: Macmillan, 1907.

———. *Myself.* Madison: Univ. of Wisconsin Press, 1963.

Condon, Edward U., and Philip M. Morse. *Quantum Mechanics.* New York: Macmillan, 1929.

Conway, Jill. "Women Reformers and American Culture, 1870–1930." *Journal of Social History* V (Winter 1971–72): 164–77.

Cook, Blanche Wiesen, ed. *Crystal Eastman on Women and Revolution.* New York: Oxford Univ. Press, 1978.

Cooper, Lewis B. *Sabbatical Leaves for College Teachers.* Univ. of Florida Education Series, I, 1932.

Cott, Nancy F. *The Bonds of Womanhood, "Women's Sphere" in New England, 1780–1835.* New Haven: Yale Univ. Press, 1977.

———. "Feminist Theory and Feminist Movements: The Past Before Us." In Juliet Mitchell and Ann Oakley, eds. *What is Feminism: A Reexamination.* New York: Pantheon Books, 1986.

———. *The Grounding of Modern Feminism.* New Haven: Yale Univ. Press, 1987.

Cowley, Malcolm. *Exile's Return: A Literary Odyssey of the 1920's.* New York: Viking, 1934.

———. "Sister Carrie's Brother." *New Republic* 116 (May 26, 1947): 23–25.

———. "Sister Carrie: Her Fall and Rise." In Alfred Kazin and Charles Shapiro, eds. *The Stature of Theodore Dreiser: A Critical Survey of the Man and His Work.* Bloomington: Indiana Univ. Press, 1955.

———, ed. *Writers at Work: The Paris Review Interviews.* New York: Viking, 1965.

Cox, Oliver C. *Caste, Class and Race: A Study in Social Dynamics.* Garden City, N.Y.: Doubleday, 1948.

Cravens, Hamilton. *The Triumph of Evolution: American Scientists and the Heredity-Environment Controversy, 1900–1941.* Philadelphia: Univ. of Pennsylvania Press, 1978.

Cronon, E. David. *Black Moses: The Story of Marcus Garvey.* Madison: Univ. of Wisconsin Press, 1955.

Curtis, L. Perry. *Apes and Angels: The Irishman in Victorian Caricature.* Washington, D.C.: Smithsonian Institution Press, 1971.

Davis, Lawrence B. *Immigrants, Baptists, and the Protestant Mind in America.* Urbana: Univ. of Illinois Press, 1973.

Degler, Carl N. "American Political Parties and the Rise of the City." *Journal of American History* LI (June 1964): 41–59.

———. *Neither Black Nor White: Slavery and Race Relations in Brazil and the United States.* New York: Macmillan, 1971.

———. "What Ought to Be and What Was." *American Historical Review* LXXIX (Dec. 1974): 1467–90.

———. *At Odds: Women and the Family in America from the Revolution to the Present.* New York: Oxford Univ. Press, 1980.

D'Emilio, John, and Estelle B. Freedman. *Intimate Matters: A History of Sexuality in America.* New York: Harper and Row, 1988.

DeKruif, Paul. "Jacques Loeb, the Mechanist." *Harper's Magazine.* CXLVI (Jan. 1923): 182–90.

Dooley, D.J. *The Art of Sinclair Lewis.* Lincoln: Univ. of Nebraska Press, 1967.

Dreiser, Theodore. *Sister Carrie.* New York: Doubleday and Page, 1900.

Du Bois, Ellen Carol. *Feminism and Suffrage: The Emergence of an Independent Women's Movement in America, 1848–1869.* Ithaca: Cornell Univ. Press, 1978.

Du Bois, W. E. B. *Philadelphia Negro: A Social Study.* Philadelphia: Univ. of Pennsylvania Press, 1899.

————. *Souls of Black Folk.* Chicago: A.C. McClurg, 1903.

————. "The Negro in Literature and Art." *Annals of the American Academy of Political and Social Science* XLIX (Sept. 1913): 233–37.

————. "Marcus Garvey." *Crisis* XXI (Dec. 1920): 58–60; (Jan. 1921): 112–15.

————. "Negro Art." *Crisis* XXIII (June 1921): 55–56.

————. "The Negro Takes Stock." *New Republic* XXXVII (Jan. 2, 1924): 143–45.

————. "Criteria of Negro Art." *Crisis* XXXII (Oct. 1926): 290–97.

————. *Three Negro Classics.* New York: Avon, 1965.

————. *The Autobiography of W. E. B. Du Bois.* New York: International Publishers, 1968.

————. *Dusk of Dawn.* New York: Schocken, 1968.

————. *Darkwater: Voices from Within the Veil.* New York: Schocken, 1969.

Dumenil, Lynn. *Freemasonry and American Culture, 1880–1939.* Princeton: Princeton Univ. Press, 1984.

Dyer, Thomas G. *Theodore Roosevelt and the Idea of Race.* Baton Rouge: Louisiana State Univ. Press, 1980.

Elbert, Sarah. *A Hunger for Home: Louisa May Alcott and Little Women.* Philadelphia: Temple Univ. Press, 1984.

Elias, Robert H. *Theodore Dreiser: Apostle of Nature.* New York: Knopf, 1949.

Ettling, John. *The Germ of Laziness: Rockefeller Philanthropy and Public Health in the New South.* Cambridge: Harvard Univ. Press, 1981.

Evans, Hiram Wesley. "The Klan's Fight for Americanism." *North American Review* CCXXIII (Mar. 1926): 33–63.

Farber, Bernard. *Guardians of Virtue, Salem Families in 1800.* New York: Basic Books, 1972.

Farley, Reynolds. "The Urbanization of Negroes in the United States." *Journal of Social History* I (Spring 1968): 241–58.

Farris, Robert. *Chicago Sociology, 1920–1930.* San Francisco: Chandler, 1967.

Fass, Paula. *The Damned and the Beautiful: American Youth in the 1920's.* New York: Oxford Univ. Press, 1977.

Feinberg, Richard. "Margaret Mead and Samoa: *Coming of Age* in Fact and Fiction." *American Anthropologist* XC (Sept. 1988): 656–63.

Fine, Nathan. *Labor and Farmer Parties in the United States, 1828–1928.* New York: Rand School, 1928.

Flexner, Eleanor. *Century of Struggle: The Woman's Rights Movement in the United States.* Cambridge: Harvard Univ. Press, 1959.

Flexner, James Thomas. *An American Saga: The Story of Helen Thomas and Simon Flexner.* Boston: Little, Brown, 1984.

Flexner, Simon. "On the Etiology of Tropical Dysentery." *Philadelphia Medical Journal* VI (July–Dec. 1900): 414–24.

———. "The Pathology of Bubonic Plague." *University of Pennsylvania Medical Bulletin* XIV (1901): 205.

———, and L. F. Barker. "Report upon an Expedition sent by the Johns Hopkins University to Investigate the Prevalent Diseases in the Philippines." *Johns Hopkins Hospital Bulletin* XI (1900): 37.

———, L. F. Barker, and F. G. Novy. "Report on the Commission Appointed by the Secretary of Treasury for the Investigation of Plague in San Francisco, under Instructions from the Surgeon-General, Marine Hospital Service, Treasury Department, U.S. Marine Hospital Service." Washington, D.C.: GPO, 1901.

Forman, Paul, John L. Heilbron, and Spencer R. Weart. "Physics circa 1900: Personnel, Funding, and Productivity of the Academic Establishment." Vol. 5. *Historical Studies in the Physical Sciences.* Princeton: Princeton Univ. Press, 1975.

Forrest, D. W. *Francis Galton, The Life and Work of a Victorian Genius.* London: Elek, 1974.

Fosdick, Raymond B. *The Story of the Rockefeller Foundation.* New York: Harper, 1952.

———. *Adventure in Giving.* New York: Harper and Row, 1962.

Frankfurter, Felix, and Nathan Green. *The Labor Injunction.* New York: Macmillan, 1930.

Frazier, E. Franklin. *Black Bourgeoisie.* New York: Collier, 1962.

Fredrickson, George M. *The Black Image in the White Mind, The Debate on Afro-American Character and Destiny, 1817–1914.* New York: Harper, 1971.

Freedman, Estelle. "The New Woman: Changing Views of Women in the 1920's." *Journal of American History* LXI (Sept. 1974): 372–93.

Freeman, Derek. *Margaret Mead and Samoa: The Making and Unmaking of an Anthropological Myth.* Cambridge: Harvard Univ. Press, 1983.

Garrison, Dee. "The Tender Technicians: The Feminization of Public Librarianship, 1987–1905." *Journal of Social History* VI (Winter 1972–1973): 131–59.

Garvey, Amy Jacques. *Philosophy and Opinions of Marcus Garvey.* New York: Universal Publishing House, 1926.

———. *Garvey and Garveyism.* London: Collier-Macmillan, 1970.

———. "The Early Years of Marcus Garvey." In John Hendrik Clarke. *Marcus Garvey and the Vision of Africa.* New York: Random House, 1974.

Gates, Henry Louis, Jr. *The Signifying Monkey.* New York: Oxford Univ. Press, 1988.

Geiger, Roger L. *To Advance Knowledge: The Growth of American Research Universities, 1900–1940.* New York: Oxford Univ. Press, 1986.

Geiss, Imanuel. *The Pan-African Movement.* London: Methuen, 1974.

Gerlach, Larry R. *Blazing Crosses in Zion: The Ku Klux Klan in Utah.* Logan: Utah State Univ. Press, 1982.

Gieske, Millard. *Minnesota Farmer Laborism: The Third-Party Alternative.* Minneapolis: Univ. of Minnesota Press, 1979.

Gildersleeve, Virginia C. *Many a Good Crusade: Memoirs of Virginia Croceron Gildersleeve.* New York: Macmillan, 1954.

Gilmer, Walker. *Horace Liveright, Publisher of the Twenties.* New York: David Walker, 1970.

Gluck, Sherna, ed. *From Parlor to Prison: Five American Suffragists Talk about Their Lives.* New York: Random House, 1976.

Goldberg, Robert Alan. *Hooded Empire: The Ku Klux Klan in Colorado.* Urbana: Univ. of Illinois Press, 1981.

Goldmark, Josephine. *Impatient Crusader: Florence Kelley's Life Story.* Urbana: Univ. of Illinois Press, 1953.

Gompers, Samuel. "We Are in to Win." *American Federationist* XXXI (Sept. 1924): 741–43.

———. "Why Labor Should Support La Follette and Wheeler." *American Federationist* XXXI (Oct. 1924): 889–93.

Gossett, Thomas F. *Race, The History of an Idea in America.* New York: Schocken, 1965.

Gould, Stephen Jay. *The Mismeasure of Man.* New York: W.W. Norton, 1981.

Graham, Otis L., Jr. *The Great Campaigns: Reform, and War in America, 1900–1928.* Englewood Cliffs, N.J.: Prentice Hall, 1971.

Gray, George W. *Education on an International Scale: A History of the International Education Board, 1923–1938.* New York: Harcourt Brace, 1941.

Gregory, Daniel Mason. "Stravinsky as a Symptom." *American Mercury* 4 (Apr. 1925): 465–68.

Griffen, Clyde C. "The Progressive Ethos." In Stanley Coben and Lorman Ratner, eds. *The Development of an American Culture.* New York: St. Martin's, 1983.

Grove, J.W. *In Defense of Science: Science, Technology, and Politics in Modern Society.* Toronto: Univ. of Toronto Press, 1989.

Hagedorn, Hermann. *The Works of Theodore Roosevelt.* New York: Scribner's, 1926.

Hall, David D. "The Victorian Connection." In Daniel Walker Howe, ed. *Victorian American.* Philadelphia: Univ. of Pennsylvania Press, 1976.

Handlin, David P. *The American Home: Architecture and Society 1815–1915.* Boston: Little, Brown, 1979.

Harbaugh, William H. *Lawyer's Lawyer, The Life of John W. Davis.* New York: Oxford Univ. Press, 1972.

———. *The Life and Times of Theodore Roosevelt.* New York: Oxford Univ. Press, 1975.

Harcourt, Alfred. *Some Experiences.* Riverside, Conn.: 1951.

Harding, Vincent. "A Black Messianic Visionary." In Rayford W. Logan, ed. *W.E.B. Du Bois, A Profile.* New York: Hill and Wang, 1971.

Hareven, Tamara K. *Family Time and Industrial Time.* Cambridge: Cambridge Univ. Press, 1982.

Harrison, Cynthia. *On Account of Sex: The Politics of Women's Issues, 1945–1968.* Berkeley and Los Angeles: Univ. of California Press, 1988.

Hartman, Mary S., and Lois Banner, eds. *Clio's Consciousness Raised.* New York: Harper, 1973.

Hartmann, Susan M. *From Margin to Mainstream: American Women and Politics Since 1960.* New York: Knopf, 1989.

Hawley, Ellis W. "Herbert Hoover and Economic Stabilization, 1921–22." In Hawley, ed. *Herbert Hoover as Secretary of Commerce.* Iowa City: Univ. of Iowa Press, 1981.

Hemingway, Ernest. *Death in the Afternoon.* New York: Charles Scribner's Sons, 1932.

Hendrick, Burton J. *The Life and Letters of Walter H. Page.* Garden City, N.J.: Doubleday, Page and Co., 1923.

Hershberg, Theodore, ed. *Philadelphia Work, Space, Family, and Group Experience in the Nineteenth Century.* New York: Oxford Univ. Press, 1981.

Herskovits, Melville. "The Racial Hysteria." *Opportunity* II (June 1924): 166–68.

———. "Some Effects of Social Selection on the American Negro." *Publications of the American Sociological Society* XX (1926): 77–80.

———. "Some Physical Characteristics of the American Negro Population." *Journal of the Social Forces* VI (Sept. 1927): 93–98.

———. *The American Negro.* New York: Knopf, 1928.

———. "Race Relations." *American Journal of Sociology* XXXIV (May 1929): 1129–39.

Hicks, John D. *Republican Ascendancy 1921–1933.* New York: Harper, 1960.

Higham, John. *Strangers in the Land, Patterns of American Nativism, 1860–1925.* New Brunswick: Rutgers Univ. Press, 1955.

———. "The Reorientation of American Culture in the 1890's." In John Weiss, ed. *The Origins of Modern Consciousness.* Detroit: Wayne State Univ. Press, 1965.

———. "The Schism in American Scholarship." *American Historical Review* LXXII (Oct. 1966): 1–21.

Hill, Joseph A. *Women in Gainful Occupations, 1870–1920.* U.S. Census Monography IX. Washington: 1929.

Hill, Robert A., ed. *The Marcus Garvey and Universal Negro Improvement Association Papers.* Vol. I. *1826–August, 1919.* Berkeley: Univ. of California Press, 1983.

Hill, Thomas E. *Hill's Manual of Social and Business Forms.* Chicago: Quadrangle, 1971.

Hoffman, Frederick J. *The Little Magazine: A History and Bibliography.* Princeton: Princeton Univ. Press, 1946.

———. *The Twenties: American Writing in the Postwar Decade.* New York: Viking, 1955.

Hofstadter, Richard. *Social Darwinism in American Thought, 1860–1915.* Philadelphia: Univ. of Pennsylvania Press, 1945.

———. *Anti-Intellectualism in American Life.* New York: Knopf, 1962.

———, and Walter P. Metzger. *The Development of Academic Freedom in the United States.* New York: Columbia Univ. Press, 1955.

Hooks, Janet M. *Women's Occupations Through Seven Decades.* U.S. Department of Labor. Women's Bureau. Bulletin No. 218. Washington, D.C.: GPO, 1947.

Horowitz, David A. "The Klansman as Outsider: Ethnocultural Solidarity and Antielitism in the Oregon Ku Klux Klan of the 1920's." *Pacific Northwest Quarterly* LXXX (Jan. 1989): 12–20.

———. "Order, Solidarity and Vigilance: The Ku Klux Klan in La Grande, Oregon." In Shawn Lay, ed. *The Invisible Empire in the West: Toward a New Historical Appraisal of the Klan in the 1920's.* Forthcoming from the Univ. of Illinois Press, 1991.

Houghton, Walter E. *The Victorian Frame of Mind, 1830–1870.* New Haven: Yale Univ. Press, 1957.

Howard, Jane. *Margaret Mead: A Life.* New York: Simon and Schuster, 1984.

Howe, Daniel Walker, ed. *Victorian America.* Philadelphia: Univ. of Pennsylvania Press, 1976.

Howells, William Dean. "A Modern Instance." In H.S. Commager, ed. *Selected Writings of William Dean Howells.* New York: Random House, 1950.

Huggins, Nathan Irving. *Harlem Renaissance.* New York: Oxford Univ. Press, 1971.

Hughes, Langston. "Negro Artist and the Racial Mountain." *Nation* 122 (June 23, 1926): 692–94.

———. *The Weary Blues.* New York: Knopf, 1926.

———. *Fine Clothes to the Jew.* New York: Knopf, 1927.

———. *The Big Sea.* New York: Knopf, 1940.

Hughes, Langston, and Arna Bontemps, eds. *Book of Negro Folklore.* New York: Dodd, Mead, 1958.

Jackson, Kenneth T. *Ku Klux Klan in the City, 1915–1930.* New York: Oxford Univ. Press, 1967.

James, Henry. *Notes and Reviews.* Cambridge, Mass.: Dunster House, 1921.

Jammer, Max. *The Conceptual Development of Quantum Mechanics.* New York: McGraw-Hill, 1966.

Jenkins, William D. "The Ku Klux Klan in Youngstown, Ohio: Moral Reform in the Twenties." *Historian* XLI (Nov. 1978): 76–93.

John, Arthur. *The Best Years of the Century: Richard Watson Gilder, Scribner's Monthly, and the Century Magazine, 1870–1909.* Urbana-Champaign: Univ. of Illinois Press, 1981.

Johnson, Charles S. *The Shadow of the Plantation.* Chicago: Univ. of Chicago Press, 1966.

Johnson, James Weldon. "Harlem: The Culture Capital." In Alain Locke, ed. *The New Negro.* New York: Albert and Charles Boni, 1925.

———. *Black Manhattan.* New York: Knopf, 1930.

Jonas, Gerald. *The Circuit Riders: The Rockefeller Money and the Rise of Modern Science.* New York: Norton, 1989.

Jones, A.M. *Studies in African Music.* London: Oxford Univ. Press, 1959.

Jones, E.K. "The Negro's Struggle for Health." *Proceedings of the National Council on Social Work, 1923.* Chicago: Univ. of Chicago Press, 1923.

Jordan, Winthrop D. *White Over Black: American Attitudes Toward the Negro, 1550–1812.* Chapel Hill: Univ. of North Carolina, 1968.

Kahn, Sholom. *Mark Twain's Mysterious Stranger: A Study of the Manuscript Texts.* Columbia: Univ. of Missouri Press, 1978.

Kaminsky, Max. *My Life in Jazz.* New York: Harper, 1963.

Kaplan, Justin, ed. *Mark Twain: A Profile.* New York: Hill and Wang, 1967.

Karl, Barry D. *Charles E. Merriam and the Study of Politics.* Chicago: Univ. of Chicago Press, 1974.

———, and Stanley N. Katz. "The American Private Philanthropic Foundations and the Public Sphere, 1890–1930." *Minerva* XIX (1981): 236–70.

Kazin, Alfred, and Charles Shapiro, eds. *The Stature of Theodore Dreiser: A Critical Survey of the Man and His Work.* Bloomington: Indiana Univ. Press, 1955.

Keating, Edward. *The Story of "LABOR."* Washington, D.C.: Edward Keating, 1923.

Keenleyside, H. "The American Political Revolution of 1924." *Current History* XXI (Mar. 1925): 833–40.

Kellogg, E.E. *Studies in Character Building, A Book for Parents.* Battle Creek, Mich.: Good Health Publishing, 1905.

Kennedy, Louise Venable. *The Negro Peasant Turns Cityward: Effects of Recent Migrations to Northern Centers.* New York: Columbia Univ. Press, 1934.

———, and Frank A. Ross. *A Bibliography of Negro Migration.* New York: Columbia Univ. Press, 1922.

Kessler-Harris, Alice. *Out to Work: A History of Wage-Earning Women in the United States.* New York: Oxford Univ. Press, 1982.

Kett, Joseph F. "Adolescence and Youth in Nineteenth-Century America." *Journal of Interdisciplinary History* II (Autumn 1971): 283–98.

Kevles, Daniel J. *In the Name of Eugenics.* New York: Knopf, 1985.

Key, V. O. *Politics, Parties and Pressure Groups.* New York: Thomas Y. Crowell, 1964. Fifth edition.

Klein, Viola. *The Feminine Character: History of an Ideology.* London: Routledge and Kegan Paul, 1971.

Klineberg, Otto. "An Experimental Study of Speed and Other Factors in 'Racial' Differences." *Archives of Psychology* No. 93 (1928): 5–111.

―――. *Race Differences*. New York: Harper, 1935.

―――, ed. *Characteristics of the American Negro*. New York: Harper, 1944.

Kohler, Robert E. "A Policy for the Advancement of Science: The Rockefeller Foundation, 1924–29." *Minerva* XVI (Winter 1978): 480–515.

Kohlstedt, Sally G. *The Formation of the American Scientific Community*. Urbana: Univ. of Illinois Press, 1976.

Kraditor, Aileen S. *The Ideas of the Woman Suffrage Movement, 1890–1920*. New York: Columbia Univ. Press, 1965.

Kuehland, John, and Jackson R. Bryer, eds. *Dear Scott/Dear Max: The Fitzgerald-Perkins Correspondence*. New York: Scribner, 1971.

Kusmer, Kenneth L. *A Ghetto Takes Shape*. Urbana: Univ. of Illinois Press, 1976.

La Follette, Belle C. and Fola. *Robert M. La Follette*. New York: Macmillan, 1953.

Laidlaw, Walter, ed. *Population of the City of New York*. New York: The New York City 1920 Census Committee, Inc., 1923.

―――, ed. *Statistical Sources for Demographic Studies of Greater New York*. New York: The New York City 1920 Census Committee, Inc., 1923.

Larcum, Lucy. *A New England Childhood*. Boston: Houghton Mifflin, 1889.

Larson, Edward J. *Trial and Error: The American Controversy over Creation and Evolution*. New York: Oxford Univ. Press, 1985.

Lasch, Christopher. *The New Radicalism in America, 1889–1963: The New Intellectual as a Social Type*. New York: Knopf, 1965.

Laslett, John H., and Seymour Martin Lipset, eds. *Failure of A Dream? Essays in the History of American Socialism*. Garden City, N.Y.: Doubleday, 1974.

Laurie, Bruce, Theodore Hershberg, and George Alter. "Immigrants and Industry: The Philadelphia Experience, 1850–1880." *Journal of Social History* IX (Winter 1975): 219–48.

Lay, Shawn. *War, Revolution and the Ku Klux Klan: A Study of Intolerance in a Border City*. El Paso: Texas Western Press, 1985.

―――, ed. *The Invisible Empire in the West: Toward a New Historical Appraisal of the Klan in the 1920's*. Forthcoming from the Univ. of Illinois Press, 1991.

Leach, Paul R. *That Man Dawes*. Chicago: The Reilly & Lee Co., 1930.

Leavitt, Judith Walzer. *Brought to Bed: Childbearing in America: 1750–1950*. New York: Oxford Univ. Press, 1986.

Lebow, Richard Ned. *White Britain and Black Ireland: The Influence of Stereotypes on Colonial Policy*. Philadelphia: Institute for the Study of Human Issues, 1976.

Lemons, J. Stanley. *The Woman Citizen: Social Feminism in the 1920's*. Urbana: Univ. of Illinois Press, 1973.

Leonard, Neil. *Jazz and the White Americans: The Acceptance of a New Art Form*. Chicago: Univ. of Chicago Press, 1962.

Lerner, Gerda. *The Majority Finds its Past: Placing Women in History*. New York: Oxford Univ. Press, 1979.

Leuchtenburg, William E. *The Perils of Prosperity, 1914–32*. Chicago: Univ. of Chicago Press, 1958.

―――, ed. *The Unfinished Century*. Boston: Little, Brown, 1973.

Levine, Lawrence W. *Black Culture and Black Consciousness: Afro-American Folk Thought From Slavery to Freedom*. New York: Oxford Univ. Press, 1977.

Lewis, Dio. *Our Girls*. New York: Harper and Bros., 1871.

Lewis, Sinclair. *Arrowsmith*. New York: Harcourt Brace, 1925.

———. *From Main Street to Stockholm*. New York: Harcourt Brace, 1952.

Lichtman, Allan J. "Critical Election Theory and the Reality of American Presidential Politics, 1916–1940." *American Historical Review* LXXXI (Apr. 1976): 317–51.

———. *Prejudice and the Old Politics, The Presidential Election of 1928*. Chapel Hill: Univ. of North Carolina Press, 1979.

Link, Arthur S. *Wilson: The Road to the White House*. Princeton: Princeton Univ. Press, 1947.

———. *Wilson: The New Freedom*. Princeton: Princeton Univ. Press, 1956.

Locke, Alain, ed. *The New Negro*. New York: Albert and Charles Boni, 1925.

Logan, Rayford W., ed. *W.E.B. Du Bois, A Profile*. New York: Hill and Wang, 1971.

Lomask, Milton. *Seed Money: The Guggenheim Story*. New York: Farrar, Strauss, 1964.

Lomax, Alan. *Mister Jelly Roll*. Berkeley: Univ. of California Press, 1973.

Lonn, Ella. "Academic Status of Women on University Faculties." *Journal of the American Association of University Women* XVII (Jan.–Mar. 1924): 5–11.

Lorimer, Douglas A. *Colour, Class and the Victorians: English Attitudes to the Negro in the Mid-Nineteenth Century*. Leicester: Holmes and Meier, 1978.

Lowitt, Richard. *George W. Norris: The Persistence of a Progressive, 1913–1933*. Urbana: Univ. of Illinois Press, 1971.

Lunardini, Christine A. *From Equal Suffrage to Equal Rights: Alice Paul and the National Woman's Party, 1910–1928*. New York: New York Univ. Press, 1986.

———, and Thomas A. Knock. "Woodrow Wilson and Woman Suffrage: A New Look." *Political Science Quarterly* XCV (Winter 1980–81): 655–71.

Lutz, Alma. *Created Equal: A Biography of Elizabeth Cady Stanton, 1815–1902*. New York: John Day, 1940.

———. *Crusade for Freedom: Women of the Antislavery Movement*. Boston: Beacon Press, 1968.

Lyman, Stanford M. *The Black American in Sociological Thought, A Failure of Perspective*. New York: Capricorn, 1973.

Lynd, Robert S. and Helen M. *Middletown: A Study in Modern American Culture*. New York: Harcourt Brace, 1929.

Lynn, Kenneth S. *William Dean Howells: An American Life*. New York: Harcourt Brace Jovanovitch, 1970.

McCormick, Richard L. "The Discovery that Business Corrupts Politics: A Reappraisal of the Origins of Positivism." *American Historical Review* LXXXVI (Apr. 1981): 247–74.

McDannell, Collean. *The Christian Home in Victorian America, 1840–1900*. Bloomington: Univ. of Indiana Press, 1986.

MacDonald, Dwight. "Mark Twain: An Unsentimental Journey." In Justin Kaplan, ed. *Mark Twain: A Profile*. New York: Hill and Wang, 1967.

McDougall, Mary Lynn. "Working-Class Women During the Industrial Revolution." In Renate Bridenthal and Claudie Koonz, eds. *Becoming Visible: Women in European History*. Boston: Houghton Mifflin, 1977.

McDowell, Nancy. "The Oceanic Ethnography of Margaret Mead." *American Anthropologist* LXXII (June 1980): 278–302.

MacKay, Kenneth Campbell. *The Progressive Movement of 1924*. New York: Columbia Univ. Press, 1947.

MacKenzie, Norman and Jeanne. *The First Fabians*. London: Weidendeld and Nicolson, 1977.

Madison, Charles A. *Book Publishing in America*. New York: McGraw-Hill, 1966.

Malia, Martin. *Alexander Herzen and the Birth of Russian Socialism 1812–1855*. Cambridge: Harvard Univ. Press, 1961.

Maney, Patrick J. *"Young Bob" La Follette*. Columbia: Univ. of Missouri Press, 1987.

Mannheim, Karl. *Ideology and Utopia: An Introduction to the Sociology of Knowledge*. New York: Harcourt Brace, 1949.

Mansbridge, Jane J. *Why We Lost the ERA*. Chicago: Univ. of Chicago Press, 1986.

Mansergh, Nicholas. *The Irish Question 1840–1921*. Toronto: Univ. of Toronto Press, 1966.

Marable, Manning. *W. E. B. Du Bois: Black Radical Democrat*. Boston: Twains Publishers, 1986.

Marcus, Steven. *The Other Victorians*. New York: Schocken, 1966.

Martin, Tony. *Race First: The Ideological and Organizational Struggles of Marcus Garvey and the Universal Negro Improvement Association*. Westport: Greenwood Press, 1976.

May, Elaine Tyler. "The Pressure to Provide: Class, Consumerism, and Divorce in Urban America, 1880–1920." *Journal of Social History* XII (Winter 1978): 180–93.

May, Henry F. *The End of American Innocence: A Study of the First Years of Our Own Time: 1912–17*. New York: Knopf, 1959.

Mead, Margaret. "The Methodology of Racial Testing." *American Journal of Sociology* 31 (Feb. 1926): 657–67.

———. *Coming of Age in Samoa: A Psychological Study of Primitive Youth for Western Civilization*. New York: William Morrow, 1928.

———. *Growing Up in New Guinea*. New York: William Morrow, 1930.

———. *Blackberry Winter: My Early Years*. New York: Simon and Schuster, 1972.

———, ed. *An Anthropologist at Work: Writings of Ruth Benedict*. Boston: Houghton Mifflin, 1959.

Meier, August. *Negro Thought in America, 1880–1915*. Ann Arbor: Univ. of Michigan Press, 1963.

Meier, Norman C. "Motives in Voting: A Study in Public Opinion." *American Journal of Sociology* XXXI (Sept. 1925): 199–212.

Meyer, D. H. "American Intellectuals and the Victorian Crisis of Faith." In Daniel Walker Howe, ed. *Victorian America*. Philadelphia: Univ. of Pennsylvania Press, 1976.

Mezzrow, Mezz. *Really the Blues*. New York: Random House, 1946.

Miller, Stuart Creighton. *The Unwelcome Immigrant: The American Image of the Chinese, 1785–1882*. Berkeley and Los Angeles: Univ. of California Press, 1969.

Mintz, Stephen. *A Prison of Expectations: The Family in Victorian Culture*. New York: New York Univ. Press, 1985.

Mitchell, David. *The Fighting Pankhursts: A Study in Tenacity*. London: Jonathan Cape, 1967.

Mitchell, Juliet, and Ann Oakley, eds. *What Is Feminism: A Reexamination*. New York: Pantheon Books, 1986.

Monroe, Paul. *Founding of the American Public School System*. New York: Macmillan, 1940.

Morlan, Robert L. *Political Fire, The Nonpartisan League, 1915–1922*. Minneapolis: Univ. of Minnesota Press, 1955.

Moses, Wilson J. "The Poetics of Ethiopianism: W.E.B. Du Bois's Struggle to Reconcile Folk and High Art." Reprinted in William L. Andrews. *Critical Essays on W.E.B. Du Bois*. Boston: G.K. Hall, 1985.

Mott, Frank Luther. *History of American Magazines*. Cambridge: Harvard Univ. Press, 1957.

Nash, Gary B. *Red, White and Black: The Peoples of Early America*. Englewood Cliffs, N.J.: Prentice Hall, 1974.

Nash, Gary, and Richard Weiss, eds. *The Great Fear*. New York: Holt, Rinehart and Winston, 1970.

Nelli, Humbert S. *The Italians in Chicago, 1880–1930: A Study in Ethnic Mobility*. New York: Oxford Univ. Press, 1970.

Newby, I.A. *Jim Crow's Defense: Anti-Negro Thought in America, 1900–1930*. Baton Rouge: Louisiana State Univ. Press, 1965.

Newcomber, Mabel. *A Century of Higher Education for American Women*. New York: Harper, 1959.

Norman, E.R. *Anti-Catholicism in Victorian England*. London: George Allen and Unwin, 1968.

Novick, Peter. *That Noble Dream: The "Objectivity Question" and the American Historical Profession*. New York: Cambridge Univ. Press, 1988.

Oestreicher, Richard. "Urban Working-Class Political Behaviour and Theories of American Electoral Politics, 1870–1940." *The Journal of American History* LXXIV (Mar. 1988): 1257–86.

Oliver, Paul. *The Meaning of the Blues*. New York: Macmillan, 1969.

———. *Savannah Syncopators: African Retentions in the Blues*. New York: Stein and Day, 1970.

Oppenheimer, J. Robert. *Science and Common Understanding*. New York: Simon and Schuster, 1953.

Osofsky, Gilbert. *Harlem: The Making of a Ghetto*. New York: Scribner's, 1963.

Otten, Charlotte M., ed. *Anthropology and Art: Readings in Cross-cultural Aesthetics*. Garden City, N.Y.: Natural History Press, 1971.

Ottley, Roy, and William J. Weatherby, eds. *The Negro in New York: An Informal Social History, 1626–1940*. New York: Praeger, 1967.

Ovington, Mary White. *Half a Man: The Status of the Negro in New York*. New York: Longmans, Green, 1911.

Paige, D.D., ed. *The Selected Letters of Ezra Pound, 1907–1941*. New York: New Directions Publishing Co., 1971.

Painter, Leonard. *Through Fifty Years with the Brotherhood Railway Carmen of America*. Kansas City, Mo.: Railway Carmen, 1941.

Parr, Carol C. "Women in the Military." In Irene Tinker, ed. *Women in Washington: Advocates for Public Policy*. Beverly Hills: Sage Publications, 1983.

Pelling, Henry. *A Short History of the Labour Party*. London: Macmillan, 1961.

———. *The Origins of the Labour Party, 1890–1900*. London: Oxford Univ. Press, 1965.

Piper, Henry Dan. *F. Scott Fitzgerald: A Critical Portrait*. New York: Holt, Rinehart and Winston, 1965.

Pivar, David J. *Purity Crusade: Sexual Morality and Social Control, 1868–1900*. Westport, Conn.: Greenwood Press, 1973.

Poirier, Philip P. *The Advent of the British Labour Party*. New York: Columbia Univ. Press, 1958.

Proceedings, Conference for Progressive Political Action Convention held at Cleveland, Ohio, July 4–5, 1924.

Proceedings, Democratic National Convention, held at New York, N.Y., June 24–July 9, 1924. New York: n. p., 1924.

Proceedings of the Women's Rights Conventions, held at Seneca Falls and Rochester, New York, July and August, 1848. New York: R.J. Johnston, 1870.

Putnam, Carleton. *Theodore Roosevelt, the Formative Years, 1858–1886*. New York: Charles Scribner's Sons, 1958.

Rampersad, Arnold. *The Art and Imagination of W.E.B. Du Bois*. Cambridge, Harvard Univ. Press, 1976.

———. *The Life of Langston Hughes, 1902–1941*. Vol. I. *Too, Sing America*. New York: Oxford Univ. Press, 1986.

Reichenbach, Hans. *Philosophic Foundations of Quantum Mechanics*. Berkeley and Los Angeles: Univ. of California Press, 1944.

Reingold, Nathan, ed. *The Sciences in the American Context: New Perspectives*. Washington, D.C.: Smithsonian Institution Press, 1979.

Report of the Proceedings of the Thirty-ninth Annual Convention of the American Federation of Labor, 1919. Washington, D.C.: Law Reporting Co., 1919.

Report of the Proceedings of the Forty-second Annual Convention of the American Federation of Labor, 1922. Washington, D.C.: Law Reporting Co., 1922.

Report of the Proceedings of the Forty-third Annual Convention of the American Federation of Labor, 1923. Washington, D.C.: Law Reporting Co., 1923.

Riley, Glenda Gates. "The Subtle Subversion: Changes in the Traditionalist Image of the American Woman." *The Historian* XXII (Feb. 1970): 210–27.

Robinson, Ronald, John Gallegher, and Alice Denny. *Africa and the Victorians: The Climax of Imperialism.* New York: St. Martin's Press, 1961.

Roosevelt, Theodore. *The Winning of the West.* New York: G.P. Putnam's Sons, 1889.

———. "Character and Success." *Outlook* LXIV (1900): 745.

Rosen, Ruth. *The Lost Sisterhood, Prostitution in America, 1900–1918.* Baltimore: Johns Hopkins Univ. Press, 1982.

Rosenberg, Rosalind. *Beyond Separate Spheres, Intellectual Roots of Modern Feminism.* New Haven: Yale Univ. Press, 1982.

Ross, B. Joyce. *J.E. Spingarn and the Rise of the N.A.A.C.P., 1911–1929.* New York: Atheneum, 1972.

Ryan, Mary Patricia. *Cradle of the Middle Class: The Family in Oneida County, New York, 1790–1865.* New York: Cambridge Univ. Press, 1981.

Salvatore, Nick. *Eugene V. Debs, Citizen and Socialist.* Urbana: Univ. of Illinois Press, 1982.

Sapir, Edward. "Culture, Genuine and Spurious." *American Journal of Sociology* XXIX (1924): 401–29.

Saxon, Martha. *Louisa May: A Modern Biography of Louisa May Alcott.* Boston: Houghton Mifflin, 1977.

Saxton, Alexander P. *The Indispensible Enemy: Labor and the Anti-Chinese Movement in California.* Berkeley: Univ. of California Press, 1971.

Scheiner, Seth M. *Negro Mecca: A History of the Negro in New York City, 1865–1920.* New York: New York Univ. Press, 1965.

Schlesinger, Arthur M., Jr., ed. Vol. VI. *The History of American Presidential Elections.* New York: Chelsea House, 1971.

Schnore, Leo F., and Eric E. Lambard, eds. *The New Urban History: Quantitative Explorations by American Historians.* Princeton: Princeton Univ. Press, 1975.

Schorer, Mark. *Sinclair Lewis: An American Life.* New York: McGraw-Hill, 1961.

Schuller, Gunther. *Early Jazz: Its Roots and Musical Developments.* New York: Oxford Univ. Press, 1968.

Scott, Emmett J. "Letters of Negro Migrants of 1916–1918." *Journal of Negro History* IV (July 1919): 290–340.

———. "Additional Letters of Negro Migrants of 1916–1918." *Journal of Negro History* IV (Oct. 1919): 412–65.

———. *Negro Migration During the War.* New York: Oxford Univ. Press, 1920.

Sedgwick, Catharine. *Home.* New York: J. Munroe, 1850.

Seligman, Herbert J. *The Negro Faces America.* New York: Harper and Bros., 1920.

Shapley, Harlow. *Galaxies.* Cambridge: Harvard Univ. Press, 1961.

Shils, Edward. "Intellectuals and Their Discontents." *American Scholar* XLV (1976): 181–203.

Short, James F., Jr., ed. *The Social Fabric of the Metropolis: Contributions of the Chicago School of Urban Sociology*. Chicago: Univ. of Chicago Press, 1971.

Singleton, Gregory H. " 'Mere Middle-Class Institutions': Urban Protestantism in Nineteenth-Century America." *Journal of Social History* VI (Summer 1973): 489–504.

———. "Protestant Organizations and the Shaping of Victorian America." *American Quarterly* XXVII (Dec. 1975): 549–60.

———. "Fundamentalism and Urbanization: A Quantitative Critique of Impressionistic Interpretations." In Leo F. Schnore and Eric E. Lambard, eds. *The New Urban History: Quantitative Explorations by American Historians*. Princeton: Princeton Univ. Press, 1975.

Sinkler, George. *The Racial Attitudes of American Presidents from Abraham Lincoln to Theodore Roosevelt*. Garden City, N.J.: Doubleday, 1972.

Sklar, Kathryn Kish. *Catharine Beecher: A Study in American Domesticity*. New Haven: Yale Univ. Press, 1973.

Sklar, Robert. *F. Scott Fitzgerald: The Last Laocoon*. New York: Oxford Univ. Press, 1967.

Smith, Henry Nash. *Mark Twain: The Development of a Writer*. Cambridge: Harvard Univ. Press, 1962.

Smith, Thomas V., and Leonard D. White, eds. *Chicago, An Experiment in Social Science Research*. New York: Greenwood, 1929.

Smith-Rosenberg, Carroll. "The Hysterical Woman: Sex Roles and Role Conflict in 19th-Century America." *Social Research* XXXIX (Winter 1972): 657–77.

———. "The Female World of Love and Ritual: Relations Between Women in Nineteenth-Century America." *Signs* I (Autumn 1975): 1–30.

———. *Disorderly Conduct, Visions of Gender in Victorian America*. New York: Knopf, 1985.

Solomon, Barbara Miller. *Ancestors and Immigrants*. Cambridge: Harvard Univ. Press, 1956.

Sombart, Werner. *The Quintessence of Capitalism*. New York: Dutton, 1915.

Sopka, Katherine. *Quantum Physics in America, 1920–1935*. New York: Arno Press, 1980.

Spear, Allan H. *Black Chicago: The Making of a Negro Ghetto 1890–1920*. Chicago: Univ. of Chicago Press, 1967.

Stannard, David E. "Death and Dying in Puritan New England." *American Historical Review* LXXVIII (Dec. 1973): 1305–30.

———. *The Puritan Way of Death: A Study in Religion, Culture, and Social Change*. New York: Oxford Univ. Press, 1977.

Stanton, Elizabeth. *Eighty Years and More: Reminiscences 1815–1897*. New York: T. Fisher Unwin, 1898.

Stanton, Theodore, and Harriot Stanton Blatch, eds. *Elizabeth Cady Stanton As Revealed in Her Letters, Diary and Reminiscences*. New York: Harper, 1922.

Stein, Judith. *The World of Marcus Garvey: Race and Class in Modern Society.* Baton Rouge: Louisiana State Univ. Press, 1986.

Steinbrecher, George, Jr., "Inaccurate Accounts of Sister Carrie." *American Literature* XXIII (Jan. 1952): 490–93.

Stepanchev, Stephen. *Dreiser Among the Critics.* New York: New York Univ. Press, 1950.

Stern, Madeline B. *Louisa May Alcott.* Norman: Univ. of Oklahoma Press, 1950.

Stevens, Doris. *Jailed for Freedom.* New York: Boni and Liveright, 1920.

Stigler, George J. *Employment and Compensation in Higher Education.* Occasional Paper No. 33. New York: National Bureau of Economic Research, 1950.

Stocking, George W. *Race, Culture, and Evolution. Essays in the History of Anthropology.* New York: Free Press, 1968.

———, ed. *Malinowski, Rivers, Benedict and Others, Essays on Culture and Personality.* Madison: Univ. of Wisconsin Press, 1986.

Stowe, Harriet Beecher. *Oldtown Folks.* Boston: Fields, Osgood & Co., 1869.

Stratton, David H. "Splattered with Oil: William G. McAdoo and the 1924 Democratic Presidential Election." *Southwestern Social Sciences Quarterly* XLIV (June 1963): 62–75.

Swanberg, W. A. *Dreiser.* New York: Scribner's, 1965.

Taft, Philip. *The A.F. of L. in the Time of Gompers.* New York: Harper, 1957.

Tawney, Richard H. *Religion and the Rise of Capitalism.* New York: Harcourt Brace, 1947.

Tebbe, John. *George Horace Lorimer and the Saturday Evening Post.* New York: Doubleday, 1948.

Thelen, David P. *Robert La Follette and the Insurgent Spirit.* Boston: Little, Brown, 1976.

Thernstrom, Stephan A. *Poverty and Progress.* Cambridge: Harvard Univ. Press, 1963.

———. *The Other Bostonians.* Cambridge: Harvard Univ. Press, 1973.

Thompson, Charles H. "The Conclusion of Scientists Relative to Racial Differences." *Journal of Negro Education* III (July 1934): 494–512.

Thompson, Robert Farris. *Flash of the Spirit: African and Afro-American Art and Philosophy.* New York: Random House, 1983.

Tinker, Irene, ed. *Women in Washington: Advocates for Public Policy.* Beverly Hills: Sage Publications, 1983.

Tobey, Ronald C. *The American Ideology of National Science, 1919–1930.* Pittsburgh: Univ. of Pittsburgh Press, 1971.

Tolbert, Emory. *The UNIA and Black Los Angeles.* Los Angeles: Center for Afro-American Studies, Univ. of California, Los Angeles, 1980.

Toll, William. "Progress and Piety: The Ku Klux Klan and Social Change in Tillamook, Oregon." *Pacific Northwest Quarterly* LXIX (Apr. 1978): 75–85.

———. *The Resurgence of Race: Black Social Theory from Reconstruction to the Pan-African Conferences.* Philadelphia: Temple Univ. Press, 1979.

Tomsich, John. *A Genteel Endeavor: American Culture and Politics in the Gilded Age.* Stanford: Stanford Univ. Press, 1971.

Toy, Ekard V. "The Ku Klux Klan in Oregon." In G. Thomas Edwards and Carlos A. Schwantes, eds. *Experiences in a Promised Land: Essays in Pacific Northwest History.* Seattle: Univ. of Washington Press, 1986.

——. "Robe and Gown: The Ku Klux Klan in Eugene, Oregon." In Shawn Lay, ed. *The Invisible Empire in the West: Toward a New Historical Appraisal of the Klan in the 1920's.* Forthcoming from the Univ. of Illinois Press, 1991.

Trachtenberg, Alan. *The Incorporation of America, Culture and Society in the Gilded Age.* New York: Hill and Wang, 1982.

Tracy, Steven C. *Langston Hughes and the Blues.* Urbana: Univ. of Illinois Press, 1988.

Troeltsch, Ernst. *The Social Teachings of the Christian Churches and Sects.* New York: Macmillan, 1931.

Tuckey, John S. *Mark Twain and Little Satan: The Writing of the Mysterious Stranger.* West Lafayette: Purdue Univ. Press, 1963.

Turner, Darwin T. "W.E.B. Du Bois and the Theory of a Black Aesthetic." Reprinted in William L. Andrews. *Critical Essays on W.E.B. Du Bois.* Boston: G.K. Hall, 1985.

Tuttle, William M., Jr., *Race Riot: Chicago in the Red Summer of 1919.* New York: Atheneum, 1972.

Vale, Vivian. *Labour in American Politics.* London: Routledge and Kegan Paul, 1971.

Valelly, Richard M. *Radicalism in the United States: The Minnesota Farmer-Labor Party and the American Political Economy.* Chicago: Univ. of Chicago Press, 1989.

Van Voris, Jacqueline. *Carrie Chapman Catt: A Public Life.* New York: Feminist Press, 1987.

Veysey, Laurence R. *The Emergence of the American University.* Chicago: Univ. of Chicago Press, 1965.

Wald, Kenneth D. "The Visible Empire: The Ku Klux Klan as an Electoral Movement [on Memphis, Tennessee]." *The Journal of Interdisciplinary History* XI (Summer 1980): 217–34.

Waldron, Edward E. "The Blues Poetry of Langston Hughes." *American Literature Forum* V (Winter 1971): 140–49.

Walkewitz, Judith K. *Prostitution and Victorian Society: Women, Class, and the State.* Cambridge: Cambridge Univ. Press, 1980.

Walters, Ronald G. *Primers for Prudery, Sexual Advice to Victorian America.* Englewood Cliffs, N.J.: Prentice Hall, 1974.

Warner, Sam Bass. *The Private City: Philadelphia in Three Periods of Its Growth.* Philadelphia: Univ. of Pennsylvania Press, 1968.

Warren, Austin. "Some Periodicals of the American Intelligentsia." *The New English Weekly* I (Oct. 6, 1932): 595–97.

Waskow, Arthur I. *From Race Riot to Sit-In.* Garden City, N.Y.: Doubleday, 1966.

Waterhouse. "The Estimation of Voting Behavior from Aggregate Data: A Test." *Journal of Social History* XVI (Spring 1983): 35–53.

Waterman, Richard A. "African Influences on the Music of the Americas." In Charlotte M. Otten, ed. *Anthropology and Art: Readings in Cross-cultural Aesthetics.* Garden City, N.Y.: Natural History Press, 1971.

Weart, Spencer R. "The Physics Business in America, 1919–1940: A Statistical Reconnaissance." In Nathan Reingold, ed. *The Sciences in the American Context: New Perspectives.* Washington, D.C.: Smithsonian Institution Press, 1979.

Webb, Beatrice. *Our Partnership.* New York: Longmans, Green, 1948.

Weber, Max. *The Protestant Ethic and the Spirit of Capitalism.* London: George Allen and Unwin, 1930.

———. *Ancient Judaism.* Glencoe: Free Press, 1952.

———. *The City.* Glencoe: Free Press, 1958.

Weibel, Kathryn. *Mirror Mirror: Images of Women Reflected in Popular Culture.* New York: Anchor Books, 1977.

Weinstein, James. *The Decline of Socialism in America, 1912–1925.* New York: Random House, 1967.

Weiss, John, ed. *The Origins of Modern Consciousness.* Detroit: Wayne State Univ. Press, 1965.

Weiss, Richard. *The American Myth of Success: From Horatio Alger to Norman Vincent Peale.* New York: Basic Books, 1969.

Welter, Barbara A. "The Cult of True Womanhood." *American Quarterly* XVIII (Summer 1966): 151–74.

———. "The Feminization of Religion in Nineteenth-Century America." In Mary S. Hartman and Lois Banner, eds. *Clio's Consciousness Raised.* New York: Harper, 1973.

———. *Dimity Convictions, The American Woman in the Nineteenth Century.* Athens, Ohio: Ohio Univ. Press, 1976.

Wertheim, Arthur J. *New York Little Renaissance.* New York: New York Univ. Press, 1976.

Wiebe, Robert H. *The Search for Order: 1877–1920.* New York: Hill and Wang, 1967.

Williams, Martin. "King Oliver in New York," RCA Vintage LPV–529. Reprinted in Williams, *Jazz in Its Time.* New York: Oxford Univ. Press, 1989.

Wilson, Douglas L., ed. *The Genteel Tradition, Nine Essays by George Santayana.* Cambridge: Harvard Univ. Press, 1967.

Winch, Julie. *Philadelphia's Black Elite: Activism, Accommodation, and the Struggle for Autonomy: 1787–1848.* Philadelphia: Temple Univ. Press, 1988.

Wishy, Bernard. *The Child and the Republic.* Philadelphia: Univ. of Pennsylvania Press, 1968.

Wolf, Eric R. *Anthropology.* Englewood Cliffs, Prentice Hall, 1964.

Wolman, Lee. *The Growth of American Trade Unions, 1880–1923.* New York: National Bureau of Economic Research, 1924.

Woody, Thomas. *A History of Women's Education in the United States.* New York: Science Press, 1929.

Woofter, Thomas J. *Negro Migration.* New York. W. D. Gray, 1922.

———. *Negro Problems in Cities.* Garden City, N.Y.: Doubleday, 1928.

Wright, Helen. *Explorer of the Universe, A Biography of George Ellery Hale.* New York: Dutton, 1966.

Wyllie, Irvin G. *The Self-Made Man in America: The Myth of Rags to Riches.* New York: Free Press, 1954.

Yerkes, Robert M., ed. Vol. 15. *Psychological Examining in the United States Army.* Memoirs of the National Academy of Sciences, Washington, D.C., 1921.

Zieger, Robert G. "From Hostility to Moderation: Railroad Labor Policy." *Labor History* IX (Winter 1968): 23–38.

Zuckerman, Michael. *Peaceable Kingdoms: New England Towns in the Eighteen Century.* New York: Random House, 1970.

INDEX

973.915   Coben, Stanley.
COB
          Rebellion against
          Victorianism.

                                    29936
$21.95

DATE			